The General's Children
American Families in Occupied Japan

By

James Lamont

Dedication

…To my fifth grade classmates at Nasugbu Beach Elementary School for the school year 1949-'50: wherever you are, whatever you're up to. And a special nod to the memory of Karl ("Pat") Conley, and twins Jeannine and Rexine White: you left this world way too soon.

Douglas MacArthur

Taken in Australia in 1943, when MacArthur was a four-star general, with the stars aligned on his shirt collar. When he was made a five-star General of the Army two years later, the picture was altered to show his new rank in the pentagon-shaped orientation. This is his most-widely distributed picture, and may have been his favorite photo of himself.

Table of Contents

Photo Credits

Cover: Jim (US Army Major James) and Virginia Moynahan, with borrowed jeep at a-building "Area X" housing project, Yokohama, May 1948. Photo courtesy of Jay Moynahan.

MacArthur: MacArthur Memorial, Norfolk, VA

Yokohama views: housing projects, aerials, building exteriors and interiors: Department of Defense Dependents Schools (DoDDS), courtesy of Joe Ross.

Toyota vehicles: Stars and Stripes newspaper.

Miscellaneous aerials and other views of Yokohama and Tokyo, Dependents Guide to Japan booklet: US Army Center of Military History, Washington, DC.

Certain personal pictures of family, friends and tourist sites: Colonel James Lamont and yours truly.

Introduction: Citizen MacArthur

Once upon a time...not all that long ago, but definitely in a land far, far away...a fairly large cohort of Americans--men, women and children of all ages--did nearly everything right! And because they did, the world's consumer marketplace would be changed dramatically; if not forever-and-ever, at least for the foreseeable future.

I was a *very* minor part of this unique undertaking at a very young age, so at the time was wholly unaware of the impact we few were making. But neither was anyone else then cognizant we were laying the foundation for some significant future. Nor is what we accomplished recognized to this day. Still, perceiving and publicizing what we did, and why and how, had to begin somewhere, and for me it was at a family gathering a few years ago.

My wife and I had an out-of-town nephew and his wife to our suburban Chicago home for dinner. The couple were in the area to visit with members of her family, so when time came for them to join us, conversation naturally turned to family matters and experiences.

At one point, attention focused on me when I revealed that I had lived in Japan with my parents in 1949 and -50, when I was 10- and 11 years old, during the post-World War II occupation of the conquered Axis power. When our nephew asked what life was like for us there, I began my reply by offhandedly name-dropping that I had once played musical chairs with Douglas MacArthur, then sat smugly back to await a request for details about how this happenstance came about. But imagine my chagrin when, instead of further querying me about our time in Japan, our nephew's wife looked questioningly around the table, then asked, "Who was Douglas MacArthur?"

The rest of us squirmed uncomfortably. For my part, I sifted through my mental resources on how to explain to this bright, college-educated young lady that she had just expressed ignorance about not just one of the most preeminent figures of the twentieth century, but someone whose triumphs and missteps alike reverberate in today's world. I juggled how to describe such a multi-faceted, imperious, far-reaching (and often over-reaching) figure as MacArthur. Among many other accomplishments, he is the most-decorated figure, military or

1

otherwise, in American history, a battlefield commander and statesman who had been anointed the sole administrator of the victorious Allies' occupation of defeated Japan, which surrender in August 1945 concluded the Second World War.

MacArthur had no specific orders how to conduct the occupation other than to ensure that Japan honor the surrender terms imposed upon the ravaged nation. But he went much further: he took it upon himself to lead a resurrection of the devastated country. In just half a decade, MacArthur orchestrated the raising of Japan from the literal ashes of its defeat and placed it firmly on a par with Western Civilization, a herculean task he performed in so unprecedented and magnanimous a fashion that he came to be revered as a near-deity by the very people of whose conquest he was in large measure responsible.

Then in addition to outlining MacArthur and all he had been and done and was (and still is), I also felt compelled to explain what I was doing in the company of such an epic person in the first place, which seemed only fair given that I had brought the general into the dinner table conversation in the way I did. And this obligation in turn required that I explain how and why this five-star General of the Army came this particular afternoon in 1949 to be playing a child's game with a gaggle of squirmy grade-school kids--and cavorting so inside the United States embassy in Tokyo, of all places.

I handled the challenges by framing MacArthur and his accomplishments with respect to the occupation in a context I felt our young, affluent guests, who were just starting a family, could readily comprehend and relate to: their needs and keen passions for many and varied consumer goods. So I drew on what little I knew at the time about how the occupation helped lay the (admittedly rudimentary) foundation for today's consumer societies, and blurted outright that MacArthur was in large measure responsible for the make of cars they might be driving and the television set brands they all but surely watched.

I had no sooner spoken these words that I got blank stares from our guests. So it came to pass that the balance of the evening was devoted to my relating: a) what MacArthur did to justify my claim that the occupation and his guidance of it is somehow responsible for the current worldwide plethora of Toyotas and Toshibas, Sonys and Samsungs; b) how and why I became a part of all this; c) what life was like for our family and other American households in Japan at such a time, when the country still lay in ruins; and with no one, not even MacArthur, daring to foretell the influential role the isolated island nation would begin to assume on the world's consumer stage a scant two decades after its humiliating defeat.

Being bright and curious, the young couple of course had questions as I told them of life in the devastated Japan of that time. And while I could answer most of their inquiries, one stumped me: if American families in Japan during the occupation have had such a great and lasting impact on today's consumer-oriented societies, how come we've never heard of their contributions? Or even heard of American families being in Japan at the time? It was only long after that evening, while I was researching this book (an endeavor that included gathering background support for my own childhood memories) that I came upon, if not definitive answers to the young couple's question, at least what I consider plausible explanations for my contentions.

A principal reason no one knows of the role American families performed in the Occupation of Japan--and their input, however oblique, to present-day consumerism--is that they were never given a stated mission to do anything extraordinary. Or to do much of anything specific, for that matter. And in the absence of such a written order or directive or memoranda or what-have-you, there was never any record for historians and scholars to seize upon as evidence that the families either achieved or failed to attain some specific goal.

Scores of books have been published about the occupation, but none of the well-known, widely-published texts delve into the families' presence, involvement in and contributions to the occupation, or even bother to mention the families. Some works that do detail family life there were published at the time and so are long forgotten; or are self-published diaries, compilations of letters home, and academic examinations that never reached a general audience. I cite

3

and quote from some of these works herein where the authors' experiences were outside my own and thus add to my story.

It's also helpful to know the definition of "families" as used in the context of the occupation. Almost all the American families in occupied Japan were *military* families, and most of these were army husbands with their wives and children. I was in this group; my father was a regular army colonel, a West Point graduate and veteran of the European war. The point is that military personnel and their families alike are accustomed to following orders unquestioningly--and the orders, regulations and directives with respect to living in occupied Japan mentioned virtually *nothing* with regard to what we could and could not do.

There weren't even any cautions with respect to relations with the all-too-recent enemy. Just the reverse, in fact: we were *encouraged* to interact freely with the Japanese. And did! The most dire warning I remember from the time, and came across again in my research, wasn't to be wary of resentful, insurrection-bent war veterans and the like (although they were around), but a caution that the Japanese drive on the left side of the road.

The families weren't even called upon to put the American way of life on display. While a major goal of the occupation was to democratize Japan (or, more accurately, re-acquaint the Japanese with the democratic principles they had experimented with earlier in the twentieth century), there were no orders--nor even suggestions, for that matter--about overtly flaunting the United States' democratic traditions for the Japanese to observe and emulate. Things just happened that way naturally. We pretty much tried to live as we had back home, and while we certainly had our faults, jingoism included, they apparently weren't obnoxious enough to dissuade the locals from resurrecting democracy. By-and-large we just were ourselves, and in the ruins of immediate postwar Japan, being "ourselves" meant blending into the rubble-scape as best we could, asking little and giving where we could.

The vast majority of families simply tried to run their households as they had back home. This basic desire was augmented by the war having just ended, and during the conflict there had been numerous, sometimes onerous rationings and other privations. War production priorities meant no new cars for sale, and even if there had been, you couldn't drive too far or too often due to gasoline rationing. Food and other basic household staples were either rationed or hard to come by, so when the war ended and normal production of consumer goods resumed, there was a rush to acquire what had for the previous half-decade been largely unavailable.

We families in Japan were no different from any back home; we wanted long-suppressed goodies, and we wanted them *now*! Thing is, shipping restrictions made even taken-for-granted necessities difficult to obtain; priorities were instead given to supplies the Japanese desperately needed. So occupation administrators turned to slowly recovering Japanese industries and contracted with them, plus makeshift cottage industries, to provide American households with appliances, tools and utensils familiar to Americans--but more often than not, wholly *un*familiar to the Japanese.

But the natives learned quickly what we wanted and needed! The occupation lasted six and one-half years, from the late summer of 1945 to the spring of 1952--and the families were present in varying yet growing numbers for all but the first nine months of that period. And during that time, in many ways and varying degrees, the men, women and children who came to Japan and lived openly in the process provided the conquered people an unprecedented look deep inside America's consumer soul.

Japanese worked for us and provided to us in myriad ways, certain of which could be considered menial and even demeaning; and later accounts about the occupation have vilified us for this aspect of our presence. True enough and fair enough. But in the process, the Japanese sold us their cameras and radios and cookers and lighting fixtures even as they clerked in the very exchanges that carried such items. As servants in our homes and clubs, they learned to operate coffee makers and ovens and pop-up toasters and food mixers, but they also learned how to manufacture and market those very same and many other common American household gadgets and appliances. And of course, they serviced American-made automobiles, in the process becoming familiar with our driving tastes and habits.

MacArthur oversaw all this. But not overtly. To the occupation forces under his command--soldiers, sailors and civilians alike; American and representing the other victorious Allies--he was the Supreme Commander Allied Powers, his official title, abbreviated simply as SCAP. To the families, however, he was also the epitome of another authority figure: *paterfamilias.*

Looking back, he really was a father figure, although I'm not sure many of us, even the adults who worked for him, realized the connection at the time. Yet everyone followed his examples! MacArthur set the standards by his personal behavior as much as by the orders he issued and the remarks and speeches he made for the historical record. Total authority in all ways to all things, whether expressed openly or not. His very demeanor said it all, the very standard of the autocrat from an earlier age he very much was. And acted. And likely relished being.

I feel he was something else as well: a closet romantic. He in many ways yearned for the past, specifically his own, very young boyhood in Arizona and New Mexico in the 1880s, decades before the two territories became states, when Native Americans could still be hostile. He showed this aspect of his character is subtle ways, among them being a devoted fan of Western movies. He also reveals these longings in his own autobiography: *Reminiscences*, hand-written and published shortly before he died in 1964. An early chapter in the book has several pages devoted to his primal youth on what was still the American frontier, a long ago experience he writes about using caressing words, as if wistfully recalling a more peaceful and accommodating time.

I can empathize with MacArthur here. We're both "army brats," products of upbringing in a military atmosphere. We were both born on army posts long given over to other uses: he in a fort that would later become Little Rock, Arkansas, I in the Presidio of San Francisco that overlooks the Golden Gate Bridge, once the headquarters of the entire Pacific army, now a national park. We both moved around a lot before becoming adults; we both lived in exotic locales at impressionable ages; we both had career army officer fathers who were often gone from home for long periods of time, leaving us with a single older sibling and a firm and resolute, if also at times overly-indulgent and -protective mother; we both had experiences most other children never shared or could envision. And so we sometimes can get very nostalgic about our unusual, often unique childhood experiences.

I therefore believe that MacArthur had and held closely and privately a "Rosebud." The reference is to the central theme of legendary film maker Orson Welles' masterpiece, *Citizen Kane*, which pivots on the search for whatever it was in Kane's background that caused him to mutter the word "Rosebud..." at the moment he died. The answer, revealed only at the film's end, was a reference to a childhood treasure. I feel that MacArthur's "Rosebud" was not to a single object, but rather a way of life the general once lived, cherished and wished for the Japanese to follow as an example of how to rebuild their shattered lives and country. And it would seem he got his wish.

I cannot cite definitive proof of my assertion; I'm neither a historian nor a scholar. Furthermore, I viewed Japan through a child's eyes, so my contentions could be faulted on the grounds that I lacked the experience and sophistication to weigh judgments and observations properly. And in addition, MacArthur himself had little to say or write about the matter of what influence we families may have had. But he did express this opinion on occasion, and his few words appear to link what I believe he meant the families to contribute with actual achieved goals.

Chapter 1: A Man and a Mission

In the late summer of 1964, the first rumblings of a momentous, earthshaking event occurred in Japan that would alter the course of the world's economies, changing consumer buying habits for the decades to come. The venue for this milestone was the Summer Olympic Games, held in Tokyo that year, and the events plus all the ancillary excitement that accompanies an Olympics served as a showcase for what amounted to a coming out party for Japan. Here for the first time since its defeat in World War II, Japan's wholly new industrial prowess, with all of its diversity, ingenuity and inventiveness, was put on display for the world at large to gaze upon, marvel over, and ultimately consume ravenously.

The tidal waves of Japanese consumer products did not well up instantly in the wake of those Olympics, cascading over world markets and washing away competitors like some economic tsunami. While Japanese skill in optics, demonstrated in their cameras and lenses, had been known and coveted since the 1920s, a decade would pass until the oil embargo crises of the 1970s first brought wide attention to their reliable, gasoline-sipping automobiles.

And it would take several more years and the advent of the personal computer age in the early 1980s before their innovations in consumer electronics, led by television sets, began to be fully appreciated. Altogether, almost twenty years would pass before Japan's effect upon consumer buying habits would become fully realized--coincidentally, about the same amount of time it took the country to arise from the ashes of its defeat and despair at war's end to the takeoff stage it displayed at those Tokyo Olympics.

The crucible for Japan's re-emergence upon the world stage was the six-and-a-half-year postwar occupation of the island nation by the victorious World War II Allies who had battled Japan in that theater of the conflict. The occupation lasted from September 1945 to April 1952, and is most famous and remembered for having democratized Japan, exemplified in the country's constitution, which was ratified overwhelmingly in a national referendum in September 1947--a scant two years following war's end. For better or worse, the occupation is also cited--and criticized--for the Americanization of Japan, to the extent that the Japanese adopted generally Western but specifically American cultural icons such as fashions and styles, modes of living, and business practices.

No such imprint was made upon defeated Nazi Germany during its concurrent occupation, for the reason that the two tenancies were quite different in character and composition. The occupation of Germany was a truly joint, balance-of-powers venture by the European Theater's four victorious Allies: the United States, Great Britain, France and the Soviet Union, each with its own sector. Under this arrangement, any American influences were diluted in the multinational political and cultural mishmash that inundated postwar Germany.

The occupation of Japan, on the other hand, while officially and ostensibly a collective Allied endeavor, was overwhelmingly an American-dominated venture, a *de facto* if not *de jure* undertaking. This preeminence threw wide the door for unimpeded introduction of all manner of American character traits, from cultural quirks to consumer buying habits to home- and private-life customs and idiosyncracies, certain of which the Japanese surely resented and found offensive and intrusive, but all of which left indelible marks to some degree or other.

The long-term, contrasting effects of the two postwar occupations can be glimpsed in Germany and Japan to this day, most visibly in the respective major metropolitan areas. Even excepting the presence of such ubiquitous American franchise outlets as KFC (more popular in Japan than McDonalds), Neiman-Marcus and other restaurant chains and general and specialty merchandisers, Japanese cities reflect far more American influences than do corresponding German metropolises. Downtown Tokyo, Osaka and Yokohama especially have both a look and persona--a fast-paced, buttoned-down, dark-suit-and-tie bustle--that is far more evocative of New York, San Francisco or Chicago than can be discerned in present-day Berlin, Frankfurt, Bonn--or any other European city, for that matter.

It almost didn't happen that way. As originally conceived by the Allies, the Occupation of Japan would have had scant if any American influence. Under one proposal, the country, or at least a significant portion of it, would have more resembled communist East Germany than any Western model. And if that had transpired, the world today-- the consumer marketplace especially--would be vastly different than what developed.

This near-divergence of the occupation occurred at the Yalta Conference in February 1945. The main purpose of the meeting was to finalize the impending four-power Allied division and occupation of postwar Germany. But President Franklin D. Roosevelt also wanted a commitment from Soviet Union leader Josef Stalin to enter the Pacific war; and FDR was willing, anxious even, to grant Stalin a piece of Japan in return for Russian help in the Far East.

In a private meeting with Stalin, Roosevelt specifically offered the Soviet dictator the Kurile Islands and the southern half of Sakhalin Island (Russia already held the northern half), entities Japan had held as prizes of their victory in the Russo-Japanese war forty years earlier.[1] A quadripartite occupation of Japan that would involve China and Great Britain in addition to America and the USSR also was allegedly discussed, but nothing was committed to paper. Under this scheme, Stalin would have gotten the northern Japanese home island of Hokkaido in addition to return of the aforesaid islands as a price for entering the war against Japan; China would be given the southern portion of the main island of Honshu, plus Kyushu, Shikoku and Okinawa; and the US and Britain would have split what was left of the main island of Honshu.[2] In any event, had a postwar Occupation of Japan been implemented along the lines of that done for postwar Germany, it is doubtful that American influence would have been as profound as it became.

But the occupation idea introduced at Yalta never advanced. Instead, a plan evolved for a joint postwar Occupation of Japan

---

[1] John Toland, *The Rising Sun*, Vol. 2, Chapter 25, "Our Golden Opportunity," pp. 787-'90.

[2] *The Rising Sun*, Vol. 2, Chapter 37, "The Voice of the Crane," p. 1066.

consisting solely of the principal Allies who had from the beginning fought the war in the Pacific Theater: the United States, British Commonwealth nations engaged in that region (Great Britain, Australia, New Zealand and India), and China. Several factors then coalesced to arrive at the occupation being an America-dominated enterprise, beginning with the fact that the United States had almost single-handedly won the war against Japan.

The Central Pacific Campaign especially was a wholly American venture, as was Midway and the encounters in the Aleutian Island chain stretching westward from Alaska. The same was nearly true for the Southwest Pacific Campaign. There, a multi-national effort consisted of sea, air and ground forces from the United States, Australia, New Zealand, the Netherlands and New Guinea, but it was under American command, and American personnel and materiel dominated. Geography also played a major role in enabling the United States-favored outcome. The four-power occupation of Germany was facilitated by that country's easily-accessed, endo-continent locale; Japan, on the other hand, is an isolated archipelago.

Finally, of all the Allies, America alone still had the manpower, logistical means, economic wherewithal and backup resources to field a *de facto* national police force--all by itself if need be--to ensure that Japan would abide by the surrender terms. India, Australia and New Zealand had no neo-colonial ambitions whatsoever, but did send token troop contingents, who were garrisoned on the island of Shikoku and western Honshu. Great Britain had more pressing matters at home, notably rebuilding wartime destruction and restoring critically depleted shortages, but did send a substantial occupying force, which at its peak in 1947 totaled some fifty-six thousand troops plus dependents. The British contingent was responsible for much of southwestern Honshu--including, significantly and symbolically, the Hiroshima Prefecture.[3] China withdrew altogether from any occupation obligation. The country was entangled in a civil war, which had gone on even during the near-decade Japan had occupied a

---

[3] A prefecture is somewhat like an American state, but different in that it is an incorporated entity, thus has more autonomous powers.

sizeable portion of the land, and so was altogether too war-ravaged to offer any assistance.

Stalin briefly threatened to send troops to join the occupation, but recanted when informed through an emissary that Moscow would have no decision-making authority; and that the troops, along with the other Allied military forces, would be strictly under American command. This acquiescence was the only occasion during the World War II era that Stalin conceded to an American ultimatum. He had some two million troops massed in the region, which he used to attack the few remaining Japanese forces in Manchuria after the Soviet Union formally declared war against Japan on August 8, 1945, exactly one week before Japan surrendered. But he lacked the naval power in the Pacific region to force the issue. Besides, Stalin already had and was busily subjugating the prize he coveted most: Eastern Europe, plus half of Austria and the northeastern third of Germany. (Soviet forces did, however, occupy North Korea--and the United States Army South Korea as a buffer against that threat--during the immediate postwar period.)

Then there was the matter--and manner--of the man who had so brusquely rebuffed Stalin through the emissary: General of the Army Douglas MacArthur, leader of the Allied victory in the southwest corner of the Pacific Theater. In April 1945, just days before he died, President Franklin Roosevelt tapped MacArthur to command what seemed at the time an unavoidable invasion of Japan. Then at the Potsdam Conference in late July, with Harry Truman now president but Japan's surrender still somewhat in doubt, it was agreed among all the Allies that MacArthur should head the occupation.

Truman made this decision official on August fifteenth, the very day Japan did surrender, when he formally anointed MacArthur with the title Supreme Commander Allied Powers--SCAP. MacArthur used this authority, which gave him total power over every aspect of the occupation, to brush aside Stalin's threatened intrusion. (Truman actually had designated MacArthur SCAP at least three days before Japan surrendered, on or about August twelfth. This is known because China's leader, Generalissimo Chiang Kai-Shek, sent MacArthur a congratulatory wire dated August thirteenth.)

Like the occupation composite itself, the naming of MacArthur to be its overseer also almost didn't happen. Earlier that year, powerful interests in Washington and elsewhere felt that Fleet Admiral Chester Nimitz, Commander of the Central Pacific Campaign, should head the occupation by virtue of the Pacific Theater's internal boundaries, which placed Nimitz's area of responsibility squarely between Japan and the upper edge of MacArthur's sector, which halted just north of the Philippines.

One of those powerful interests was Admiral of the Fleet Ernest King, Chief of Naval Operations, who personally disliked MacArthur and had vowed to keep the general's area of influence far from Japan. Brigadier General Bonner Fellers, MacArthur's Chief of Psychological Operations, writing in a diary, cited King as expressing his intention to keep MacArthur "...south of the Equator."[4] When MacArthur vigorously opposed the Nimitz nod, one of the admiral's aides fired off an exasperation-laden message to the general that ticked off in bullet points why his naval boss should be in charge of the occupation, then concluded with a sarcastic reference to the principal transportation mode (meaning the United States Navy) used to support MacArthur's campaigns: "Who do you think got you there?"[5]

But in the end, the Joint Chiefs of Staff and the Allies together decided that only a large occupying army could guarantee that Japan would abide by the surrender terms. Nimitz himself agreed; he did not have such a land-based force, just his six triumphant but also exhausted US Marine Corps divisions, numbering barely one hundred thousand men. MacArthur, by contrast, had two full armies totaling more than half a million men under his immediate command, plus more who had been assembled back on the west coast of the United States in anticipation of having to invade Japan.

---

[4] MacArthur Memorial Library, RG-44, Papers of Brig. Gen. Bonner Fellers.

[5] MacArthur Memorial Library, RG-3, Records of Headquarters, Southwest Pacific Area (SWPA), 1942-1945.

Roosevelt's death certainly sealed the deal in MacArthur's favor. Some historians have opined that had Roosevelt lived, Nimitz may have been named to head up the occupation in any event: first because FDR was such a stalwart navy supporter that his wartime acronymic code pseudonym was "SK" for "Sailor King;" and second because he also otherwise disliked, distrusted and feared MacArthur on a personal level. Truman likewise was no fan of MacArthur's on a personal level (he some years later regretted giving MacArthur so much authority), but otherwise was very much a pragmatist.

MacArthur took the SCAP title, its honor and implied responsibilities very literally and made of it--and himself--a unique position in history: never before nor since has any American held such absolute power over another foreign nation. For nearly six years, from Japan's surrender until April 1951, when Truman fired the general for insubordination over his conduct of the Korean War and ordered him home, MacArthur ruled Japan like a benevolent despot: he literally had life-and-death control over every Japanese citizen, members of the occupation, and visitors.

It is one of history's greatest ironies that principal credit for the occupation's stupendous success went to the very same man who had in large part directed the conquest of the far-flung empire, and would have led an invasion of the country's home islands had the Japanese not surrendered. In managing the occupation in the way he did, MacArthur also became one of history's greatest anomalies: a conqueror who treated his vanquished foe munificently, then directed its recovery. Even MacArthur's detractors admit that he prevented Japan from isolating itself from other nations, as it had done for much of its history, or turning westward and falling under the communist influence then engulfing mainland Asia. He is esteemed today more for democratizing Japan and directing the country's resurgence than for his considerable military achievements in both world wars and the Korean conflict--and he wanted it that way.

There was no comparable position or person in postwar Germany, not from any of the four occupying Allies. General of the Army Dwight Eisenhower, who had directed the conquest of the Nazi regime from the European western front, was, in power and position, akin to

MacArthur only in the similarity of their titles: the future president was named Supreme Commander Allied Forces, SCAF--but that designation gave him command over the American, French and British *military* contingents only; separate military governors presided over the occupation zones themselves.

At the outset of the occupation of Germany, Eisenhower, in addition to his SCAF post, was also the first military governor of the American Zone of Occupation, which included most of west central and southern Germany plus the northern port cities Bremen and Bremerhaven--but that was as close as he would come to equilibrium with MacArthur in terms of territory overseen and people governed. When Eisenhower was recalled home in December 1945 to become the army's new Chief of Staff, replacing General George C. Marshall who had moved up to become Chairman of the Joint Chiefs of Staff, Lieutenant General Lucius Clay became both commander of the American Seventh Army *and* military governor of the American sector. But Clay never led all the Allied forces, just the American army. The Supreme Commander designation in Europe vanished with Eisenhower's return to Washington.

Matters were wholly different on the other side of the world. While SCAP's organization included an American-dominated military government that had jurisdiction over Japanese affairs, there were no individual military governors presiding over the prefectures. Allied military overseers weren't needed on local levels, because Japanese prefecture and municipal governmental entities had emerged intact from the ravages of war, and thus were able to perform public service functions, including especially municipal police and court duties. Their ability to perform these responsibilities in traditional fashions therefore relieved occupation forces of civic chores.

By contrast, Nazi government philosophy and structure had permeated every aspect of German life, all the way down to the most seemingly insignificant *burgermeister*, so all German governmental units had to be rebuilt from scratch. While this was going on in Germany, Japanese civil affairs, now bolstered with their new democracy, simply kept functioning as if nothing untoward had only recently occurred, which of course relieved the SCAP bureaucracy of the day-to-day niggling burden of governmental responsibilities, which in turn left MacArthur free to focus upon raising up Japan Phoenix-like from the literal ashes of its destruction in a manner pretty much of his own choosing.

And that's exactly what he did! From organization to outcome, virtually everything about the occupation of Japan was unprecedented, beginning with the formal relationship between MacArthur and President Truman. The chain-of-command from any American military commanding officer to the commander-in-chief normally would pass upwards through military channels, first to the army's chief of staff, then perhaps the Joint Chiefs of Staff as a whole, and finally even the relevant cabinet secretary before reaching the president's desk. In Eisenhower's SCAF situation, that was how the system worked: Ike's immediate superior was General Marshall, and all SCAF official business went first to him.

That procedure wasn't followed on the other side of the world. MacArthur, acting as SCAP and the man himself, didn't contend with any intermediaries; he reported directly--and only--to Truman. The president, for his part, didn't so much issue MacArthur specific must-do orders as provide him interpretable guidelines based upon work done elsewhere. Yet the nature and tenor of the directions smack of the thirty-third president's feisty, get-it-done-and-never-mind-the-consequences, character. Most notably, there is strong evidence that Truman was so concerned about the four-power partitioning of Germany that he took pains to see to it that no similar fate would befall the other major defeated Axis power, that the United States would manage the occupation of Japan pretty much as it saw fit.

The basis for this American prerogative was the Allies' four-power joint agreement on the pending occupation of Japan. The leaders of the victorious Allied nations in the war against Nazi Germany met in the German village of Potsdam from mid-July until early August 1945 to hammer out an arrangement on the occupation of defeated Germany, which became known as the Potsdam Agreement.

That done, the meeting turned its attention to yet-to-surrender Japan, and issued the Potsdam Declaration. This document reiterated the Allies' demand for unconditional surrender, specified to Japan the surrender and disarmament terms the victors insisted upon, outlined how the Allies were to conduct the occupation and treat the former enemy, and encouraged introduction of democratic principles in a broad sense. Truman included the declaration in a general policy communiqué he forwarded to MacArthur right after Japan surrendered, and this action with the declaration as the principal inclusion has been cited as the impetus and authority MacArthur used as his basis for managing the occupation and democratizing Japan.

Well, not quite. As matters turned out, the Potsdam Declaration would *not* be the final word about the occupation. At least not where the Truman White House was concerned. Specifically, United States' hegemony over the occupation would be firmly implanted, and democratic characteristics the United States expected Japan to adopt would be expanded and delineated. As a result, while history rightfully credits the Potsdam Declaration as being the *official* source and authority for MacArthur's subsequent actions, the Truman administration's audacious contributions settled the issue about which of the victorious Allies would be in charge, bolstered MacArthur's authority, and also likely emboldened the general to push those authoritative responsibilities to their maximum limits.

Truman's determination to forge the occupation on strictly American terms is shown in a news release that accompanied a press conference the president held on September 22, 1945. The key element of that release stated, in no uncertain terms:

> *The statement of intentions contained in the Potsdam Declaration will be given full effect. It will not be given effect, however, because we consider ourselves bound in a contractual relationship with Japan as a result of that document. It will be respected and given effect because the Potsdam Declaration forms a part of our policy stated in good faith with relation*

> *to Japan and with relation to peace and*
> *security in the Far East.*
>
> – Harry S Truman Library:
> President's Secretary's Files>Foreign Affairs>Japan

MacArthur wasted little time taking care of any ambiguity with respect to the democracy question. In mid-October, barely a month after Japan's surrender, he interpreted the Potsdam Declaration as a commandment and declared democracy by fiat. He literally *ordered* the country to adopt the hallmark political feature of Western Civilization, simultaneously released a list of sweeping political and social reforms, then dispatched hundreds of Japanese-speaking civil affairs teams throughout the island nation to teach people everywhere what democracy, American style, was all about.

In response, the Japanese took to their new form of government near-instantly. By Christmas of that year, the Japanese Diet had formally adopted democracy and created a new word for it in their vocabulary, *Minshushugi* ("the way of democracy"); while on the street, ordinary citizens had their own new word for their nascent political system: "demokrashi."[6]

Japan's eye-blink conversion to democracy, as dramatically earth-shaking as it was, was but one element, albeit the basic essential one, that contributed to the country's eventual Americanization. Other, often very divergent factors poured into the mix that lay the foundation for today's market where Americans (and indeed the free world at large) drive more Toyotas than Volkswagens, watch television on Toshiba or Panasonic and not Grundig sets, and take pictures with Nikons and Canons and not Leicas. Involved were ancient mysticisms, modern fears, the postwar communist threat, a huge outpouring of charitable good will, a grand ambition that failed--and not least of all, MacArthur's own instincts, prejudices, fears, concerns, beliefs...even his boyhood memories. And it all began with the fortuitous and timely confluence of three powerful factors, a veritable "perfect storm" of harmonic coincidences: Japan's existing familiarity and experience

---

[6] William Manchester, *American Caesar*, Chapter VIII

with democratic principles and ideals, MacArthur's personal character and demeanor, and the Japanese national character.

Japan had been feudal in nature for most of its history, and while trade had begun with the Portuguese in the sixteenth century and the Dutch in the seventeenth, the Japanese didn't begin to fully accept Western nations' political thought along with their goods until after the arrival of United States Navy Commodore Matthew Perry in 1854. The Treaty of *Kanagawa*, named for the tip of the prefecture where Perry had landed and did business, and which capital is Yokohama, was signed that same year. The agreement specifically opened Japan to trade and exchange of ideas, including democratic principles, with the United States.

Twenty-four years later, the *Meiji* regime (1868-1912) even fashioned a constitution of sorts that delineated certain individual liberties and freedom of assembly, but which otherwise had more in common with England's thirteenth century Magna Carta than any modern, democratic constitution. Most especially, the Meiji creation failed to provide the grass roots individual freedoms, property ownership rights, and comprehensive legal protections that encourage the rise of a middle class, without which wide distribution of wealth, the economic hallmark of any true democracy, cannot develop and flourish.

Democratic principles were implemented more universally following the death of the last Meiji emperor in 1912. The succeeding *Taishō* regime soon found itself governing one of the world's most economically sound, respected and technologically advanced nations by the time World War I ended in 1918, principally because the regime had chosen not to engage materially in the conflict that otherwise was so destructive to all its participants, winners and losers alike.

That same year, Hara Takashi, a protégé of a deposed prime minister, became the first commoner to be named prime minister, and he expanded all manner of democratic practices that had already been gathering steam under the Meiji regime. These hallmarks of democracy included more universal suffrage, some women's rights, new election laws and redistricting, establishment of labor unions, and tolerance of formation of a broad range of political parties–including a nascent communist party, which active, agitating presence and appeal would dramatically affect MacArthur's policies and practices a quarter-century later.

Unfortunately for Japan and successive history, Hara[7] was assassinated in 1921--ironically, given the democratic practices he had implemented and encouraged, by a disgruntled railway worker. Democratic policies were weakened but continued to be practiced following Hara's death, only to be brutally crushed, along with all other forms of dissent, communism of course included, by the *shoguns* who regained power under the succeeding Shōwa regime of Hirohito, who became emperor on Christmas Day 1926 and ruled until his death in 1989.

Thus when the American army entered Japan in the late summer of 1945, it found a country that had thrown aside all traces of democracy and reverted to vestiges of its feudal past: real power in the hands of regional oligarchs, the shoguns, rather than the central government in Tokyo, farmers bound to rural landlords in the manner of medieval serfs, and a people conditioned to rigid, unquestioning, top-down obedience of authority.

Whether MacArthur knew all this and more about Japan's history and people is, after all these years, still subject to debate. Historians and his biographers alike disagree on how much scholarly knowledge he held about Japan, or, conversely, how much he relied upon instinct, advice of others, and just plain good luck in making his decisions.

To cite two examples of this extreme: William Manchester, writing in *American Caesar*, contends that MacArthur had been an ardent, even voracious student of Japanese history, culture and people since his first, brief visit there in 1905-'06, and as a result likely knew more about the country than any other Occidental layman or scholar at the time. On the other hand, John Dower, author of the Pulitzer Prize-winning *Embracing Defeat*, dismisses such assertions, claiming that MacArthur knew little about Japan beyond what he read about in dispatches or heard in briefings.

---

[7] Surnames are listed first in Japanese.

James Zobel, since 1993 the chief archivist at the MacArthur Memorial in Norfolk, Virginia, often worked closely with the general's widow, Jean, and so knew the family well. He says, "The truth lies somewhere in between." MacArthur's personal library, which is shelved in the Jean MacArthur Research Center across a courtyard from the Memorial Museum, unfortunately offers few clues. The hugely extensive and varied collection, some five thousand volumes, represents only those tomes MacArthur acquired *after* he was forced to flee the Philippines in early 1942; the invading Japanese army burned his original library when it sacked his Manila headquarters. Some two score books about Japan are included in the post-escape library, indicating MacArthur certainly knew *something* about the country before becoming its overseer, but perhaps not as much as he may have led others to believe.

In any event, whether intuitively or with certain prior knowledge, MacArthur seemed to know beforehand that the surest way to get the people to accept democracy was to parlay their nature with his own and simply declare democracy to be the new law of the land. That pairing was seamless because MacArthur and the Japanese were a natural fit, a casting director's dream. The Japanese, having for centuries literally and figuratively bowed to autocratic individuals, instantly recognized MacArthur's no-nonsense, authoritarian persona, and so accepted his decree unquestioningly.

For his part, MacArthur didn't have to role-play an autocrat because he already was one: in tone and visually, whether speaking or writing, a throwback to the Edwardian Era, a natural aristocrat who looked and acted the part. Historians have noted that MacArthur's haughty, overbearing manner was perfect for the time, the place, and the people; that a less overtly patrician figure--the folksy Eisenhower, for example--could never have commanded the universal respect, admiration, devotion, and eventually literal worship among the Japanese that MacArthur attained just by being his supercilious self.

All manner of opinions, from scholarly to streetwise, have been used to portray MacArthur's unique relationship with the Oriental people over whom he had total dominion. Perhaps no one captured the accord (and MacArthur's nature) more succinctly than did Lorena

Treadway, who worked in the SCAP office from early 1946 until just weeks before Truman fired the general. In a self-published compilation of letters she had mailed home, and memoirs of her time in Japan, *By the Grace of God and MacArthur: A Department of the Army Civilian in Occupied Japan*, she wrote, "The Japanese and General MacArthur have a symbiotic relationship: they adore him, and he loves to be adored."

The third and final ingredient in the democratization success formula was provided by Japan's overwhelming national characteristic: homogeneity. Japan is the most homogeneous of major, industrial nations; there simply is little cultural or ethnic diversity there--and in 1945, with the sole exceptions of a small Chinese community in Yokohama and a tiny enclave of Dutch traders and fishers on the island of Deshima in Nagasaki Bay on Kyushu, both still extant, there was virtually none. This remarkable uniformity of character made (and may still make) the entire population susceptible to sudden, unpredictable, and highly traumatic mood swings, a *de facto* national schizophrenia of various personalities, each with its own term.

The Japanese of the time experienced *four* of these engulfing traumas. All occurred within the two decades that bracketed the war years, and each was distinct: at one extreme, riling up a vicious, conquering people; at the other, enabling a docile, conquered people.[8]

In the 1930s, the shoguns whipped the population into a hyper-aggressive, ultra-nationalistic and -racist frenzy called *zangyaku-sei* (zang-guy-yah-koo-say),, cited as the violent emotion that drove Japan to wage war, and the underlying psychological reason Japanese soldiers were so contemptuous of, and unmercifully brutal to, the peoples they conquered and prisoners of war they held. This trait prevailed into the spring of 1945, when the horrendous death and destruction raining down upon Japan began to cast a pall over the savage spirit, fomenting a nationwide malaise termed *ensei* (en-say), meaning literally a "weariness of living." The country plunged further into ensei after the two atomic bombs were dropped, yet more

---

[8] Manchester, *American Caesar*, "Last Post," p. 465.

conventional bombs rained down, the threat of invasion from both the United States *and* the Soviet Union heightened, and there was even a call for national suicide.

All these factors combined to cause Japan finally to surrender on August fifteenth. That same day, Hirohito himself instigated the third shift in the national mood--but this time, to one that enabled the occupation to proceed unhindered: *shikata ga nai* (she-kah-tah-gah-nye), loosely translated as acceptance of fate, a resignation to the way things are and will be. This deeply pessimistic mind-set was caused by the emperor making a radio address to his subjects at home and, via shortwave radio, Japan's few remaining armed forces abroad. Reception was poor, and he spoke in an ancient dialect that few modern Japanese understood. Still, that the emperor addressed the populace at all was unprecedented. Since earliest Japanese history, the *mikado* had been worshiped as a deity, and in the 1930s, the Japanese were told that they were going to war because of the emperor's divine inspiration.

Now in that dismal summer, Hirohito sealed his nation's fate, first by acknowledging that he was not a god after all, then by uttering the oft-quoted words that are cited for bringing on shikata ga nai: "We have resolved to endure the unendurable, and suffer what is insufferable." When the American army came ashore less than two weeks later, it met no resistance in large part because shikata ga nai had become firmly ingrained.[9] It would not be a stretch to state that Hirohito's publicly-expressed repudiation of his divinity, together with his admonition that the country accept defeat and occupation gracefully, smoothed the way for acceptance of American presence and influence more so than any other single factor, MacArthur's presence, character and demeanor included.

MacArthur may or may not have been aware of the underlying reason for this abysmal state. What he and all the other American

---

[9] Certain Japanese forces resolved to fight on. One air force commander led a final airborne suicide attack that disappeared, but otherwise did no damage. Toland, *The Rising Sun*, Vol. 2, Chap. 37, "The Voice of the Crane," pp. 1057-'58.

soldiers could easily discern, in the coastal areas at least, was that the country was a bombed-out, blackened mess occupied by a wretchedly depressed people who were not at all disposed to resisting the invaders. It has also been opined that Japanese cultural peculiarities played a minor role, that the people were simply fed up with sacrificing for a cause they now knew had been a lie, and so were more than willing, anxious even, to turn their allegiances to anyone and anything that held out promise for redemption.

And that's where the democracy edict had its effect: its proclamation launched the fourth traumatic shift in the national mood, albeit this time one heralding a brighter future: *mono-no-aware* (mo-no-no-ah-wah-ray), an optimistic cognizance of the world's transience and man's mortality. This characteristic dwelt alongside shikata ga nai for the occupation's duration--at least on the surface, for the benefit of the "occupationaires," as the American occupation contingent informally termed itself.

Thus the way was clear for MacArthur to rule Japan just as he envisioned. But not quite. He had one nemesis: the Far Eastern Commission (FEC), a wholly civilian bureaucracy that had oversight with respect to occupation goals and strategies. FEC was composed of representatives from thirteen Allied governments, this time including China--plus the Soviet Union. This organization could have stymied the democratization process, but MacArthur finessed that possibility by hurrying along the constitution's approval, here-and-there offering points to keep things humming along--notably retaining the emperor as a figurehead regent, and abolishment of declaring or otherwise engaging in warfare.

Occasionally, acronym-happy news reports would confuse FEC with FECO (later FECOM), the cipher for the Far Eastern Command, a mostly-United States Army entity that included the Japan-based US Eighth Army plus military installations and operations elsewhere in the Western Pacific, all under MacArthur's command. These occasional mix-ups irked the general, who had a lifelong disdain for civilian government bureaucracies that sometimes overflowed into tangible contempt. He also and characteristically resented his military forces being mistakenly associated with FEC, or for that matter with any civilian governmental entity with the notable (and understandable) exception of his own SCAP offices.

But the FEC annoyance aside, MacArthur was otherwise free from accountability to any other of the victorious Allies, encouraged by his commander-in-chief and with a direct line to him, unfettered by any further order prohibiting him from reshaping Japan politically or socially in the manner he chose, and respected and admired by the Japanese people and Americans back home alike (according to a 1946 Gallup poll, the second most admired American military leader, behind only Eisenhower).

So he set about creating not just a democracy in Japan, but also an entirely new cultural direction–specifically, he wanted the Japanese to build their new society on the example of the *American Christian home*! And that archetype precisely; he said so--and acted so--often during the occupation.

In early 1948, his certainty this ambition was working is revealed in a portion of a letter he sent to a Marjorie Benson of Macon, Georgia, in response to her concern that Christianity was being slandered in a Japanese school book. In his response, MacArthur promised that the offending passage had been stricken from the textbook, then added his opinion on how and why Christian principles were taking hold. His response was published in several Christian religious publications plus the Jewish *Brooklyn Tablet*, and included this key portion:

> *Through daily contact with our American men and women who are here engaged in the reshaping of Japan's future, there is penetrating into the Japanese mind the noble influences which find their origin and their inspiration in the American home. These influences are rapidly bearing fruit, and apart from the great numbers who are coming formally to embrace the Christian faith, a whole population is*

26

*coming to understand, practice and
cherish its underlying principles and
ideals.*

> – Toshio Nishi, *Unconditional Democracy:
> Education and Politics in Occupied Japan,
> 1945-1952,* Chapter 3, MacArthur's Japan

But of course, in order for the Japanese to be able to experience American-style homes and living styles, Christian and otherwise, those very same homes, complete with their American families, would have to be gotten to Japan. This of course would be done at MacArthur's personal bidding--but in a manner that reveals rarely if ever shown opposing extremes of the general's character: at one limit, his arrogant presumptuousness; at the other, his longing for the innocence of childhood.

Chapter 2: The MacArthur Way

MacArthur laid out his strategy for converting Japan into a Christian nation in the same first October of the occupation he proclaimed the country a democracy. He began by inviting leading American evangelical Protestant church officials to Tokyo to plan a "crusade" (MacArthur's term, oft repeated) throughout the country.

His principal reason for wanting to spread Christianity throughout Japan was revealed during the confab when he thundered, "Japan is a spiritual vacuum. If you do not fill it with Christianity, it will be filled with Communism. Send me one thousand missionaries!"[10] Later in the occupation, he implored American missionary societies to send "Bibles, Bibles and more Bibles," then in 1950 tagged a specific value to that demand when he called upon the Gideons to distribute ten million English and Japanese language Bibles throughout Japan. As a result of his entreaties, a Protestant evangelical missionary program was begun, became a mainstay of the occupation, and eventually transcended it, not peaking until the year of the Tokyo Olympics when 1,245 Protestant missionaries were scattered throughout the islands.

However, while some two million Japanese were baptized Protestant Christians during the occupation, once that era ended, nearly all the converts reverted to their traditional Oriental beliefs: primarily Buddhism and the Japanese-bred, highly nationalistic and often racist Shintoism, or simply lost interest in Christianity. Japan today has an indigenous Christian population of about one-seventh of one percent, virtually equivalent to its prewar level; and the overwhelming majority of that small number are Roman Catholics, a legacy of the missionary efforts of Jesuit priests, led by Francis Xavier, who had accompanied the Portuguese traders four hundred years earlier.

The high regression rate among the mid-twentieth century converts indicates the Japanese shrugged off Protestant Christianity as casually as they shed the last vestiges of shikata ga nai once the

---

[10] William P. Woodard, *The Allied Occupation of Japan and Japanese Religions,* p. 243.

occupation was over, and the American presence began to wane following the end of the Korean War in 1953. Also, a large number of Japanese allowed themselves to be baptized in order to obtain Bibles-- not to read but for their thin paper pages, which the "converts" would tear out and use for rolling smoking tobacco in place of then-expensive cigarette papers. Whatever, the only prominent remnant of this missionary effort in Japan today is the International Christian School in Tokyo, considered one of Japan's most prestigious private academies, and one of several such schools scattered throughout Asia.

While the missionaries may not have left a lasting impression in Japan in terms of a convert head count, their efforts nevertheless contributed immeasurably to Japan's postwar recovery, in large measure because the program ignited the most tremendous outpouring of charitable goodwill in world history.

When the first missionaries sent home reports of the horrendous poverty, starvation, rampant disease, and overall desperate living conditions in the country, churches back in America responded by mounting unprecedented charity drives that Americans responded to with unparalleled generosity. Throughout the occupation and continuing into the mid-1950s, cargo ships laden with thousands of tons of donated foods, clothing, household goods, toys, drugs, and medical supplies crossed the Pacific for distribution among destitute Japanese. American businesses donated equally massive tons of capital goods for the rebuilding of Japan's industrial infrastructure. One ship's entire manifest was several hundred head of dairy cattle, plus support equipment and feed, donated by a Wisconsin cooperative to help Japanese dairymen restart their own industry.

This incredible outpouring of charity became so huge and comprehensive, and did so much both to ease Japan's postwar human suffering and create good will between the two recent enemies, that the missionary program became an *ex officio* auxiliary of the occupation, with the army providing logistical support and even supplies to missionary outposts, the navy ferrying church personnel between the various Japanese islands, and the air force giving church officials gratis lifts on transport planes. And MacArthur would always make it a point to visit with church leaders of any faith or denomination who happened to be in Japan.

At first glance, MacArthur's call for widespread Christian proselytizing seems totally out of character. SCAP almost always considered Japanese culture and sensitivities foremost in making his major decisions--yet here he was taking a course that was highly parochial, invasive, and marked with pejorative comments. Most especially--and potentially risky to his reputation with the Japanese--he was highly critical of Japan's indigenous Shinto culture, which, taken to its extremes, had been instrumental in instigating zangyaku sei, the fanatical national mind-set that had led Japan to wage war.

MacArthur's endorsement of Christianity as savior of the Japanese soul was also surprising because his public persona had never been that of a model Christian. He was not known to have attended a Sunday church service even once since his cadet days at West Point, where chapel attendance is mandatory, nor was he known to have engaged in any organized religious activities. US Treasury Secretary Henry Morgenthau, for one, was stunned when MacArthur wrote him, in the context of brushing aside the secretary's insistence that Japan be punished for its wartime role, "If the historian of the future should deem my service worthy of some slight reference, it would be my hope that he mention me not as a commander engaged in campaigns and battles, even though victorious to American arms, but rather as one whose sacred duty it became, once the guns were silenced, to carry to the land of our vanquished foe the solace and hope and faith of Christian morals."[11]

In seeking to explain the general's embrace of the American Christian home example as the model for Japan's new democracy, MacArthur's biographers have noted that while he did not practice religion formally, he was nevertheless a devout Episcopalian who prayed daily, invoked God often (and usually verbosely) in public addresses, correspondence, and published materials, and led his family and any staff members who happened to be present in ersatz Sunday morning worship services in the American embassy in Tokyo, where

---

[11] William Manchester, *American Caesar*, "Last Post," p. 466.

31

he lived throughout the occupation. But MacArthur's religious feelings--and prejudices--apparently went far deeper.

William P. Woodard, a prewar missionary to Japan who after the war worked for SCAP as director of the occupation's Religious Research unit, wrote in his book, *The Allied Occupation of Japan and Japanese Religions*, that MacArthur had "...something of a messianic complex, a consciousness of being called of God for the hour, and a confidence that God was on his side." Woodard also noted that MacArthur viewed Japan's traditional religions, Shintoism especially but not exclusively, as inferior and even dangerous schools of thought.

What Japan needed, MacArthur once declared in a speech quoted by Woodard, was a "...spiritual recrudescence and improvement of human character that will synchronize with our almost matchless advance in science, art, literature, and all material and cultural development of the past two thousand years." That elegant if overblown rhetoric deeply impressed President Truman, who quoted the passage in the official letter of endorsement he penned for the American clergymen to carry during their October 1945 visit to Japan.

MacArthur's biographers have also opined that the sheer challenge of the uniquely imposing task of managing the occupation brought out a latent messianic complex in the man. Guests of MacArthur, colleagues, and staff members alike have written that when talk turned to SCAP's goals for the occupation that the general would often pace back-and-forth restlessly, wave his arms and otherwise animate his orations with what amounted to evangelical Bible-thumping, missionary-style zeal.

Given MacArthur's high degree of personal faith, it follows he would consider Christianity a natural bulwark against communist propaganda--and he had reason to be concerned about what was then called the "Red Menace," for communism had resurfaced in Japan with a vengeance following its two decades of suppression. A major reason for its appeal of course was the desperate living conditions, under which communist ideologies traditionally have flourished. Another was the largess, including especially freedoms of expression, granted by Japan's new, quite liberal constitution. So there was little to stop street corner harangues and clandestine cell gatherings, which traditionally have served to advance the communist cause. Communism continued to be a major threat to Japan's nascent democracy into the 1950s and early -60s, only to fade away when Japan's booming industrial might enlarged, enriched, and strengthened the country's middle class.

And as likely as it seems MacArthur relied upon the Christian standard to withstand communism, it appears equally likely that while he of course appreciated, lauded and encouraged the incredible charity once it was underway, there is no indication he issued the call for the missionaries in the first place with the idea in mind their presence in Japan would engender the amazing magnanimity; that was all the doing of churches back in America.

But in seeking to explain MacArthur's rationale for wanting to force Christianity upon postwar Japan, historians and his biographers alike seem to have overlooked yet another compelling reason he was so adamant about the missionary program and the importance of the American home in portraying the Christian ideal: the influences of his early childhood.

MacArthur was born in 1880 in what is today Little Rock, Arkansas, and spent the first nine, impressionable years of his life in what was then territorial Arizona and New Mexico--the still-Wild West, the rugged and relentless frontier--moving from one isolated army post to another with his army officer father, mother, and older brother, Arthur III.

Life was a rough-and-tumble existence (the family even traveled in that iconic symbol of the old west, a covered wagon), but young Douglas reveled in it, and in his later years he would romanticize the period. During the occupation and after, he would regale others with reminiscences of squatting beside an evening campfire with cavalry troopers, still dusty from their day's ride, listening to them tell of their adventures. He even claimed to have once seen Geronimo, the legendary Apache chief. Small wonder his preferred movies were Westerns, especially the cavalry horse operas directed by John Ford and starring John Wayne. His favorite was *She Wore a Yellow Ribbon*, released in 1949, the second of the Ford-Wayne so-called "Cavalry

Trilogy" movies (the first, *Fort Apache*; the third, *Rio Grande*), which he would watch over-and-over.

And on at least one occasion right after Japan's surrender, his love of the Old West even permeated an official action. When the Eighth Army first entered Tokyo following Japan's capitulation, its immediate objective was to reopen the American embassy, abandoned since the Pearl Harbor attack, but seen to by the Swiss Embassy, which had remained open throughout the war. The first unit of the Eighth to reach the embassy was a company from the Fifth Cavalry Regiment of the First Cavalry Division, and according to custom, this outfit would have had the honor of hoisting the American flag above the compound, in this case for the first time in nearly four years. The ceremony was all set when MacArthur suddenly intervened and ordered the flag-raising honor to go instead to a detachment from the division's *Seventh* Cavalry Regiment--the same unit once famously commanded by George Armstrong Custer.

MacArthur's early childhood in the lusty, charged atmosphere of the American frontier filled him with more than an abiding sense of awe of the period and the place; it also instilled him with a strong and equally long-lasting belief in the power of religious faith when the going got tough. His model for the value of religious devotion was not the cavalry troopers, whose adventures he doted upon and whom he idolized; nor was it even his father, whom he lionized: Arthur MacArthur, Jr., a Civil War hero awarded the Congressional Medal of Honor for his gallantry at the Battle of Missionary Ridge above Chattanooga, Tennessee, in November 1863.

The model was his mother, a tenaciously devout Episcopalian. To young Douglas, his mother was the pillar of strength he looked to through good times and bad, especially when his father would be gone on patrol for weeks at a time but even when he was home--and the support she turned to almost without exception was Jesus Christ. The tougher things got, the more she relied upon her Episcopalian faith, and she instilled her two sons with the value of prayer and devotion as durable stanchions during times of hardship.

The lessons stuck, and six decades later, the devoted younger son of that frontier wife and mother equated conditions in devastated

Nippon with the roughshod American frontier he had known as a child, and concluded that the faith that had upheld his family and the families of his friends during their times of travail would equally well serve the Japanese as they labored to rebuild their country. All he needed was a model of the American Christian home for the Japanese to look to for inspiration, the only question being from where, or whom, the example would come.

Democracy alone could not have provided the model. While Japan's constitution is liberal and innovative--theirs contains more defined guarantees of freedom than does America's own with all its amendments--Japan is a constitutional monarchy, and thus its government is parliamentary; it is not based upon the American republican constitution. If anything, the parliamentary structure, absent the American home prototype, might have caused the Japanese to follow the example of typical home life in Great Britain or the life styles under some other Western nation's parliamentary system in building their new society--or no model at all--but in any event, not the American home example.

Nor could the American missionaries who came to Japan during the occupation have provided the typical American home model, because their living conditions in the war-torn country were more akin to those encountered--and endured--by today's Peace Corps volunteers than to typical American middle class families of the time. Also, the vast majority of these missionaries were single young men fresh out of colleges, seminaries, or the military. A few missionaries were young married couples, and some of them bore their first children in Japan, but they were a distinct minority.

And no missionaries, married or single, lived as they had back in America. While the manner of the missionaries was surely Christian, and they showed the friendly, forgiving face of America and contributed to the general spirit of good will with the recent enemy, they had to live in the same, often ramshackle domiciles as occupied by their Japanese hosts--and quite often *with* those same hosts. Their living quarters had virtually no familiar American accouterments like easy chairs and familiar electrical appliances. They brought from

America their Bibles, study guides, communion kits, spiritual enthusiasm--and that was about it.

By much the same token, the Americanization of Japan would not have occurred had just American troops been present throughout the occupation, because garrison soldiers, no matter how open and egalitarian they may be, are still a military force; and a military contingent, especially at that place and time when it was all male, is in no way an example of a typical homespun environment.

This factor aside, the American soldiers who first went ashore and fanned out over Japan did smooth the way for the rest of the occupation by setting a friendly, forgiving example. Before the American soldiers arrived, Japanese leaders had told the people to expect barbaric conduct from their conquerors and to flee certain rape and pillage. Thousands of Japanese did just that; they abandoned the heavily populated coastal regions of their country for the mountains north and west of the Kanto Plain--but soon returned when, instead of rampaging through the country, the American GIs set up soup kitchens, opened their mess halls to whole communities, took in orphans, and passed out meal rations, Cokes, and Hershey bars by the pallet load.

MacArthur himself contributed to the early good will even before he first set foot in the country. Shortly after capitulation was agreed to by the Japanese hierarchy, a formal surrender order calling for Japanese military personnel to lay down their arms and offer no resistance was to have gone out from American army headquarters to Japanese military forces at large. MacArthur intervened, and instead directed that the surrender order go solely to Japanese military commanding officers, directing *them* to give the surrender orders down the line, rank-by-rank and unit-by-unit. This procedure meant that the Japanese officers would not be embarrassed--would not, in their terms, "lose face"--by having their command authority shoved perfunctorily aside. Word of the courtesy spread quickly around the country and helped contribute to a wellspring of admiration that was quickly building toward MacArthur.

MacArthur moved into the just-reopened American embassy on September eighth, to be joined there ten days later by his wife, Jean, and seven-year-old son, Arthur IV, who were flown in from Manila, itself liberated from Japanese forces just six months earlier. The MacArthurs were free to use their embassy home unencumbered by ambassadorial business, because terms of the occupation meant that the United States and Japan would not resume diplomatic relations until after the formal peace treaty was signed in April 1952. So the First Family of the occupation settled in, ready to do business and socialize.

While the MacArthur family was getting settled, occupation business was getting underway in a Japanese insurance company building the occupation had appropriated to serve as SCAP's headquarters, commonly referred to as "GHQ" (General Headquarters). Like many other ferro-concrete structures in Japan's major cities, this imposing edifice had survived the incessant firebombing scorched but otherwise unscathed.

Significantly, the building stood directly across a wide boulevard from the main entrance to the imperial palace grounds. Equally significant, and also symbolic, the insurance company that had occupied the building was named *Dai Ichi*, meaning "Number One," and thus quickly became associated with MacArthur's unique position and persona. American civil service workers together with Japanese and American consultants soon filled the headquarters building, plus others still intact in Tokyo, Yokohama and elsewhere appropriated by the occupation, and fell to the task of putting Japan back together.

One section of the occupation organization was devoted not to managing the occupation, but to providing housing, supplies, and amenities for married American servicemen stationed in Japan whose wives and children would fairly soon come to join them. Once reunited, these families would constitute the first denizens of the model of the American home, Christian and otherwise, MacArthur seems to have long planned to establish in the conquered nation for the Japanese to observe and emulate. All that was needed was for the man in charge to give the formal go-ahead, and the wives and children would begin coming over. But even that was carried out in a particular MacArthur-esque manner.

Another high-ranking officer with a strong interest in the dependents' program was Lieutenant General Robert Eichelberger, the occupying Eighth Army's commanding officer, a long-time personal friend and confidant of MacArthur's, who would often discuss all manner of issues with his boss, including personal ones such as details of a dependents' program.

Like many of the officers and men who had been overseas for some time and had experienced combat, it was Eichelberger's habit to write multi-page letters home, usually daily when he could. A letter to his wife back in Asheville, North Carolina, dated November 13, 1945, seems to constitute the first written evidence, official or otherwise, of the possibility of reuniting families in occupied Japan. Following a lengthy paragraph wherein he talks about himself and others retiring, and the possibility of getting back to America in time for Christmas, he writes:

> *There is still a lot of talk about wives coming out here and I have made my recommendations to SCAP based on the length of time overseas, which I suggested be two years and a half. And policy must include the availability of quarters and must include not only officers but enlisted men; otherwise there will be a hell of a row. My own staff tried to get me to approve a recommendation which would include special consideration for generals which I turned down.*
> – MacArthur Memorial Library, RG-41, Selected Papers of Lieutenant General Robert L. Eichelberger, 1942-1948

Naturally, only MacArthur could authorize bringing wives and children over to Japan. But as Eichelberger would soon find out, SCAP had done just that a week or two before he speculated about the prospect in his letter home. Of course, MacArthur being MacArthur, he inaugurated the program in a way that was distinctively his: he gave the order, such as it was, *orally*! MacArthur never wrote anything down, or had any staff member make any formal, written record of the action. He just told an official visitor that he wanted soldiers' and officers' wives and their children to come live in Japan, and that was that; the job got done in a completely offhanded yet effective manner.

The occasion for SCAP to broach the subject of the dependent program with someone outside his immediate circle who could transmit his wishes back to Washington and get them fulfilled occurred during a meeting he held in late October. Assistant Secretary of War John J. McCloy had come to Tokyo to conduct an inspection of the occupation for purposes of making a report to Congress, and of course spent some time with MacArthur.

The timing of their meeting is significant because it occurred less than two weeks after MacArthur had met with the evangelical Protestant delegation, and launched his plans for Christianizing Japan. Thus while meeting with McCloy, he may have mentioned his vision of using the American Christian home and family as a model for his Japanese minions. Or not. All this and more regarding their discussion is pure speculation, because no secretary was present with the two men to take notes, and neither ever wrote anything about it.

MacArthur and McCloy likely discussed how reuniting families in Japan would raise morale and help curb the wanton and surging prostitution problem, which even that early in the occupation was vexing Japanese and American administrators alike. And they surely must have discussed logistics, supplies, housing for families, and similar must-see-to matters. They might have also talked about the reason wives and children were going to be brought over to the American Sector of occupied Germany, which, as one planner had put it, was to present a "softer, feminine" face of the American army before the German people.

But it's problematic whether MacArthur confided his deepest-felt reasons for wanting the families in Japan. This is because while McCloy was a civilian, he also had been a combat veteran of World War I, and so would have fit within MacArthur's approval parameters. SCAP felt strongly that combat validated a man's character, which means that McCloy was someone with whom MacArthur would have felt comfortable sharing his innermost feelings. Then again, MacArthur was never wont to believe he had to give reasons for his actions, whether to subordinates, visitors, superiors, or equals (if indeed he ever felt he had "equals"); he just did what he did and never mind what anyone else might think.

The two almost certainly discussed family support and accommodation issues, including especially the critical logistics involved in bringing over, housing, and otherwise seeing to the welfare of the wives and children. This is known because shortly following McCloy's return to Washington, SCAP briefed Eichelberger about the session. Eichelberger mentions this briefing in his customary lengthy letter to his wife: written that evening, dated November fourteenth. Eichelberger raises the dependents' issue as a brief, this time somewhat gossipy aside to rambling on about other matters:

> *By the way, SCAP told me he had recommended to the War Department that wives be allowed to come out here and join their husbands. When McCloy asked how he would take care of them, he said, "We'll find a way some way." The only stipulation he made was that the officer or soldier should have time still to serve over here. I told him if there was any question of cutting it down I would suggest they bring in the length of time overseas. With the limited quarters here, it doesn't seem to me right that an officer just leaving his family should immediately have them come over. Of course Dick* (Colonel Richard Marshall, SCAP's Deputy Chief of Staff) *does not want his wife over here; in fact I imagine*

he would like to lose that baby and take
on that other one.

–Ibid

While Eichelberger's letter makes it seem that he and MacArthur just chatted about the family program, circumstances surrounding the occasion indicate their discussion was more formal and pointed. This is because Eichelberger couldn't just walk down a hallway and knock on his boss's door to get a meeting; he would have had to make a deliberate trip of some distance and trouble.

Reason: while MacArthur's headquarters, the nerve center of the organization charged with reshaping Japan politically, philosophically and economically, was located in Tokyo; the headquarters of the Eighth Army, the organization charged with assuring that any insurrections were suppressed and in general seeing to it that Japan didn't return to a belligerent posture, was based in the Yokohama harbor area, more than thirty miles distant. This wide physical division of the headquarters of the two entities was deliberately meant to drive home the idea that the force charged with policing Japan was not intertwined with the force responsible for rebuilding the country. Ironically, and despite this separation intent, the Eighth Army's largest unit, the First Cavalry Division, was based in a Tokyo suburb located on a far side of the capital from Yokohama.

To complicate matters, motoring between Tokyo and Yokohama was no casual drive then. The *Kawasaki* Industrial District separated the two metropolitan areas, and still does--only in 1945, more than eighty percent of it had been bombed into rubble, and the area would remain largely in ruins for the occupation's duration. Naturally, roads also had been struck by bombs, so a large portion of the drive between the two headquarters meant navigating a slalom course of craters and generally ravaged pavement of what before the war had been a majestic four-lane boulevard.

The point is that any meeting between Eichelberger and MacArthur would usually mean the former's having to plan out a goodly portion of his workday to include the two- or three-hour round-trip commute it would take him to be driven between the two cities.

Additionally, it is clear that MacArthur used the occasion of the November fourteenth briefing session to formally charge Eichelberger with getting the dependent program underway from the Japan end. This is known because, a few days later, Eichelberger took the requisite, procedural step of sending MacArthur--not as SCAP but as Commander in Chief, Army Forces Pacific--an official request that read, in part, "The morale and general well-being of this command would best be served by the establishment of a policy at this time to permit the quartering of families in the occupied areas consistent with available transportation and housing accommodations." MacArthur forwarded the request to the War Department, which got around to approving the program the following February.

Still, the whole dependent program got underway with what must have been off-handed talk between MacArthur and McCloy–who also, upon his return to Washington, filed a glowing report to Congress about SCAP's conduct of the occupation.

(For his part, John McCloy would go on to much greater accomplishments than being MacArthur's errand boy for getting families together in Japan. Most especially, he would distinguish himself seven years later as High Commissioner of (West) Germany, during which tenure he was responsible for overseeing creation of the Federal Republic of Germany. In other words, McCloy became, in a very real sense, the MacArthur of West Germany with respect to forming a new political system. He later on was also a World Bank president.)

MacArthur's methodology for inaugurating his dependents' program stands in sharp contrast to Eisenhower's, who from the outset *did* go procedurally through channels to request the family program for the American sector of occupied Germany. In mid-June 1945, scarcely a month after Germany had surrendered, Eisenhower sent a somewhat plaintive letter to General Marshall saying that he missed wife Mamie, wished she could join him, and then requested that a program be set up to bring wives and children to Germany. At one point in the letter, "Ike" wrote, "I will admit that the last six weeks have been my hardest of the war, (but) part of my trouble is that I just plain miss my family."[12] Ike's request was similarly honored, and dependents began embarking to the American sector of Germany in the spring of 1946.

MacArthur never expressed any similar sentiment to have his family join him because he didn't have to; his wife and son were with him throughout the war (first in the Philippines, then in Australia, then back to Manila) except for when he chose to be in a combat zone. Which doesn't mean he simply shrugged off the worth of getting families reunited where others were concerned.

In selecting American military families as the archetype of the American way of life, MacArthur reached back not only to his boyhood as the product of an army family--an "army brat," to cite the term commonly used by and for Army and Air Force dependent children (Navy and Marine Corps dependent children are called "juniors")--but also to his entire, by that time, sixty-five-year life spent in the company of such households. Intrinsically and with certainty, because he had come from such roots, MacArthur believed that no other form of family life could better portray the highest values of the American Christian household than the families of American military personnel. The otherwise crusty General of the Army revealed these feelings in his sole public acknowledgment of the dependents' program and how he envisioned the families would live in the devastated country. In a press release dated February 11, 1946, he wrote:

> *Plans are proceeding to open the theater for Army wives and families on or about May 1. I hope sincerely that Congress will broaden the base to include free transportation for all ranks. Living conditions, of course, will be those of the occupied areas and are not comparable in many ways with those of continental America. It will represent a*

---

[12] Donna Alvah, *Unofficial Ambassadors: American Military Families Overseas and the Cold War*, pp. 22,23.

*type of pioneering reminiscent of the
pioneer days of our own west during the
nineteenth century, but just as those days
developed the best of American
womanhood, so it is believed the wives
of our officers and soldiers will welcome
the opportunity of sharing the hardship
with their husbands.*
– MacArthur Memorial Library, RG-5, Supreme Commander
for the Allied Powers (SCAP); 1945-1951, Vol 4

The release is remarkable for the nostalgia MacArthur exhibits in
it: he all but invites the families to join him in a contemporary version
of the romanticized past he had known as a young boy on the
American frontier. Then there's the subtle homage to his own mother
where he likens the army wife to her pioneer forebears, and singles out
the homemaker as the key family member in making life in Japan
palatable. With the sole exception of his famous farewell address to
Congress in 1951 and its oft-quoted "Old soldiers never die, they just
fade away." conclusion, the terse note is perhaps the only sentiment
MacArthur ever publicly displayed in his long and often contentious
career. One can almost imagine tears welling up in his eyes as he
wrote it. Almost.

In response to the announcement, more than seven hundred
families volunteered to be aboard the first shipload to Japan. And not
just army families, but navy and marine dependents as well. In fact,
the first families to be reunited in Japan weren't army at all, but the
wives and children of twenty-two married navy and Marine Corps
combat veterans based at the Yokosuka Naval Base that guards the
entrance to Tokyo Bay.

These dependents arrived at the base aboard the navy attack
transport USS *Charles Carroll* (not to be confused with the navy's
destroyer escort USS *Carroll*, which saw combat in the Pacific toward
war's end) on June 21, 1946. The first *army* families to be reunited
were the 312 wives and children (General Eichelberger's wife among
them) of 180 family heads. They arrived in Yokohama aboard the US

Army transport ship *Ainsworth* three days later, after a ten-day crossing of the North Pacific from Seattle. In both cases, due to space allotments, all but the passengers' barest necessities, including most household goods, had been left behind.

The *Ainsworth* was greeted by an army band, an Army Air Corps flyover, and young Japanese dancing women clad either in white *kimonos* or their less-formal, more comfortable summertime equivalent, *yukatas*. Or so reported *Stars and Stripes*, the official GI daily newspaper. Sally Amos Graessler, who was just six years old when she arrived in Japan with her mother and a younger brother on that seminal voyage, remembers white-clad Japanese men and women not dancing, but demonstrating against the dropping of the atomic bombs. Ms. Graessler's childhood memory-contention likely is at least partially accurate, since strict press censorship, including any criticism of SCAP, was rigorously enforced; thus mention of an anti-American demonstration might well have been stricken from the official account of the dependents' arrival.

The wives and children disembarked, were met by their husbands and fathers, all of them at this juncture veterans of the Pacific war, then dispersed to set up their new homes in the war-ravaged land. That the dependents were greeted with open arms--and then some where the wives were concerned--is starkly revealed in the official Eighth Army historical monograph for the next year. Under the heading "Chaplains" is found a table of baptisms held in army chapels in occupied Japan for the calendar year 1947. Eighteen baptisms were conducted in the year's first three months, likely the offspring of married missionaries, and perhaps also children of Japanese-American servicemen liaisons. This figure rises to a total thirty-eight baptisms in the April-June quarter, followed by thirty-one baptisms in July alone, twenty-one in August, and thirty-two in September.

MacArthur might have smiled had he done the math: a dramatic leap in infant baptisms immediately following the one-year anniversary of the first arrival of dependents, time enough for a child to be conceived, delivered, and reach baptismal age. This upsurge was near-replicated in the year's final quarter, each month featuring baptisms in the twenties and thirties, which may be attributable to arrival of the *second* shipload of dependent wives and children in mid-August 1946.

And they were just the beginning. Over the next six years, the number of families would increase exponentially by more than one hundred-fold. At their peak during the 1949-50 school year, more than eight thousand American military dependents were living in Japan, and for the entire occupation period, some thirty-six thousand dependents, plus their servicemen (and occasional servicewomen) household heads, rotated through. In the late 1940s, the average American family size consisted of just over three-and-a-half persons, so extrapolating that figure to the occupation meant that at least twelve thousand military families lived in Japan during the six-year period households were included in the occupation.

Numerically, the military families constituted the occupation's third largest cohort, behind the British Commonwealth military contingent, which included some families of its own, and the total number of troops in the Eighth Army itself. Symbolically, however, the effect of the families' presence far outweighed their numbers-- because just like MacArthur wanted, they lived in American-style households (if not always American-style houses), and were closely observed by the Japanese, providing the former enemy a glimpse of the families' homeland wholly separate and distinct from the occupation's formal organization and purpose.

Families came and went on a regular basis. Prior to the 1930s and the Great Depression, military personnel were rotated from one assignment to another on a three-year basis; but tight budgets during the Depression caused this schedule to be doubled to six-year rotations. Then right after the war ended, the three-year rotation policy was resumed. This resumption of the three-year tradition meant that rotations stepped up in mid-1948 as the last of the war veterans of the Pacific Theater left Japan and elsewhere in the Far East, to be replaced by personnel who had served either on the American home front or in the European Theater.

One of those veterans of the war against Nazi Germany was my father, a graduate of the United States Military Academy Class of 1928. During World War II, he had served first in North Africa and

Sicily on the staff of the legendary General George S. Patton, Jr., then in the Italian campaign on the staff of General Mark Clark. In 1948, he was a forty-four-year-old full colonel in the Quartermaster Corps (supply), with a Master's in Business Administration from Harvard University, earned at the army's expense a year earlier, in addition to his West Point bachelor's degree. Just before Christmas that year, he boarded the troop transport *Patrick* in Seattle for what turned out to be an especially stormy crossing of the North Pacific. The *Patrick* arrived in Yokohama on January 2, 1949. Typical for the port city at that time of year, it was chilly and rainy.

Like MacArthur and many other high-ranking American officers before him, dad stayed temporarily in the New Grand Hotel, which was convenient to his office, located in the nearby harbor area. He was the newly-appointed Procurement Officer for the Eighth Army, the official army for the occupation's duration--and still on duty in Japan. In this position, he was responsible for making sure that all occupation forces, military and civilian, were adequately supplied, and also that supplies for the rebuilding of Japan were properly appropriated and allocated. It was a challenging but also fascinating and intriguing position, because it required him to travel throughout Japan in search of resources for occupiers and occupied alike. Plus, when he had the time, he had to prepare for the arrival of his wife and ten-year-old son later that winter. It would be a new adventure for our family, the latest in a continual string of at times unique experiences. And now I was to be a part of it.

Chapter 3: The Long Voyage Home

I'm certain anyone can vividly and intimately remember exactly what they were doing when they first learnt of an earth-shaking, traumatic event: the time, the surroundings, the place, details, who was doing what...even the exact spoken words. This truism applies whatever your generation or the circumstances. My parents, for example, could until they passed away recite exactly what they were doing and said the moment they heard of the Japanese attack on Pearl Harbor. People of my generation can precisely detail what they were doing when news broke of President Kennedy's assassination. And everyone reading this can pinpoint their circumstances when the 9/11 attack occurred. All and more frozen in time.

What goes for world-wide calamities may also apply to personal traumas: a bad accident, the sudden passing of a loved one, the sudden gain or loss of a coveted job, an un-anticipated marriage proposal...any number of events that personally strike to the core of an individual. In my case, while I can remember numerous bits and pieces from my early childhood, a sunny September evening in 1948, when I was just nine years old, marks the first time I sharply recall everything--everything!--about an event that was so traumatic to my young, secure world, that it would change my life forever.

Our family lived in Silver Spring, Maryland, a close-in suburb of Washington. Dad worked downtown, in the Office of the Quartermaster General. My older sister (and sole sibling) and I were preparing the dining room table for dinner, with mother fussing in the kitchen and within our view. I was setting plates around, then paused and looked up when dad came in the front door, walked solemnly across the living room and up to us, set his briefcase on the table before him, then looked around and said matter-of-factly, without a hint of emotion one way or the other, "We're moving to Japan."

Jeanne and I looked quickly and intently at each other from across the table as mother walked out hurriedly to join us, wiping her hands on a towel. I was nonplussed. I knew my father was in the army; I saw him in uniform every work day and even bragged of his job to friends. But while many other military families lived on bases, we did not, nor

49

did we socialize with any who did. So I knew nothing of being yanked away from familiar surroundings, torn from friends and schools and playgrounds and playmates I would never see again. It had never occurred to me that my comfortable, familiar, pristine childhood was about to be traumatized. Now, just like that, I wasn't so sure.

My sister knew what was up. Just shy of eighteen, Jeanne had that June graduated from high school and had a steady boy-friend, a Marine Corps lance corporal from Mississippi just months older whom she had met at a teen-age canteen mixer for servicemen, a holdover from the war years and still very popular then. Her reaction to the news of our move (sullen), which puzzled me at the time, became all too clear in a couple of months. As for mother...She reacted brightly, full of anticipation, even glee, as, once again, she would be off on some adventure to an unfamiliar destination with the man she had married with expressly that purpose in mind.

The balance of that evening remains bright in my memory. Jeanne got a world atlas so we could pinpoint where we would live in Japan (Yokohama). Dad briefed us on the job he would have and how we would live (fairly luxuriously, in the manner of the conquerors we were). When he mentioned we would have servants, he sternly admonished me never to order any of them to do anything, a rebuke which startled and embarrassed me and puzzles me still because, to the best of my knowledge, I had never ordered any adult to do anything, and had only the vaguest idea what servants were. Altogether, he gave us a briefing--yet a briefing unsupported by any printed material or visual aids other than that atlas: no pamphlets, no pictures, no books, no slide show--nothing whatsoever with respect to Japan and its culture.

This absence of support materials might be inconceivable now but that's the way it was then. Everything I was to learn about Japan before setting foot on her soil I learned that evening from my father, and that was near totally about how we would live there and would be expected to conduct ourselves. Nothing--*nothing*--was mentioned of how Japan had been a very recent and ferocious enemy, nor did my mother express concerns in this regard or ask questions; for example, whether we were to live in some enclosed compound separated from Japanese people to protect us from reprisals.

The subject simply never came up! There had been a war, the war was over, a new world was in the making--and that was that. For all practical purposes, end of lecture (or more accurately, end of a lecture that never occurred). Any neighbor who had wandered into our family gathering that portentous evening and not been told the precise subject of the occasion might have thought we were moving to Kansas and not some completely alien land on the other side of the world.

Practical matters were of course covered because my father was, above all else, a pragmatic and organized person. He had brought papers home with his orders that designated what household goods and other paraphernalia we could pack for shipment to Japan, what we could take with us, what furniture we could designate to have in our Yokohama home (quite a bit, given dad's high rank and designated position), and what we would have to leave in storage back in America.

Much that was designated one way or the other was based upon a single word that would continue to affect my childhood until I graduated from high school soon after my father's retirement from the army: allotments. There were all manner of allotments: housing allotments, shipping allotments, personal effects allotments, expense allotments, currency allotments (a special form of American money was then used in Japan and the occupation in Germany alike), entertainment allotments, transportation allotments, travel expense allotments, and probably more that I have long forgotten.

While certain allotments were based upon family size, assignment locale and the like, individual allotment status was based near-solely upon rank; and because dad was a full colonel by then, this meant we could ship over most of our furnishings. The living and dining room furniture I was familiar with (and being so young, the only such I had ever known) would be shipped to Japan, as would our bedroom furniture, which of course pleased me. We could also take our car with us, a rare privilege, granted only to the higher-rank personnel.

Personal items were another matter. I was given two pasteboard packing boxes to fill with whatever toys, books, comics and other personal items excepting clothing I wished to have with me in Japan. This occupied me for some time, as I was and remain something of a pack rat, and so could not bring myself to leave anything behind. No contest on the hardest toy to leave, however: my brand-new American Flyer electric train set that I had received just the previous Christmas. I could not take it because Japan's 100-volt, 50-cycle direct current electrical power system (still the norm there) was not compatible with American 110-volt, 60-cycle alternating current.

This electrical incompatibility also meant that we couldn't take any electric appliances, which distressed mother because it meant she had to leave behind such vital kitchen appliances as our toaster, coffee maker and waffle iron, plus her sewing machine and iron, and our household radios (television sets were extremely rare then). That said, some families did bring select electrical appliances, but even with then-rare converter plugs, they didn't function correctly on the tepid Japanese current pulse. Among other annoyances: clocks ran slowly, light bulbs didn't burn brightly, anything that ran on a reciprocating electric motor didn't function properly, and radios had to have their volume turned way up, if indeed a station could even be tuned in. American households weren't as electric appliance-giddy then as they grew to be, so while mother, and certainly other Japan-bound wives, may have regretted leaving this-or-that electrical appliance behind; once settled in Japan, compensations and substitutions generally proved adequate, if also occasionally quirky.

Another strong memory of that autumn is my last days of school with my friends and schoolmates. I had just entered the fourth grade at a brand-new school much closer to our home that I could walk to. I recall the morning my mother wrote a note for me to take to school, attached a copy of dad's orders to it, and sent me off. In my home room, I dutifully presented the papers to my teacher who then announced aloud to the class, "Listen up, boys and girls, Jamie is going to Japan!" Lots of oohs and ahs and stares followed, making me self-conscious and in the same stroke jumping me from being somewhat shy to the extrovert I remain today.

There was a large globe at the front of the room (well, large for a nine-year-old), and our teacher gathered us all around it. I remember her first showing us all where we then were, then slowly turning the globe and indicating where Japan was. This brought even more oohs and ahs and caused me to puff up my chest in pride because now everybody was staring at me as if I had suddenly sprung a third arm. Altogether, my coming adventure quickly made me a celebrity among fellow students and teachers alike. I was inundated with questions about Japan, but of course could give no information for I knew virtually nothing of my home to be; although our teacher did locate a picture book or two on Japan, so I at least gained an idea of what the country and its people looked like.

All I knew was that my days at the new school among friends I had known since earliest memories were quickly fading with the last traces of summer greenery. A unique adventure awaited me, and I faced it as a blank wall, a void into which I would be plunged. I went through motions: studied as directed, did as I was told, packed away familiar belongings and bid sad good-byes, little aware that this nondescript suburban grade school would be the first of three I would attend in the fourth grade, separated from one another by a total of some eight thousand miles, which may be something of a record even among service brats.

The moving van came sometime in October. I recall standing numbly outside our town home with my three closest friends (I still remember their names), just watching the movers empty out the last familiar trappings of my life. It was a day of losses, even of our family pet, as with so much else the only one I had ever known: a long-haired black cat who was given to close friends of my parents. No family pets of any kind were allowed to be brought into occupied Japan, although you could acquire one or more once there. The family to whom we gave Skippy returned him to us three years later after we were resettled back in the US; he would live to age twenty.

The day we left, my three closest friends came to see me one last time. Our car was a green, 1940 two-door Chevrolet coupé that would be shipped to Japan on the same troopship dad took. For the drive, I took my usual place behind my father's driver's seat, next to my (still sullen) sister. As we drove away, I turned and looked out the tiny rear window at my friends, who stood in the middle of the cul-de-sac, slowly waving good-bye. Like that evening my father announced we would be moving to Japan, the image remains sharply frozen in time.

And so we were off to...Michigan! That's right. Both my parents were from Michigan; my father from Bay City, and my mother from Middleton, a tiny farming community in the center of the Lower Peninsula palm that struggles to make the official state map–and that's where we were headed. We left familiar, suburban Washington not for Japan, but for my widowed grandmother's home in Middleton, there to spend the winter while my father went on to Japan. Why leave Washington when we weren't due in Japan until the following March? Because dad's quarters and living allowances for the Washington area were cancelled effective the time he was to depart for Japan, more than three months before mother and I were due, and we could not then afford to remain in Silver Spring. Plus, dad took our only auto with him, so we would have been isolated.

Grandmother lived in the last house on the edge of town; a village, really, of just some eight hundred people and a chicken processing plant. Mother and I were left there while my sister rode on with dad to Mississippi, where he was to drop her off to spend some time with her Marine Corps boyfriend, then hurry on to San Francisco to catch the ship to Japan, leaving Jeanne to take a bus back up north. But she instead took advantage of dad's favor by eloping! Jeanne was a month shy of her eighteenth birthday, and her marine lance corporal little more than a year older. But the marriage had a satisfactory enough result for a pair of runaway teenagers, only ending when she was widowed fifty-five years later.

Meantime, there I was in backwater Michigan, for the very first time in the state my parents were from, and where their total of eight siblings and their myriad children, my cousins I had never before met, had spent all their lives up to that point. It was unusual then that one branch of a family tree be so separated from the others, because families tended to stay in the same general area where they were reared. So my cousins were no more familiar to me than someone I would encounter casually. Or I to them. I was treated politely enough, but distantly, as if I had some latent genetic defect they feared they might someday contract. It's been the same way since. I only keep in touch with two of my fifteen or so cousins, and they just by Christmas cards. And I never once met one aunt and her family, my father's younger sister.

But that's the way it is with service brats. Whether cousins or neighbors or school mates, we're always having to make new friends and acquaintances; it's a requisite of the life style. From time-to-time, we must enter a strange school room for the very first time, be introduced formally to the other students ("Class, this is Jamie Lamont. He comes to us from Washington, D-C--our nation's capital!"), then with books tucked under your arms march steadfastly to your indicated desk, the while being stared at (sized up, really) by the entire class. It's a little easier when the school you're entering is an on-base facility, for there all of you have shared the same experience. Yet it's still awkward, still a challenge, still a case of agonizing over who will like you and who won't; still a matter of deciding how outward you should be balanced against any reticence about seeming too forward, too much of a wise guy or gal.

One thing you cannot be (and I learnt this quickly in Michigan that winter) is shy and withdrawn, for that will get you flat-out ignored: the last one chosen to participate in playground games, the one to be left out when study groups are formed. So, you become the one the teachers fuss over just because you *are* a stranger in a strange land--kindly actions well-meant, but ill-served because they act to separate you even more from your peers.

Small wonder service kids usually if not often grow up to be extroverts. That's true in my case: I can walk into a room full of strangers, size up the situation, then enter just about any conversation I choose. But even if you're not outgoing, you soon learn that if you're going to have a social life at all, that you had better tuck your reservations away and let people know you want to be part of the scene.

Meantime, there I was. And there my mother was. Living with my grandmother in a stark prairie village through a long Midwestern winter. My second-floor bedroom faced south, across a corn field which browned and broken stalks shown upward through the sheen of ice and snow like beard stubble on a worn and tired face. A gas station-cum-general store stood at the intersection of the only road into Middleton and the two-lane state highway that ran east-west. Often at night I would just lie in bed and gaze out at that lonely sentinel of another time now gone, a more familiar life with the friends I had left behind. Occasionally (very occasionally) a single auto would pass by, and I would follow its headlights and shout silently in my head, "Take me! Take me!," only to watch its taillights fade mockingly, disdainfully.

A winter routine settled in. Mother's older brother would come by every morning to stoke the coal-fired furnace, and I would sometimes help him, hauling buckets of coal from the side of the house. Mother would handle the kitchen stove, a huge, cast iron contraption that originally was wood-fired, proving if nothing else that rural Michigan in those days, or at least in that house, remained very fundamental, very prairie-esque.

Grandmother did have a radio, an AM affair that could only pick up a station or two. Other than that, I learned, at age nine, to read adult books and also books for older children, bought for my mother and her siblings when they were scarcely older than I was at the time. I recall going through her *Tom Swift and...* collection several times. This was necessary to keep from becoming too bored, because all my books from Maryland were packed away, either en route to Japan or back in storage.

I did make a few friends at school (not a romanticized Prairie Gothic one-roomer, but close to it), none of whose faces I can still see clearly, plus a girl named Karen who had a crush on me, proving if nothing else that rural kids do, in fact, mature earlier. Needless to say, I was oblivious of her intentions, so it's perhaps curious that I still remember her name--and hers alone.

The school itself was nearly two miles away in the next village east, requiring me to take a school bus with other children, although we sometimes would walk home when the weather was clear and not too cold. The walk was along a high-crowned, barely two-lane affair that paralleled a railroad track. This right-of-way quickly became my sole attachment to my electric train set back in storage in Maryland. Only occasional freight trains ran along it, but they were excuse enough for me to stand and watch them puff by, wondering as I did when I gazed at the cars rumbling past whether one would someday, hopefully bear me away.

We did leave Middleton now and then with my uncle and aunt who still lived there, to spend time with other relatives within driving distance, in Flint, Lansing or Durand. One of those times was Christmas, a big, noisy, happy affair with loads of goodies to eat, and where I for once felt close to and accepted by my cousins. I remember one present from that Christmas: a Kodak Baby Brownie Special, a simple point-and-shoot camera that I took on to Japan and kept for years. That winter, I used it mostly to take pictures of the steam-powered freight trains that chuffed through town.

Besides my grandmother and a few other relatives, the only adult I remember from that time is a tall, lean dairy farmer my mother's age (mid-forties at the time) with whom she had attended school in Middleton and who dropped by our house a couple of mornings a week, each time bearing a glass quart bottle or two full of milk. Some may remember when milk was sold this way: un-homogenized, with a layer of pale yellow cream nestled perhaps an inch or two thick atop the milk's whiteness. The milk this man brought was radically different even from that: it was *raw* milk: un-pasteurized, still warm, straight-from-the-cow-that-morning milk. And the cream atop this milk was not a token offering for a cup of coffee or two, but occupied the upper half of the bottle!

I remember mother ensuring me that the milk was safe to drink, as I had been enough urbanized even at that young age and time to question anything that was not supermarket-identifiable. This milk was incredibly rich; I have not seen its like since. Mother would skim off some of the cream for her coffee or for baking, then shake the rest together and serve it to me. This man also brought us eggs. Like the milk he brought, the eggs were always fresh from the source: still warm, often straw-covered. Huge eggs! And often fertilized eggs ("The blood's good for you," grandmother would say brusquely when I hesitated eating them). With all the loneliness and melancholy, I remember from that winter of 1948-49, I probably never ate so well or heartily or healthily before or since, and this continuing movable feast was one of the few memories I cherished from that winter once we were in Japan with its restricted commissary-provided rations.

I remember this farmer for one other reason: he was always deferential to my mother; exquisitely polite, excessively so. "How are you today, Bernice?" he would ask. "May I do something else for you before I have to leave?" "Is there something I can bring you from town?" "May I take you to Carson City for some shopping?" Mother would always demur, always look away, always say, "Thank you, Frank, everything's fine." Yet he would linger, following mother with his eyes, hanging about the edges of the living room or kitchen like a butler, silently watching mother go about her business, stepping forward gingerly yet eagerly when she reached to get something or to move something.

Years later I would learn that this man had proposed to my mother shortly before she left Michigan for New York to be near her husband-to-be, who was a cadet at West Point. He was the only other man besides my father to have proposed to my mother. He never married and died sometime in the mid-1980s, coincidentally about the same time my father died. His dairy farm with its warm eggs and incredibly rich and delicious milk is long gone.

The winter crept on, and as it does in the upper Midwest, deepened. Then in early March 1949, mother and I packed up my clothing and few personal belongings (I hand-carried my prized camera), then very early one cold morning bid farewell to grandmother, climbed into my uncle's car and left Middleton for the last time: to catch the first of two trains that would take us west to Seattle, and the ship to Japan. The first train ride was in a simple coach to Chicago, where we took a taxi from our arrival station to Union Station, there to board a long, colorful and sleek brown-and-orange train: the Great Northern Railway's "Empire Builder," then one of the supreme passenger trains in the United States or anywhere.

We boarded in the afternoon into a Pullman car, where mother took the bottom berth and consigned me to the top. The train pulled out and we ate that evening in the dining car, an elegant affair with thick white linens and heavy silver. I ordered from the special children's menu and gawked at how the motion of the train caused the water in the crystal goblets to shimmy. I marveled as well at how the silver implements would gently jostle one another in what amounted to music, Thomas Wolfe's "tintinnabulation" of the silverware. Water dancing to gently jingling silver, the music of a train in motion. At each setting, I would purposely gather the flatware together, then watch the water shimmy to the silver serenade.

Early the next morning, I explored the train with my mother and quickly settled into my favorite seat for the entire two-and-one-half-day ride to Seattle: the rearmost chair in the rearmost car, a streamlined observation car. I would sit in that chair for hours--*hours!* --as the train swept across first snow-covered prairies then into the mountains of Montana and Idaho. I was enthralled; I had never seen scenery like this and was anxious to take in all I could, quickly exhausting what film I had brought with me for my Baby Brownie Special. I recall how mother would sit just behind me and chat with the businessmen in the observation car and how these men would look at me and chuckle and marvel at how my attention could be held so rapturously for such long periods of time. No matter. I didn't care; I was off in my own marvelous world, a world I had never seen. I don't recall Japan entering my mind; I don't recall any hesitation; I only knew the adventure of it all, and I reveled in it.

Soon (too soon) we arrived in Seattle and another taxi ride, this time to dingy greyish-white dormitory-like buildings at the port. I remember this facility was on a low hill above the wharves, and from there I would see this huge, grey, twin-funneled passenger ship. I well remember mother clutching my shoulder when I first stared at it and explaining to me that we would be boarding that ship and crossing a vast ocean. More adventure--only this time, I was numbed.

We boarded the ship sometime the next day, then sat in port overnight, then set out the next morning, for which would be a near-constant, storm-buffeted crossing of the North Pacific Ocean. Mother confirmed this much later: no passengers, mostly dependents like us, were allowed on open decks at any time once outside Puget Sound, until we entered the calm embrace of Tokyo Bay ten days later. Which was just as well, because I was seasick most of the way. As apparently were a number of fellow passengers, because the dining room was often near-empty at mealtimes.

One thing from that crossing does remain firmly in my memory. While we could not go on deck, we were free to roam interior spaces not off-limits to passengers. I quickly staked out my favorite viewing locale: as far forward on our deck that I could go to peer out in the direction we were headed. In a reverse of the cross-country train ride, where I spent most of my time viewing where we had been, the ocean voyage was characterized by my viewing where we were going, and I would take in that view whenever I was not too seasick from the constant tossing to do so.

I remember this view as vividly as the train ride. The forward bulkhead had tall windows that stretched from beam-to-beam. I would stand there, stretch up on my toes, and press my nose against the salt-streaked glass, straining to peer forward into the future of my life. From there, I could clearly see the prow of our ship, but due to the constant cloudiness not much beyond that except a grey and angry sea that seemed always to be flecked with whitecaps spitting contemptuously. Now-and-then the sea would be so rough the bow would disappear beneath the waves for a long moment. When this happened, waves would curl up synchronously from both sides of the vanished bow in huge twin rings that would hang suspended briefly in mid-air and glare at me like the eyes of some huge, malevolent owl before crashing thunderously back into the rolling waves, there to churn aimlessly before giving way to our bow, which yet again would rise triumphantly from beneath the gray seas.

Then just like that, we were there. There was no transition; my only memory is of storm-tossed seas for the entire crossing, then jump cut to gliding along water as smooth and flat as a window pane. I remember standing on the open deck with my mother and staring over the side. Once more, as she often did, she stood closely with a free arm protectively around my shoulder. It was raining still, but gently this time; the raging sea was behind us. And instead of water as far as I could see, I now saw land. It was grey, colors were dulled, yet we were slipping silently past a ridge line along which were terraced gardens and here-and-there a thatched roof hut and even occasionally a small village, all looking exactly alike in the same shade of grayish-brown. I recall I was glum, uncomprehending, and that my mother said nothing nor did she point out anything.

And then we were there, nestled alongside a wharf. Lines went out and were secured. A gangplank was moved up to our side below and to the right of where I stood with mother. And then I saw my father through the rain, standing near his staff car, his driver alongside the vehicle, both patiently awaiting. I guess my mother saw him too at the same time and may even have drawn my attention to him. I don't remember; I only knew the long journey which had begun in suburban Maryland five months earlier was finally over. Our family, less my sister, was together again.

I was home at last. A home in a land that until very recently had been a ferocious–and ferociously hated–enemy, now being transformed in a uniquely historical fashion. Mother and I disembarked into it.

Chapter 4: The Quiet Transition

One sunny day, a dignified matron dresses up in the finest equestrian attire, then heads off to a riding academy for the first time in her life. At the stables, she surveys the horses thoughtfully for a few moments, then points one out to the stable hand accompanying her. "I'll take that one," she declares resolutely. The hand stares open-mouthed at the horse, then turns to the woman and stammers nervously, "But ma'am, that horse has never been ridden before." "Well then," the woman huffs confidently, "we start out even, for I've never been on a horse before."

The occupation of Japan was very much like that drollery: Japan had never been occupied by a foreign invader, nor had the United States ever occupied the homeland of some conquered foe.[13] So when it came to occupying postwar Japan, neither party quite knew what to expect from the other--and like the stable hand, concerned interests back in America feared the encounter would turn out badly.

They had reason to be worried, because Japan and the United States had been especially bitter enemies. Virulent stereotypes typified their portrayals of each other, most especially from the American side of the Pacific, where the vitriol hurled at Japan was far worse than the propaganda directed toward Nazi Germany, in large part because it was laden with blatant racism. For their part, the Japanese, under the sinister spell of zangyaku sei, directed virtually all their racist diatribes toward their fellow Asians, Koreans and Chinese especially, whom they literally considered sub-human.

The militarists often characterized their American and British foes as "hairy devils" when addressing their own people; but such stereotyping aside, about the only propaganda of a racial, but not racist, nature Japan aimed at America was meant for African Americans--not to denigrate them, but to point out their misery in the then-largely segregated United States. Following a lynching in

---

[13] The United States did occupy the Philippines for a half-century as a prize of the Spanish-American War; but in that case Spain had been the enemy, not the occupied country.

Mississippi in June 1942, the Japanese aimed a fusillade of short wave radio broadcasts at America's Negroes, prodding them to rise up in revolt.

The nature of the attack on Pearl Harbor had much to do with the American attitude toward wartime Japan. For decades afterwards, the sudden, unexpected strike was viewed as an especially sneaky, underhanded, and typically "inscrutable Oriental" (as the racist stereotype once put it) way of beginning a war--and indeed, Japan had previously conducted two similar, unannounced and unsuspected attacks: against China in 1898 and Russia in 1904.

My own mother-in-law typified this suspicious attitude. Alice was twenty-four years old on December 7, 1941, and she and her husband delayed buying a Japanese-made television until the mid-1990s, when they had no other choice once reliable American manufacturers had conceded the market. And she resisted buying a car from a Japanese manufacturer until after the turn of the new century, even then succumbing only after being assured her Toyota had been made in America by American workers using many if not mostly American parts.

Japan and the United States had not always been so viciously acrimonious. Until the decade before Pearl Harbor, relations between the two nations were very friendly and had been since the mid-eighteen hundreds, when Perry's visits and increased contact with the West in general encouraged Japanese to travel and study abroad freely. Most of this travel was of course undertaken by the upper levels of Japanese society, who could afford the luxury of international jaunts; but even the lower classes were exposed to Western and American ways because they had accompanied the noblemen as staffers and servants.

Japan's relations with America broadened early in the twentieth century following the United States' takeover of the Philippines, and America's subsequent naval and trading thrusts deep into the western Pacific regions. For the first two decades of the century, cultural exchange was very active between the two countries. Much evidence of this goodwill can be seen to this day across the United States and Japan alike, from houses and other structures designed by celebrated architect Frank Lloyd Wright, who spent six months in Japan designing Tokyo's Imperial Hotel and whose Prairie School style renderings sharply reflect Japanese architecture; to one of America's foremost tourist attractions: the cherry trees surrounding the Tidal Basin in Washington, D.C., donated by the Japanese government in 1912.

Also during this twenty-year period, several thousand Japanese immigrated to the United States, settled primarily in Hawaii and California, and became naturalized citizens. These immigrants' children who were born in America became the sub-culture known as the *Nisei*, Japanese for "second generation," although the term mistakenly came to include their parents, plus any siblings born back in Japan. This was the society, parents and children alike, interned in concentration camps during World War II because they were considered a threat to the United States.

Despite this harsh, illegal treatment, including non-compensated seizure of their homes and businesses, the Nisei put together a special wartime army unit, the 442nd Regimental Combat Team, that fought in the Italian Campaign and became the most decorated combat outfit of World War II. In 1951, the 442nd's exploits were made into a widely-heralded and -popular Hollywood movie, *Go For Broke*, that starred Van Johnson. A veteran of the unit who was awarded the Medal of Honor for his bravery was the late United States Senator Daniel K. Inouye of Hawaii.

Relations between Japan and the United States deteriorated following Japan's invasion of Manchuria in 1931. Cultural exchanges ceased, diplomatic visits diminished, and words between the two countries became increasingly rancorous, then deteriorated more rapidly when Japan invaded China in 1937, and finally all but collapsed in the wake of the so-called "Rape of Nanking" later that year and the next, when Japanese troops slaughtered nearly a half million Chinese soldiers and civilians, enraging the American public.

Respective diplomatic staff comings-and-goings quickly became the only official travel between the two countries, although some trade and even passenger travel between Japan and Hawaii, at least, continued right up to December 1941. The Pearl Harbor attack of course bluntly terminated *all* travel and communication between the two countries; even the Japanese embassy staff in Washington was caught flat-footed and could not return home until the following July, when Japanese diplomats marooned in America were exchanged for the American diplomatic staff stranded in Japan.

Once the war was fully underway, reports from the Pacific Theater of Japanese aggression and atrocities inflamed American passions. Much of this emotion arose from frustration at the Allies' announced grand strategy for winning the war: first defeat Nazi Germany, and only then turn full resources and attention to crushing Japan. Americans who had friends and relatives fighting in the Pacific became incensed at this decision and began referring to the struggle with Japan as a "second class war." Of course, the Allies' two primary reasons for their war-winning chronology could never be announced: concern that the Soviet Union would collapse under the Nazi onslaught, leaving the Western Allies to fight on alone; and fear that Hitler's scientists would develop an atomic weapon before America's could be made ready.

Blatantly racist opinions and comments worsened as the war progressed in the Pacific, even after it became apparent that the tides of victories had turned against Japan. Racist epithets like "Jap" and "Nip" and "slanty-eyed..." this-or-that became commonplace in even the most staid and respected publications. Serio-comic caricatures of Japanese soldiers and others in editorial cartoons, propaganda materials and elsewhere compounded the racial stereotypes, invariably depicting the enemy with extremely slanted and squinty eyes, hugely comic eyeglasses, ape-like noses and outrageously oversized buck teeth, all atop generally simian bodies.

Feelings against Japan reached an apogee of sorts in 1944, much of the hostility in the wake of revelations of Japanese executions of American prisoners-of-war. A Gallup Poll conducted in November showed that thirteen percent of Americans favored killing all Japanese. About the same time, military analyst George Fielding Eliot urged in the New York *Herald Tribune* "...complete destruction of Japan so that not one brick of any Japanese factory shall be left upon another, so that there shall not be in Japan one electric motor or one steam or gasoline engine, not a chemical laboratory, nor so much as a book which tells how these things are made."[14] Further fanning the flames, Professor Harold Hooton, a noted Harvard University anthropologist, recommended that American authorities "exile, imprison and sterilize all members of the Japanese royal family and all their blood relations." Even British Prime Minister Winston Churchill encouraged reduction of Japan "to ash."

Many of the racist outpourings against the Japanese emanated from the United States Office of War Information (OWI), the government's official propaganda arm during the conflict. A film released in 1943 entitled *Our Enemy: the Japanese* termed them "primitive, murderous, and fanatical." And a widely-screened War Department training film, *Know Your Enemy Japan,* included the warning, "We will never know the tough little mind of the Japanese completely." This viewpoint came to be prescient, because once the occupation got underway, the Americans quickly discovered there was no need to even try to understand the Japanese mind, since from the first the occupiers were met with cooperation and acceptance.

Curiously, with the war raging on all fronts and before even the worst of all the diatribes against Japan, racist and otherwise, there appeared what amounted to a conciliatory note about the Japanese people themselves if not their leaders. It came from Hollywood, in the context of one of the most popular movies of the war years: *Destination Tokyo.* Starring Cary Grant and released on New Year' Eve 1943, the story was the (supposedly fictional) account of an American submarine sneaking into Tokyo Bay to gather intelligence to be used in support of the famed initial bombing raid over Tokyo in April 1942 that was led by the legendary Jimmy Doolittle and immortalized in the best-selling book and movie, *Thirty Seconds Over Tokyo.*

About midway through the film there's a scene aboard the sub where four characters (including screen legend-to-be John Garfield) are musing about how the Pacific war got going in the first place. The executive officer, played by character actor Warner Anderson, reveals

---

[14] John Dower, *War Without Mercy*

the fact that Japan had been experimenting with democratic principles when the overlords took over and assassinated everyone connected with the pro-democracy movement, then thoroughly subjugated and otherwise browbeat the people into often unwilling tools of their expansionist ambitions.

The film otherwise doesn't portray Japanese as ape-like characters, although the dialogue is surfeit with the usual for-the-time scurrilities "Jap" and "Nip" and a bit more. Nor is there any indication the movie helped assuage feelings against the Japanese once the occupation began, although it certainly didn't hurt. What the film did do was encourage budding movie star Tony Curtis to apply for submarine duty after enlisting in the navy shortly after Pearl Harbor (he instead served on a submarine tender), and leading man Ronald Reagan to accept the role of a submarine commander in the 1957 film, *Hellcats of the Navy*.

Certainly, the final months of the war offered no indications the Japanese would acquiesce so suddenly and completely. Quite the opposite was the case. As Japan's once-mighty empire collapsed back in upon the home islands, their ancient *samurai* code of death before dishonor reached a crescendo of ferocity in such classic campaigns as the final struggle to recapture the Philippines, Iwo Jima, and Okinawa. On Iwo Jima alone, a mere 1,083 Japanese soldiers survived a defense force originally estimated at some twenty-two thousand.

And then there were the *kamikaze*, the "divine wind," the suicidal air strikes by neophyte pilots in flimsy, single-engine aircraft armed with a single torpedo, taking no evasive action as they flew straight through curtains of flak toward their targets. The pilots had been trained merely how to take off and maneuver their aircraft, not land them, and their planes carried only enough fuel for a one-way trip. The kamikaze first appeared at the Battle of Leyte Gulf in October 1944, where they were dismissed as an aberration in what otherwise was history's largest naval engagement in terms of total tonnage of vessels involved. Okinawa was another matter. The damage the suicidal pilots inflicted upon the American fleet--warships, support vessels and troop transports alike--disrupted the campaign ashore and nearly halted it.

Come the early summer of 1945, reports of the enemy's suicidal mania were keenly felt back on the American home front, where the suspicion that the Japanese might prefer the specter of self-genocide on a national scale to surrender clouded the celebratory aura that briefly arose following the collapse of Nazi Germany early that May. Families became used to welcoming their soldier sons and husbands home from Europe, only to have them spend but a few weeks in the company of their loved ones before shipping out to the West Coast to join the massive invasion force being assembled in ports from San Diego to Anchorage.

Citing Japanese fanaticism, pundits and military analysts glumly predicted it would take until 1947 to finally defeat Japan; some opined the war would drag on another five years. There were pessimistic forecasts of a shaky peace riven with guerilla warfare once Japan eventually did capitulate, and even MacArthur warned of an insurgency should the victorious Allies depose the emperor.

Then, just like that, the war ended. In the span of a mere nine days beginning with the dropping of the "Little Boy" atomic bomb on Hiroshima August sixth, the Soviet Union declared war on Japan and sent troops against Japanese forces in Manchuria; the second atomic bomb, "Fat Man," was dropped on Nagasaki--and on the fifteenth (the fourteenth back in the United States, due to the time zone difference), Japan accepted the Allies' demands. Surrender negotiations had been underway since May through neutral countries, including especially the respective American and Japanese embassies in Moscow, and mostly swirled around conditional vis-a-vis unconditional capitulation terms, with the latter demand being the final determinant.

The swiftness, scope, and implications of the surrender chronology together with the realization that a new and frightful age had dawned stunned the American people as much as had the Pearl Harbor attack. The effect of the atomic bombs and the implications of the Atomic Age future overshadowed all other considerations regarding how and why the Japanese surrendered. Details about Japan's reluctant trudge toward accedence would only be revealed piecemeal in the years to come, including that an internal struggle had been ongoing in Tokyo for months between the imperial entourage and the military hierarchy, and among the militarists themselves, over whether to surrender or fight on.

Altogether, no information that may have served to portray the Japanese as other than suicidal fanatics was released to the American public in the immediate wake of the surrender. The atomic bombs were cited as *the* reason Japan capitulated; little else was written or said to show that the Japanese had simply had enough, and so were reasonable human beings after all. And it has been only recently revealed that Japan may have surrendered to the Allies in order to deflect the possibility of the Soviet Union invading their homeland. In any event, no columnists pontificated on how ensei might have helped bring Japan to surrender terms; no radio commentators bloviated over the airwaves about whether shikata ga nai was real or a ruse. The war was over; that was all that mattered, and never mind complex reasons behind Japan's surrender.

Soon enough, though, comprehension would emerge, beginning with changing attitudes on the part of America. First to go was the torrent of racist propaganda; it vanished instantly, swept away with the celebration debris from VJ (Victory over Japan) Day that August fifteenth. Then as the occupation began and true peace became evident, other hardened opinions evaporated, replaced by understanding. Into the autumn and over the winter of 1945-'46, and especially after the desperate conditions in Japan were made clear, analysts weighed in with compassionate, solicitous commentary, often with the theme that the militarists, the shoguns, alone were responsible for the war, not the Japanese people.

Joseph Grew, the prewar ambassador to Japan, urged separating "the sins of the leaders from the actions of the masses," noting that the *real* criminals were the military cliques that began the war, not the emperor. Another highly-regarded Japanese authority, Lawrence K. Rosinger, said that Japanese regimentation and chauvinism were neither psychologically induced nor racist, but came from political, economic, and social conditions, and so could be subject to change.

MacArthur offered little beyond general assurances that the occupation was going as planned; he otherwise let his democratization of the country with its accompanying reforms speak for themselves.

Letters home from American soldiers in Japan also helped ease concerns. Their missives spoke of the beautiful country that lay beyond the devastated coastal cities, of the gentle and accommodating people--and not least of all, how the occupation was proceeding without so much as a hint of guerrilla warfare, an insurgency, or even individual, last-ditch-stand fanaticism.

One incident that was reported in *Stars and Stripes* and elsewhere was particularly assuaging. A couple of days after Tokyo had been seized, two American army officers were reconnoitering a region northeast of Tokyo, presumably somewhere around where Narita International Airport is now located, when they happened upon a still fully-armed, combat-ready Japanese tank column that was heading south to turn itself in.

To give the column room, the Americans drove their jeep onto the shoulder, where they instantly became stuck in soft muck. At this, the lead tank jerked to a halt, and the column's commander, a Japanese major, bounded out and dashed over to the stranded jeep, bubbling over with bows and apologies spoken in fairly good English. After assessing the situation, the Japanese soldiers linked a chain from the jeep's bumper to one of the tanks and quickly pulled it free. More apologies, smiles all around and bows. As thanks, the Americans handed over several packs of cigarettes, which engendered even more smiles and bows. Finally, the tank column and the American jeep went their respective ways, this time to smiles and waves.

Other than the letters from their husbands and fathers already in Japan, those first dependents who crossed the Pacific the following June knew little more about the land that would be their home for the next year or more than any other average Americans. For the most part, they arrived in Japan without having received so much as a single familiarization briefing prior to their departure.

Just like all other Americans at the time, much of the dependents' recent knowledge of Japan had been strained through the racist screen of wartime propaganda. For nearly four years, their minds had been flooded with images of a ruthlessly vicious--and viciously caricatured--enemy. And yet they were expected to leave their wartime prejudices, stereotypic images, and misconceptions back on American soil, and go live among the Japanese as if nothing had happened.

And by and large, they did just that! They and all the other American military personnel and their dependents who followed. Today, there might be all manner of familiarization briefings, sensitivity classes, indoctrination courses, foreign language training, and more prior to embarking on such an adventure. Back then, nothing was required or even recommended; there were no up-to-date briefings, brochures, pamphlets, handouts, talks, training films, or travel guides.

This just-drop-in approach to the occupation on that side of the world was in stark contrast to how American dependents were handled in the postwar occupation in the American sector of Germany. On arriving in Germany, all American wives and children over the age of fourteen had to attend a mandatory four-hour indoctrination briefing. In Japan, on the other hand, we dependents were simply waved through the gate, so to speak. Individual commands within Japan had the right to sponsor their own, individual familiarity briefings; the Kyoto-based contingent, for one, held such sessions. But nothing specific was mandated occupation-wide.

The only written material everyone received upon arrival in Japan (or sometimes before departure) was a thirty-two-page booklet, *Dependents Guide to Japan*, which colorful cover featured a sketch of a leggy young American woman, swinging a suitcase and tugging a toddler, striding resolutely past a rendering of a Japanese pagoda. The booklet's topics were just as offhandedly casual. It covered practical topics such as housing, transportation, health issues, shopping for necessities, desirable personal belongings and the like, but it also was very much a journeyman tourist brochure, touting the chance to see Japan's scenery and shrines as a once-in-a-lifetime, never-to-be-forgotten experience.

(Original in color)

And that was about it where up-to-date written materials about the country and its people were concerned. Most publicly available books about Japan were pre-war and so hopelessly outdated, largely travelogue-like surface sketches depicting a quaint Oriental culture that bore little resemblance to the rapidly evolving postwar realities of the country. The first postwar writings tended to be pejorative, describing Japanese as being beaten, humiliated and submissive. Even the initial issue of *Dependents Guide to Japan* was guilty of this affront, albeit mildly so. The booklet's last page entitled "Summary" carried the assuring words, "They (the dependents, wives and children) will be guarded by the United States Army, although there is little to fear from the Japanese who are a subservient, beaten people."

There was one notable exception to this lack of up-to-date information about the Japan that was emerging from the war, a book published just after the first dependents had left for Japan that would become a landmark study of the country--and it came from an unlikely source: the Office of War Information, the same agency that had produced much of the virulent wartime propaganda.

In 1944, OWI created a special section, composed of prominent sociologists, psychologists, and anthropologists of the time, to perform in-depth studies of Japan's and Germany's national characteristics to determine what caused their bellicose motives, how to neutralize or reverse those traits, and to prepare both official America and the public at large for the anticipated postwar occupations of the two defeated Axis powers. A prominent member of this distinguished group was a Columbia University anthropologist, Ruth Benedict. Dr. Benedict was one of the giants of her field in the twentieth century, best known for her landmark work, *Patterns of Culture*, published in 1934, and she stood astride two other titans of anthropology: Franz Boaz, as his student and protégé, and Margaret Mead, her teacher and mentor.

In the OWI section, Benedict at first focused her studies on Germany and was planning a research visit there after the European war ended, but ill health (she died in 1948) prevented her from going. So she turned instead to Japan, and in 1946 published *The Chrysanthemum and the Sword: Patterns of Japanese Culture*, regarded as *the* definitive work on immediate postwar Japan and still a valid guide to the country's character.

Benedict's fellow anthropologists criticized her work because she never visited Japan to do direct research. Benedict did, however, make it to California, where she did exhaustive interviews among the interned Nisei. She also relied upon extensive indirect sources for her materials, including personal diaries taken from captured and slain Japanese soldiers that revealed their dreaded fight-to-the-death zealotry was more often than not forced upon reluctant troops by fanatical officers, who would have them shot if they did not obey. Through mining these and other obscure channels, Benedict demonstrated deep insight into Japanese character and culture, which she covered from the seventh century through the war years.

Germane to the time and place, hers was the only work then available offering a definitive explanation of what had driven Japan to wage war, then reverse course and become subservient seemingly overnight. The book's first two sentences illustrate her keen perception of the postwar situation: "The Japanese were the most alien enemy the United States had ever fought in an all-out struggle. In no other war with a major foe had it been necessary to take into account such exceedingly different habits of acting and thinking." Clearly, Benedict's book would have been useful to military families and others assigned to the occupation, and it became a best-seller, so some families likely did read it--but the book was never made available by the government to Japan-bound Americans, nor was its reading mandated or even suggested. MacArthur had a copy of the book in his personal library, but there is no indication even he ever read it.

Interestingly, her book became a bigger seller in Japan than it did in the United States because it revealed aspects of the Japanese character the Japanese themselves had not fully recognized. In any event, instead of embarking across the Pacific with thorough background knowledge of their destination, the American military families of the occupation period--husbands, wives, mothers, pregnant wives, babies, toddlers, grade schoolers and teenagers--went to Japan quite literally as wide-eyed innocents abroad.

Our family was no exception. I don't remember much about my father's briefing that September day in 1948 other than where we would be living and what personal items we could or could not take. That and his admonishment that I was never to order a servant to do anything (and I don't recall even once doing so). During the lengthy interview of my mother about our time in Japan, she confirmed my own memories of preparing for the move: nothing beyond what dad told us that early autumn day. I also remember going to Walter Reed Hospital for all manner of inoculations in preparation for the sordid health conditions in Japan, and that is all.

I was similarly unprepared for the Japanese people themselves. Our life in Silver Spring in the late 1940s was pretty much a white picket fence, Andy Hardy version of the American home: very innocent, very middle class, very suburban, very Caucasian. Because we often journeyed into downtown Washington, I had seen African Americans ("colored people" was the term we used, commonly accepted then without a trace of racism), but no people of any other race that I can recall, so I clearly remember my first ever view of a Japanese: that day at school when it was announced I would be moving to Japan.

In addition to showing us kids where Japan was in relation to where we were, our teacher also pulled out a book containing illustrations of peoples of the world in their native costumes, flipped it open to the page on Japan, and pointed out a picture of a comely young Japanese woman wearing either a yukata or kimono, standing next to a blasé-looking young man similarly attired in a male's kimono or yukata. I remember staring at the picture numbly.

Several months and some eight thousand westward miles later, I got my second ever look at a Japanese: a man dressed in tatters, bent over and slowly pushing a heavily-laden cart along the dock in Yokohama where mother and I had just landed. Like all else about my time in Japan, my education about the land and its people began at that moment--and also like so much else about my time there, the image remains sharply detailed. All my contemporaries with whom I have spoken who lived in Japan then report the same experience: they arrived knowing little or nothing about what awaited them, and all retain vivid memories of their time there, beginning with the very first step ashore.

The families' lack of familiarity about Japan prior to moving there was neither intentional nor unintentional on the part of occupation administrators; it just happened. And it happened in the way it did because the families were part of the military, and any order to a service member involving his or her family is still meant to be obeyed unquestioningly. Following that logic, unless the order *specified* that certain familiarization books be read or briefings attended prior to moving to Japan, the serviceman would have no reason to ask about them; he--and she--would consider the order all-encompassing.

An example would be the orders my father received: they did not direct us to familiarize ourselves about Japan prior to departure, so we did not. On the other hand, they specified that we receive certain immunizations before departing, and so we did. Call it the military mind set: if the order doesn't spell something out, the unmentioned subject can be said not to be considered, questioned, required--or even to exist.

Once families were reunited in Japan, briefing and familiarization materials in addition to *Dependents Guide...* were made available to them; not so many at first, but more--and more specific--as the occupation progressed. From the beginning, a single theme was evident--and emphasized: this occupation would be no exercise in neo-colonialism, with the invaders keeping their distance from the local populace, ruling arrogantly and condescendingly.

MacArthur wanted his American home model out front and tangible, within easy reach of the Japanese. He also meant his home example to nestle cozily inside yet another paradigm, one that would ensure the Japanese experienced the total breadth of the American character. And in designing this encompassing archetype that would simultaneously embrace and display his American Christian home model, MacArthur once again looked to his own family--only this time, the inspiration came not from his devoutly religious mother, but his pragmatic, egalitarian father.

Chapter 5: Bulls on Tiptoe

When the Spanish-American War broke out in 1898, Arthur MacArthur, Jr., was by then a brigadier general, nearing the end of a long and distinguished career, including, in 1890, receipt of the Congressional Medal of Honor for his gallantry in the Civil War battle twenty-seven years earlier.

In the Spanish-American conflict, MacArthur commanded a brigade sent to the Philippines as part of a larger force to claim the country from the Spanish, a mission that occurred with only token resistance. As part of the Treaty of Paris in 1898 that ended the war, Spain ceded the Philippines to the United States as a military protectorate, making the country a *de facto* American colony, for the sum of twenty million dollars.

Two years later, MacArthur was made military governor of the prize--a dubious honor, since an insurrection had been underway since early 1899, driven by Filipinos who deeply resented their country being cavalierly handed from one Western imperial power to another. This internal conflict was an especially bloody affair that lasted two full years and is estimated to have cost some 160 thousand Philippine civilians their lives, many through starvation. MacArthur finally ended the ordeal by personally brokering a deal with the leader of the insurgency, a landmark agreement for its time, embodied in a declaration of rights for Filipinos.

The pact did not grant the Philippines full independence; that would not come until 1946. But it did assimilate the people into the American-led social and governmental fabric by shredding the standards of what was then called the "colonial manner," a British term for managing their empire's outposts. This approach dictated that the occupying English and the natives live wholly segregated lives with never the twain meeting (to paraphrase how Rudyard Kipling aptly put it in his classic poem, "The Ballad of East and West"). The primary American example of following this traditional British hegemonic lifestyle was the Canal Zone in Panama, where Americans lived like colonialists until 1979, when the territory was ceded back to Panama.

Arthur MacArthur would have none of this colonial tradition; he ordered American officers, non-commissioned officers (NCOs), lower-rank enlisted men, and their families under his command to assimilate with the Filipinos. Racial barriers were similarly torn down, with harsh penalties, notably including social ostracism, decreed for any American serviceman who practiced racism or otherwise demeaned the natives, with soldiers held liable for any racist misconduct by members of their families. Additionally, MacArthur established a first-ever equitable legal system in the Philippines, including *habeas corpus*, and generally granted expanded personal freedoms. He even founded the Philippine branch of the Boy Scouts.

None of his father's activities in the Philippines were lost on young Douglas, who was a cadet at the United States Military Academy throughout his father's tenure over the island country half a world away. He kept up with events there via newspaper accounts, letters from his farther, his naval officer older brother, Arthur III, and from his mother, who was literally alongside her younger son throughout his four years at West Point, living in an apartment in the Thayer Hotel, located on the academy grounds.

MacArthur was graduated in 1903 (first in his class), then in 1905 journeyed with his mother to Tokyo to join his father, who had been sent there as a special military liaison following Japan's victory over imperial Russia in their brief naval war earlier that same year. The young MacArthur spent two months in Tokyo as an aide to his father, and it was during this time that he acquired a consuming interest in Japanese history, character and culture.

Forty years later, MacArthur would incorporate key features of his father's policies in the Philippines into his own occupation, including two traits counter to the British colonial tradition that together would directly expose the Japanese to the American way of life on the most personal levels, opening the door to acceptance and even assimilation of certain American characteristics into Japanese living standards.

The first characteristic of the Philippine occupation Douglas MacArthur incorporated into his own was to create mirror images of small town America throughout the Japanese islands. This was done by having military families allotted proportionately according to predominant representation of the servicemen's ranks, not just spread equitably across all positions; or, as was the British custom, weighted toward the higher-up ranks.

Because the occupying Eighth Army, like any army, had more non-commissioned than commissioned officers, this meant there were more non-commissioned than commissioned officers' families living in occupied Japan. And because there were more junior than senior commissioned officers and NCOs alike, this in turn meant there were more families of lieutenants and captains than colonels and generals, and more families of corporals and mid-grade sergeants than families of master sergeants and senior warrant officers.

Demographically, this policy caused the total number of American military families living in Japan at any given time during the occupation to resemble a typical American community, complete with similarly constructed hierarchies, social structures, labor-management ratios, and so forth.

The policy also--and significantly--created a preponderance of young families, and thus a plethora of young, receptive, curious and adventurous children. I happened to be one of those young, curious, adventurous kids–but in a family that was a rare exception to this sociological predominance, because I wasn't born until my parents were in their mid-thirties. My sister, being eight years older than I, would have fit the pattern, but she wasn't there. So, it happened that the fathers of my friends, classmates and playmates were predominantly captains and majors and lower-ranking NCOs, not master sergeants and navy chief petty officers and colonels and generals, whose children were quite older than I, at least teenagers if not slightly older. The only other exception to this pattern I remember was a family that lived near us who had a son my age and in my grade school class–and an older son who was fourteen or so, and thus attended the American high school.

The families were disseminated throughout Japan, attached to units of varying size. And because even the smallest military unit had basically the same top-down structure as its parent, with proportionately represented military ranks and personnel allotments, the service families who were part of any single unit, however small and remote, reflected the same diverse small town demographic as the total number of American military families.

The small-town Americana paradigm provided the lifestyle foundation, the nurturing cradle, for the second policy MacArthur adopted from his father's Philippine example: unlimited assimilation of American military families, and indeed hopefully all occupation personnel, with the Japanese to show them the occupiers meant no harm, harbored no resentments, and even welcomed them into their homes. While this may have occurred naturally, all Americans assigned to Japan except the missionaries, who of course were there for the very purpose of living among the Japanese, were made keenly aware of SCAP's open doors and open hearts intentions from the moment they first set foot in the country.

During the occupation's early days, the intermingling aim was set down casually in but one of several briefing papers and familiarization publications everyone--British Commonwealth personnel and other foreigners included---was given shortly after arrival in Japan. Then in 1948, the intention was made official policy, tantamount to a set of orders, in a voluminous publication entitled, *Occupation Personnel Regulations*, first issued in 1948 and updated twice for the duration of the occupation. The heart of the assimilation directive is found in Section II, "Purpose," which begins:

> *1. The purpose of this circular is to:*
> *(a.) Establish, in general effect, the same relationship between the occupational personnel and the indigenous population of Japan as exists between United States troops and the indigenous population of the United States. (b.) Minimize restrictions on the movement and activities of occupation personnel to the maximum practicable extent, in order to promote an attitude of friendly interest and guidance toward the Japanese people which is reflective of democratic*

*ideals and devoid of unnecessary
military control.*

Much of the balance of *Occupation Personnel Regulations* was devoted to how personnel were expected to live and conduct themselves among the Japanese, and also to specific Japanese rules and laws deemed appropriate for application to Americans and other foreigners. For example, one entire section covered driving and traffic, especially crucial to the American motorists there, if not the English, because, just like in Commonwealth countries, the Japanese drove on the left (and still do). Also, certain regulations applicable to official conduct of military personnel had to be written separately as direct orders. For example, one order made it a courts martial offense for an American serviceman to strike a Japanese under any circumstances.

The assimilation intent expressed in *...Regulations* is yet another example of how the occupation of Japan differed from that of postwar Germany with respect to American involvement--and it was a critical difference where the spouses and children of American service personnel were concerned. In Germany, American families and military personnel alike weren't just not encouraged to intermingle with the Germans, they were admonished to avoid contact as much as possible! This action was taken because insurrections and terrorism were feared in postwar Germany, whereas there were no corresponding worries about postwar Japan.

These personal safety concerns initially were well-founded. As war's end loomed, Nazi diehards led by Martin Bormann, Hitler's private secretary and head of the Nazi Party chancellery, created two quasi-guerilla organizations, *Werwolf* and *Freikorps Adolph Hitler*; with the express purpose of sabotaging the pending occupation. And in the spring and summer of 1945, after Germany had surrendered and the occupation begun--and also after Bormann had committed suicide--insurrectionists succeeded in taking some three-to-five thousand lives, mostly fellow Germans they suspected of complicity with the victorious Allies, through assassinations and terrorism. *Werwolf* even seized two radio stations from which it broadcast appeals to German citizens, teenage Hitler Youth fanatics most especially, to rise up against the occupiers. But their efforts failed to gin up significant support because ordinary Germans, just like Japanese citizens, were fed up with war's death and destruction and just wanted to move on.[15]

However, and perhaps in large part because of the insurrection activities, American propaganda kept alive the specter of a Nazi resurgence. A principal vehicle for this *ex officio* campaign was a short film produced by Warner Brothers in the summer of 1945 entitled *Hitler Lives* that contained incendiary images and narration meant to make Americans fearful and wary of any and all Germans, beginning with:

> *It's still enemy country. We must still be alert. We must still be suspicious of everyone. We must take no chances. We're up against something more than tourist scenery. We're up against German history. It isn't good.*

The film then went on to contend that Germans were just lying in wait for the chance to create a Fourth Reich:

> *It can happen again...That is why we occupy Germany, to make the next war impossible. It will be no easy job. We must keep our wits about us. The German conquest is not dead; it's merely gone under cover.*

The film won the 1945 Oscar for Documentary Short Subject. It was based upon a film produced by the War Department shortly before the war ended, entitled, *Your Job in Germany*, that was even more vehemently anti-German, characterizing Germans as thoroughly untrustworthy ("Nazi training and Nazi trickery remain," was one

---

[15] Ian Kershaw, *The End: The Defiance and Destruction of Hitler's Germany, 1944-45*, "Crumbling Foundations," pp. 278-80

narration line) and the German mind as "diseased," and flatly stating, "There will be no fraternization with any of the German people."

Your Job... didn't fare well with critics and audiences alike. One commentator called it "a bitter and angry anti-German propaganda film." And legendary General George Patton, who certainly knew a thing or two about the German soldier and by extension German people, allegedly snarled "Bullshit!" while stomping angrily out of a private screening of the film held for an audience of high-ranking generals that included Eisenhower.

Another film, *Our Job in Japan*, produced in November 1945, was a sharply contrasting portrayal of that former enemy. It was frankly sympathetic, picturing the Japanese not as revenge-bent, fascist conspirators, but as an easily-guided people who had been led astray by the war lords. Instead of eschewing any-and-all contact with Japanese, this film encouraged contact with the Japanese, stating that a purpose of the occupation of Japan was to bring democratic principles and practices to the Japanese. Curiously, and despite the film's closeness to his own ambitions for Japan's future, MacArthur suppressed its distribution.

(All three of the afore-mentioned films were written by a professional Hollywood screenwriter, one Theodor S. Geisel, who was later to become famously known by his pen name, "Dr. Seuss." As a member of the Writer's Guild of America, Geisel was eligible for a screen credit, which entry would have been automatically included without any action required on his part. On the other hand, a writer can demand that he or she not be given a screen credit, and do so unquestioningly. None of the three films carries Geisel's writing credit.)

The demonizing, as it were, of Germany was to drive even wider the chasm between the two major postwar occupations with respect to the role of American military families in them. In Germany, the intent to keep victors and vanquished separated as much as possible was facilitated by housing the families in tightly-controlled and -isolated compounds, many of which were ringed by barbed wire. Meanwhile, over in Japan, very open and receptive versions of modern suburban America were erected, all without a single forbidding obstacle. This strict segregation of American families from the German people becomes wryly ironic in light of a stated intent of that occupation to de-Nazify the country by exposing the people to American suburban lifestyles.

Martha Gravois, herself an army wife who experienced three separate tours in West Germany, wrote of the irony of the situation, first by citing an official source:

> *Denazification of all areas of German life was one of the more pressing talks of the military government. By bringing American families to live in Germany, the occupation force hoped to give the Germans an opportunity to observe, and presumably be edified by, "the example of democratic American home life."*[16]

Then by offering her opinion, based upon her own experiences:

> *The extent to which the objective was achieved is debatable, and probably unprovable. The formation of self-contained military compounds precluded much close contact. But this may not have been as much of a barrier as the psychological one separating conqueror and conquered, which only time could wear down. With some exceptions, what Germans saw of American wives and children was from quite a distance, and*

---

[16] U.S. European Command, Office of the Chief Historian, *Domestic Economy: Shipment of Dependents to the European Theater and Establishment of Military Communities: Occupation Forces in Europe Series, 1945-46,* p. 12.

thus would have been largely limited to observations about clothing, health, and general appearance. One can only wonder about the feelings of German women when confronted with the sight of stylishly clad American wives clutching the hands of their healthy, robust children.

– Martha Gravois, "Military Families in Germany, 1946-1986: Why They Came and Why They Stay," *Parameters, Journal of the US Army War College*, Vol XVI, No. 4, pp. 58-59

As I write this, a Toshiba television set and Sanyo recorder rest on the desk behind me, a Nikon camera plus lenses and accessories from Konica and Canon are in a nearby closet, and I will later drive a Toyota that awaits in the garage. And we have a couple more television sets, plus other electronic this-and-that, including perhaps some inner parts of the computer this book is being composed upon that either are Japanese in origin or were inspired by some earlier Japanese innovation.

I look at them, listen to them, toy with them, drive them...and cannot help but wonder how dramatically different our world might now be had we treated the defeated Japanese in the same fearful, dismissive manner we treated the vanquished Germans. Or conversely, how much different the world would be had we opened our hearts, consciences and homes to the Germans in the same manner as we did to the Japanese.

In the same vein of making the dependents feel at home in Japan, there seems to have been a concerted effort to psychologically separate the occupation's families from the occupation's armed forces, and by extension even the very reason for the occupation. This aim can be subtly discerned here-and-there, beginning with the dependents' welcoming brochure, the aforementioned *Dependents Guide to Japan*, and the title's omission of the adjective "occupied" to denote the host country's then-current state.

Dependents Guide... otherwise nowhere mentions or even alludes to the recent nastiness between the two nations. Here and elsewhere in official publications, the idea was to portray Japan as an inviting, exotic land that always had been of that state, not some once-hostile enemy country temporarily forced to bow to the whims of a foreign power. The only publication given to new arrivals that did mention the war, including background on Japan's aggression, was *The Occupation of Japan*, a booklet issued to arriving American *uniformed* personnel only--and even it soft-pedaled Japan's reasons for starting the Pacific war by stressing Japan's need and impulse to expand its influence out of perceived economic necessity. The booklet did, however, provide a somewhat detailed history of major combat campaigns in the Pacific Theater.

Without detailing why, one significant city received terse, emphatic mention in *Occupation Personnel Regulations* and few other publications: Hiroshima. The wasted, flattened victim of the "Little Boy" atomic bomb was strictly off limits to military and civilian personnel alike as a casual destination; one only went there under specific orders. The reason, when given at all, was simply, "Out of respect....," with no further mention of the awesome destruction, what caused it, or that the city's devastation hastened the end of the war.

The other atomic bomb target, Nagasaki, was not off limits, likely because the palpable damage there was far less evident than in Hiroshima, despite the fact the nuclear device detonated over the Kyushu port city had an equivalent TNT explosive yield a third greater than the Hiroshima bomb, 20- as against some 13-to-15 kilotons. The dissimilarity in destruction was due to the cities' topographic differences: Nagasaki is characterized by ridges and clefts, which dispersed the blast wave, whereas Hiroshima lies nakedly exposed on a flat plain, wholly open to the bomb's full effect, with hills to the city's northeast and northwest that served to focus the blast. Hiroshima remained a wasteland for most of the occupation, its reconstruction begun only after being designated a City of Peace by the Japanese parliament in 1949.

While the scope and variety of print materials available in Japan clearly indicated MacArthur's vision of the occupation and how he expected Americans and other foreign nationals to conduct themselves, the second largest occupying contingent, the British, steadfastly refused to abandon their stiffly elitist colonial manner. British Commonwealth troops, and especially their families, deliberately--and coldly--eschewed the egalitarian approach to the Japanese SCAP sought. American families might have frowned upon this behavior by our ally; my parents certainly did. But in the eyes of many Commonwealth families, their open contempt was understandable and justified because of wartime treatment by the Japanese of British civilians they had held captive.

During the war, relatively few American civilians were incarcerated by the Japanese, and virtually all these were caught unawares when Japanese forces swiftly overran Guam, Wake Islands and the Philippines during the conflict's first few weeks. On the other hand, Japanese concentration camps held thousands of Commonwealth civilians, trapped when the enemy swiftly overwhelmed such venerable Empire outposts as Shanghai, Singapore and Hong Kong, plus Malaysia and Burma.

These families did not suffer as much as military prisoners of war or Asian nationals, but they nevertheless had to endure forced labor, skimpy rations, a high mortality rate, and general survival-level living conditions. Once the conflict ended, a significant number of these former internees and prisoners were assigned to Japan, where they let it be known they didn't like their wartime treatment one little bit, and never mind which individual Japanese were responsible for their discomfort.

This postwar animosity between the two former enemies was borne out in a series of interviews conducted in the mid-1950s by historian and MacArthur biographer D. Clayton James among some seven hundred middle- and upper-class Japanese on their attitudes toward both the occupation and the occupiers. I interviewed James about his interviews shortly before he died. He told me that when talking about Americans, his subjects were very open, all smiles and chatty--but when the subject turned to the British, they became markedly reserved and cautious, selecting their words carefully and generally being reluctantly communicative.

James also found that while the Japanese constitution is drawn on the English (parliamentary) model, the people viewed Americans as infinitely more egalitarian, far more representative of democratic ideals and principles in day-to-day practice, than was the case with the British, whom they viewed as being too imbued with class-consciousness to be truly representative of what democracy meant.

This revelation raised the question on my part: So did the Japanese like us because of the way we practiced democratic principles, or simply because of our demeanor and principles in general? Mr. James replied that the latter was definitely the case, that the fact we came from a preeminent democratic society was incidental. Fair enough. But from this a sociologist might infer that we were the way we were (and still are) because of our particular democratic heritage, that we would not have developed as we did with our generally relaxed, trusting and open attitudes had our particular democracy not developed as it did.

I caught a glimpse of the Japanese attitude toward the British my first full day in Japan. When mother and I arrived, dad informed us that our house, located not far from the port area, could not be occupied until the next day. So like MacArthur and my father before me, I spent my first night in Japan in the New Grand Hotel.

The next morning, mother sent me across the street to play in Yamashita Park. I took with me a small sailboat I had brought from America, to push around a pond I had been told was on the grounds. I had barely entered the park when a half dozen or so Japanese boys, about my age and all dressed in tatters, approached me on the red gravel path. On seeing one another, we all stopped and stared uneasily. After a few awkward moments, the tallest of the boys stepped forward gingerly and asked tentatively, "Engrish?"[17] I shook my head nervously and replied "No." Then he broke into a broad grin and asked

---

[17] I am trying here and elsewhere to replicate the sound of Japanese voices as I heard them. Japanese who do not learn English as small children have trouble saying the letter "L." During the war, common passwords for Allied lines were "Lollapalooza" and "Joe Palooka," because of the Japanese inability to say "Ls."

brightly, "'Merican?" "Yes," I answered, nodding quickly. "Ah, so!" he beamed, gestured for his friends to join him, and we all went off together to sail my boat in the park's small pond.

I spent, I would guess, an hour or so with the boys, none of whom could speak English coherently, but we had fun pushing the boat back-and-forth across the water, applauding gaily now-and-then when its sail would fill in the slight breeze. At one point, the one boy asked my name. I replied with my childhood moniker: Jamie. "Ah, so," he said brightly, "Jamie-san!" In a single stroke, my given name was rendered into Japanese, and I kept the sobriquet throughout our time in Japan.

When we were done playing, the boys escorted me back across the street to the hotel entrance. As we parted, they bowed to me, and I self-consciously returned the gesture, my first introduction to Japanese customs. When my mother and I discussed the occasion as part of my interviews of her in the mid-1990s, she recalled that, at her encouragement, I gave the boat to the boys as a goodwill gesture. I vaguely remember that, and definitely know that for the rest of our time in Japan I never again sailed a toy boat.

My boat sailing morning, though trivial, was indicative of many such casual encounters American family members, adults and children alike, had with Japanese during the occupation: spontaneous, friendly, open, non-committal, and non-demanding. We followed no special rules for such occasions, or at least I didn't, other than being now-and-then reminded to always be courteous, friendly, generous, and to be careful not to ask much of a people who by-and-large had little.

If we were conscious of anything, it was that we were bulls in a china shop--a wrecked china shop to be sure, but with enough artifacts and charm still remaining to provide a glimpse of the exotic land Japan once was, and slowly but steadily becoming again. And being aware of our position as both conquerors and interlopers, we tiptoed our way through the delicate surroundings, at times as awkwardly as a bull on the point of its hooves would be, but still maneuvering with a fair degree of success, leaving everything pretty much intact.

Bear in mind that I'm speaking here just of my own observations and behavior and that of the families here: my parents and their friends, my friends and playmates and schoolmates, and other families we would encounter daily. It could be--and unfortunately was--a quite different story when it came to contact with Japanese where single American servicemen and civilian personnel were concerned.

Donna Alvah, Assistant Professor of United States History at St. Lawrence University, notes in her book *Unofficial Ambassadors: American Military Families Overseas and the Cold War*, that postwar Okinawa especially was overrun by out-of-control American GIs. Rape became so prevalent that the commanding general of that contingent made rape a capital crime. An article in *Life* magazine in 1949 called the situation in Okinawa "a shameful mess."

In Japan itself, the mother of one soldier blamed her son's murder of two Japanese on "the emotional strain of a delayed homecoming." In late 1946, an American soldier went berserk for some never-understood reason and beat four Japanese to death, then took his own life. Plus there was the horror of mixed race babies being murdered and abandoned. In his book, *Embracing Defeat*, John W. Dower writes, "Although as a rule the victors conducted themselves with far greater discipline than the Japanese military had exercised in occupied areas of Asia, assault and rape inevitably occurred."

One thing we were not aware of was our position as the very embodiment of MacArthur's ideal of the example of the American home--and in retrospect, a good thing we weren't so aware, for the revelation might have made us self-conscious of some role we were obligated to play. Which was just as well, given our status in the occupation. Family member dependents and all other US Army-sponsored civilians in Japan at the time were officially classified as Department of the Army, Civilian, or more colloquially, "DACs." Dependent wives and children DACs organizationally occupied the lowest rung on the occupation's priority ladder, beneath all other DACs and even below privates first class, the lowest army rank assigned to the occupation.

Yet despite this cellar-dwelling status, plus the absence of any mandate to do something-or-other in support of SCAP's Christianizing ambition, MacArthur saw to it that we were treated specially. For one thing, the general saw to it that the servicemen's families got to Japan expeditiously.

During the occupation, Japan was literally off limits to anyone who did not have a valid reason for being there; no tourists, traveling salesmen, or the just plain curious were allowed. MacArthur would personally review visit requests, and woe betide anyone whom he admitted, then went against his grain. In one noteworthy incident, a *Newsweek* magazine correspondent already based in Japan filed a story MacArthur didn't like. Soon after, the reporter left Japan for a vacation--and SCAP refused him re-admittance. But MacArthur's strict rules for entry into Japan did not apply to the wives and children of military personnel; just being a serviceman's family was reason enough to be allowed entry without any further qualifications.

SCAP's *laissez faire* attitude toward admitting military families did not extend to the occupation's civilian employees. Civil servants, consultants, contractors, and their dependents were closely scrutinized before being admitted. Few "feather merchants"[18] bothered to try and bring their families along in any event. For one thing, most civilian assignments to Japan were for months, not three years, so separation from one's family was not viewed as a hardship. For another, housing for families, civilians and military alike, was scarce, and usually the only reason for delaying bringing over a serviceman's family.

And still another reason civilian families weren't common in the occupation could be that the man in charge simply didn't want them around. Throughout his career, MacArthur was notorious for being both distrustful and disdainful of civilian bureaucracy and authority, up to and including every American president under whom he served-- Theodore Roosevelt excepted, but Franklin Roosevelt and Truman especially. Given the general's ingrained attitude, it follows he would sneer at a civilian underling's family as much as the man himself, and so would consider such a family unworthy to portray his American home ideal. SCAP otherwise did what he could to physically separate the Eighth Army from the occupation's civilian presence and

---

[18] The military's longtime, derogatory term for someone in a position that involves little effort or responsibility, or who deliberately evades effort or responsibility.

influence, which helps further explain why Eighth Army headquarters was sited in Yokohama and not Tokyo.

There were exceptions to the practice of discouraging civilian families, notably the dependents of medical personnel, aid workers, teachers, missionaries, and others not associated with occupation administration. Their appointments usually were for a year or more, and that long a separation from one's family could be viewed as a hardship, and so reason to welcome dependents. Also, one cannot overlook that while the families of teachers and aid workers and the like lived in Japan under SCAP's aegis, they were not part of the occupation's civilian bureaucracy, and so not subject to MacArthur's scorn. In any event, any American *civilian* family, even Christian ones and those not formally part of the occupation, resided outside the model of the American Christian home MacArthur wished to present to the Japanese; that honor belonged solely to the military families.

The largesse granted servicemen's families created among our households something of the aura of an exclusive club, or perhaps more appropriately an extended family, with MacArthur as *paterfamilias*, a persona he fit as naturally--and autocratically--as the one he displayed to the Japanese people. Like any good family head, MacArthur established the standard, embodied in his design of the occupation and his goals for it, made the rules, written out in the regulations and orders, and finally set the examples, which he displayed subtly and without fanfare--but still with as great an effect and influence as if written in his own hand.

One example MacArthur set was a studied visual casualness no matter the occasion--and no matter how other American officers in attendance might be attired, which more often than not would be suitably dressy.

Nothing illustrated MacArthur's approach to his sartorial habit better than a story my father related at dinner one evening. Earlier that day, dad had gone to Tokyo to participate in some formal military ceremony attended by a large number of foreign military generals and admirals in addition to a high-ranking American officer corps contingent. MacArthur was also present as one of the speakers. Dad took pains to describe his fellow American officers, decked out in their best uniforms and sporting chests full of colorful awards, decorations and campaign ribbons--but he took greatest delight in describing the foreign military brass: all a-glitter in their formal dress uniforms, blazoned with pounds of medals, streaming sashes, glittering sabers, and elaborate epaulets. Dad then concluded with a laugh, "...and there stood MacArthur in his shirt."

He was ever thus; SCAP was usually that way. MacArthur cultivated the image of wearing just a simple open-collar uniform shirt and trousers for almost all occasions; the look personified him as surely as Eisenhower's sharply tailored waist-length jacket or Patton's gleaming pearl- handled revolvers. Statues of MacArthur erected throughout Japan by appreciative Japanese after the occupation was over all recreate the pose he liked best: plain khaki trousers and open collar shirt revealing a hint of bare chest, a simple five-star insignia on the collar the only adornment, sunglasses on, visor hat squared up, striding resolutely forward, one hand on his hip, the other arm thrust forward and gripping his trademark corncob pipe.

To gaze upon one of these statues today is to regard one of history's greatest dichotomies: a truly great military legend, the archetype of an autocrat, even at times a megalomaniac, but also as well a self-serving blowhard who saw to his own image before all else--and yet looking in his frozen casting like he's doing nothing more consequential than heading out to hoe a garden. Even the statue of him that first greets visitors to his namesake memorial in Norfolk reflects the image he cultivated: just standing there in shirt and trousers, a jacket slung casually over one arm.

Actually, MacArthur would have looked ridiculous had he ever worn all his awards, if indeed he could have squeezed them onto a single jacket. He was the most decorated individual in American history--military or civilian, male or female--with dozens of military honors plus tributes from foreign nations. His decorations included his own Medal of Honor, a controversial homage because it was given not as recognition of a single act of valor, but for his failed defense of the Philippines in early 1942.

The worthiness of the award aside, his holding of America's highest military accolade makes him a member of but one of two father-son duos to have been bestowed the Medal of Honor. The other pair are Theodore Roosevelt, awarded for leading the charge up Cuba's San Juan Hill in the Spanish-American War, and his son, Theodore, Jr., for his leadership gallantry on Utah Beach during the Normandy landings on June 6, 1944, where he turned looming disaster into victory by rallying his division after it had landed on the beach more than a mile off course.

All MacArthur's decorations are gathered into a single display in his Norfolk, Virginia, memorial. The exhibit looks like a hugely comprehensive medal collection from all manner of sources, giving one pause to consider they were all conferred upon a single recipient.

The man once actually refused being accorded a prestigious decoration--not because he didn't think he deserved it, but rather because he didn't think the medal deserved *him*! At issue was the awarding of the Legion of Merit medal for his leadership of the campaign that wrested the Philippines back from Japanese control. There are four degrees to the medal, the highest, Chief Commander, usually intended solely for a head of state. But the individual degrees of the Legion of Merit are meant solely for *foreign* recipients of the decoration; Americans get just the medal with no degrees stipulated, a policy that seems not to have set well with MacArthur.

An incident that occurred right after Japan surrendered, while MacArthur was still in Manila, reveals his feeling. On August 16, 1945, General Marshall sent MacArthur a wire stating:

> *The citation for your liberation of the Philippines has been proposed. What is your desire, another Oak Leaf for your DSM* (Distinguished Service Medal) *or a Legion of Merit? The various degrees for the Legion of Merit were cancelled for the Army and Navy and submitted only to Foreign Officers. It might be that I could secure authority from the President to have you given the degree*

*of Chief Commander. However there is
no certainty if that can be arranged.*

MacArthur wired back to Marshall:

*Very grateful to you for your
generous action. Item* (meaning himself)
*would naturally prefer the Chief
Commander grade of the Legion of
Merit. If this is impracticable* (sic), *item
would prefer an oak leaf cluster to the
Dog Sugar Mike rather than a lower
grade of the Legion of Merit.*
– MacArthur Memorial Library, RG-9
Collection of Messages, 1945-1951

In other words, MacArthur snubbed an ordinary, suitable-for-anybody Legion of Merit because he could not get one that would in effect recognize his upcoming SCAP-ship, which he may well have viewed as equivalent to being Japan's head of state. James Zobel believes MacArthur actually took the oak leaf cluster for his existing DSM. In any event, a Legion of Merit is conspicuously missing from the display in Norfolk.

(My father was twice awarded his own Legion of Merit. The first time was for some supply innovation he introduced into the Italian Campaign during World War II; my sister couldn't remember the details. The second time, commemorated by an oak leaf cluster pinned to the main medal, was for his performance in the Korean War from June 1950 to August 1951. He was awarded this medal for innovations in food service he introduced into the theater of war. Specifically, he teamed with San Francisco restauranteur and philanthropist George Mardikian to develop materials and means to serve freshly-prepared hot meals to front line troops under combat conditions. Mr. Mardikian was awarded the prestigious Medal of Freedom by President Truman for his contributions to the endeavor. He and dad remained close friends for life; for years after at every Christmas, we would receive a case of rare California wines from Mr. Mardikian.)

While all officers under MacArthur's command were of course expected *not* to follow the boss's lead and to dress suitably for official occasions, they otherwise adopted SCAP's informal vestment habits at work and home alike. My father was no exception; I never once saw him wear his ribbons, let alone the medals the ribbons represented, on his workaday uniform. And once dad got home, he would shed his uniform jacket and putter around MacArthur-like in plain khakis, often doing chores with our gardener. This intended casualness set a tone; it made the culturally-formal Japanese feel relaxed and at home with us. Or at least that was the intent. The custom prevailed throughout the families: we open, informal Americans dressed and acted the part, and I am certain our style helped ease cautions and reservations.

Another--and more critical--personal example MacArthur set was unwavering trust in the honor of the Japanese people. He didn't do this by moving constantly among the masses like a politician; that was not his style. He in fact eschewed personal contact as much as possible, rarely making formal public appearances. Nor were his illustrations of trust haphazard, *au point*, set pieces. His example of trust was far more blatant, exposed, predictable--and constant: he daily made himself an easy target for assassination.

The American embassy in Tokyo, where MacArthur lived with his wife and son, was some five miles from his Dai Ichi headquarters building. Each morning, SCAP would be driven to work at the exact same time, seven o'clock, in the most recognizable motor vehicle in Japan: a black 1941 Cadillac limousine, which he had been issued while still in the Philippines and survived the Japanese occupation unscathed. His driver followed the same route every day, sometimes under escort and sometimes not, which meant that they sometimes got caught in traffic just like everyone else. The same route and habit were followed nightly back to the American embassy, although the time the general would leave GHQ might vary. In 1950, MacArthur was issued a new black Cadillac limousine, this time equipped all around with bullet-proof glass. This auto is on permanent display at the MacArthur

Memorial; the older Cadillac is in an automobile collection in England.

MacArthur also never had a visible personal bodyguard, not for the daily commute or anywhere else, although he sometimes carried a small, concealed pistol. His disdain of personal protection together with his unwavering commuting habit agonized his staff, for it would have been the simplest task imaginable to walk up to the general's limo and dispatch him. And such an assassination scenario was entirely possible in a land where there still remained some grumbling dissenters among a population that had demonstrated in the recent war there were many who would willingly invite their own death by taking the life of an enemy combatant. And in fact, a few assassination plots were uncovered and subsequently squelched. There was one known half-hearted attempt on his life, by a deranged army veteran wielding a wooden samurai sword. He was easily intercepted and subdued.

MacArthur's commuting habit, his aplomb at the suggestion someone might want to harm him, and the general impression that he felt totally at ease among the Japanese transferred to all Americans living in Japan, including families with children, of course including our own. I was but ten and eleven years old at the time, and I never once hesitated to go anywhere alone at almost any time of the day or evening within reason. I walked and rode a bicycle among blackened ruins; I took streetcars and buses to visit friends elsewhere in Yokohama or to go to a movie or a post exchange, sometimes not returning home until after dark, never once giving a thought to my personal safety.

I even traveled alone to visit a close friend who lived some twenty miles away in Kamakura, then and now a tourist Mecca for the *Daibutsu*, the world's largest outdoor seated Buddha, located in adjacent Hase. To get to Kamakura, I had to walk about a quarter-mile to where I caught a train to Ofuna, site of the *Kannon* (female Buddha), a huge hilltop statue just across a stream and road from the train station, then hop a train to Kamakura. On these occasions, if I did not stay overnight in Kamakura, I might not return home until past nightfall.

Listeners today are stunned when, in the context of telling about my boyhood in Japan, I reveal this habit of going around on my own just about anywhere I chose at all kinds of hours. Mothers of young children are especially aghast. Weren't your parents fearful of kidnappings or reprisals? they ask. The questions finally became so persistent I brought up the subject to my mother as part of my lengthy interview with her. She was nonplused by the query. "Of course not!" she sniffed. "It (the question of your personal safety) never crossed our minds."

I pondered mother's seeming indifference about my safety for some time before her unstated reasoning struck me: it was the military mind-set--again. The possibility of crimes against persons are nowhere mentioned in *Occupation Personnel Regulations* or *Dependents Guide to Japan* or likely anywhere else, including our, and everyone's, orders to Japan. The question of being victims of personal crime therefore became like the matter of not familiarizing ourselves about Japan prior to going there: the subject was not raised, so can be said not to be required or questioned. It was not an issue, therefore the problem did not exist, nor do crimes against persons exist as a major issue in Japan to this day. The same could be said for Japan's role in the war: it was never brought up; it was not an issue; what was done was done, and nothing more need be said.

This ingrained attitude on the part of our family and others of taking orders and similar directives at face value, with no further query or explanation, might puzzle someone unfamiliar with the military lifestyle. How could you do thus-and-so without even once questioning the rationale? they might ask. The answer is: you just did! MacArthur certainly knew this; he was born into the lifestyle and never left it. And because he knew intuitively that his troops--and their families--would follow him and all other superiors unquestioningly, and because he also knew and believed in the honor of the Japanese character, he likely decided to just go ahead and direct things with as little embellishment or additional explanations he thought necessary. For the military families that were his wards, the formula worked, and it worked because he knew it would. And so he fit his *paterfamilias* role exactly: stern, aloof, demanding--but never overtly so. He never had to state the obvious; everyone just knew.

MacArthur was obviously doing a good job directing the occupation in the eyes of people back in the United States. A Gallup Poll in 1947 placed him at the top of the list of the most popular Americans, quite a feat when one considers there were so many war heroes still around then. He was perhaps the ultimate example of being the right person in the right place at the right time with the right idea and the right backing.

As evidence that MacArthur was correct in nearly everything from his image management and tone to his attitudes and policies, consider the reaction of the Japanese themselves after Truman dismissed him. When Eisenhower, leader of the conquest of Nazi Germany for the Western powers alliance, left Germany for the last time, no particular fanfare attended his departure. By contrast, when MacArthur left Japan in May 1951, the Japanese spontaneously honored the man with perhaps the longest parade in the history of the world. A throng estimated at some two to three million Japanese (and also Koreans, plus other Asians) spent all day and well into the night walking past his Dai Ichi headquarters building. To the Japanese at least, the building and the man were still very much Number One.

Chapter 6: The Chrysanthemum Frontier

When occupation administrators responsible for the well-being of servicemen's families read in MacArthur's welcoming press release to the dependents that he foresaw their lives in Japan as "...a type of pioneering reminiscent of the pioneer days of our own west during the nineteenth century," they might have cringed. The purpose of the dependents' program, after all, was to encourage wives to gather up their children and come join their husbands, not make them apprehensive about plunging into some Wild West scenario fraught with dangers and deprivations.

Like families anywhere during any era, familiar creature comforts were a primary consideration and desire for the military families bound for Japan. Additionally, they, like all other American families of the time, eagerly sought return of the consumer products and other amenities of a normal peacetime existence; familiar, material goods and conveniences that had been denied them during the wartime years of shortages and rationing.

So beginning with the arrival of those first dependents, a not insignificant thrust of occupation planning and resources was devoted to making the families feel as much at home as possible. This was done by transplanting elements of life back in America to Japan, ranging from popular consumer items Americans took for granted, like soft drinks, ice cream, and the latest fashions, to American style educational resources for the families' children.

Trouble was, getting familiar American accouterments to postwar Japan was neither expeditious nor completely thorough for the occupation's duration. The same was true for families' household goods and other belongings. Personal effects and consumer goods alike were subject to shipping allotments, and cargo space was limited because priorities had to be given to commodities vital to rebuilding and rejuvenating the country: capital goods like bulldozers and concrete, fertilizers and structural steel. As a result, life in Japan for the families was often a matter of compromises, of making do with what they could cobble together from often meager local resources combined with the few American consumer products that were made available. In the end, the degree of hardships a family had to endure depended on its status, which was determined by the breadwinner's rank, his job, the command to which he was assigned, and where in Japan the family lived.

As one would expect, proportionately more shipping space for household goods was allotted to the families of higher-ranking commissioned and non-commissioned officers. As the occupation progressed, this rank-has-its-privileges (RHIP, in military jargon) tradition produced a huge secondary market in American consumer products, as lower-ranking servicemen, bachelors and family heads alike eagerly snatched up no longer needed merchandise from homeward-bound, higher-ranking personnel, often at premium prices far above their second-hand worth back in America.

Military exchanges (post exchanges for the army, base exchanges for the air force and navy) made an early appearance, and their number and the amount and variety of goods they carried expanded as the occupation progressed. But even these were subject to shipping restrictions. American clothing articles were the most-sought items by families with growing children, followed by American-style household goods like ordinary kitchen utensils and dressings such as curtains and throw rugs.

Some desirable items were so rare that when they did manage come in to an exchange, they were auctioned off instead of just being set out for sale. Imports from India and elsewhere in Southeast Asia, Oriental rugs especially, were the most popular items put up for auction. Otherwise, housewives got into the habit of befriending exchange personnel in order to be among the first to know when new shipments of certain goods would be on the shelves. Outright bribery usually didn't ensure a place at the head of the line, because such popular inducement goods as cartons of American cigarettes and imported liquors, scotch especially but also bourbon, were commonly purloined by exchange personnel in any event, so they weren't susceptible to bribes.

American currency could buy favors--except it wasn't used or otherwise allowed. In order to keep conventional American money out of Japanese hands, the occupation resorted to printing special scrip that was backed by the United States Treasury dollar-for-dollar, and went by the formal term "Military Payment Certificates." The scrip was issued in every denomination from the nickel up to ten dollars: 5-, 10-, 25- and 50-cent "coins;" 1-, 5- and 10-dollar "bills." Japanese weren't permitted to have or spend scrip. Pennies were the only American currency allowed in circulation, ostensibly strictly for use at exchanges and other occupation outlets, but they found their way into the local economy. I've a feeling we all contributed to Japan's rehabilitation in that small way at least.

My way of handling spending money was common among my friends, and possibly adults as well. Whenever I left the house, I'd be sure to have Japanese yen notes, coins and American pennies stuffed into my left pants pocket, occupation scrip notes in my right, in order to be certain they were kept separated. Then whenever I'd visit a Japanese shop, I'd of course pay for items with the Japanese currency--and often use the pennies (never the scrip!) to make up any difference. Shop keepers were so happy to get even the pennies that I would occasionally acquire something for more than its selling price in yen. My money-toting habit became so ingrained I practice a variation of the pattern to this day: I carry all coins in my left pocket, paper currency in my right.

The black market was another means to get goods, if the participants didn't mind leaving their scruples at the doorstep and could pay the price. Black markets are a hallmark of the aftermath of any war, but the one in postwar Japan was especially vast, varied and vigorous.

First and foremost, everyone, and I mean *everyone*, participated. Not just Americans, Japanese and British Commonwealth personnel, but also the millions of people, mostly fellow Asians but some Westerners as well, that Japan had captured, incarcerated, imprisoned, kidnaped and otherwise held for upwards of a decade or more. It was estimated that one and a quarter-million Koreans alone were still in Japan at war's end, having been brought there to perform what amounted to slave labor, mostly in coal mines. These and hundreds of thousands of other nationalities, including not a few Japanese Americans, were all awaiting repatriation back to their homelands. In the meantime, they had to subsist, and the black market was by far the most popular way for people without recourse elsewhere at least to survive as sellers, buyers, procurers, thieves, confidence men...whatever it took to keep eating.

Simply because so many thousands of people became involved in the black market in one way or other, it quickly became internationally infamous, and is still regarded as the largest, most extensive black market the world has ever known. Its main outlet was on the grounds of Tokyo's main railway station, which had been heavily damaged by bombs, although branches sprouted and flourished throughout Japan. Saturdays were the primary trading day, and the main outlet in Tokyo was sometimes raided by Japanese police on that day of the week. Veteran participants were well-prepared for such annoyances, having likely been tipped-off beforehand. They would simply temporarily disguise their nefarious trading as street side stalls, then go back to business as usual once the threat passed.

Participants' nationalities dictated what they were interested in as either buyers or sellers. For example, American cigarettes were prized by everyone, smokers and non-smokers alike because of their trading value, and by Japanese and other Asians most of all because the local product was harshly distasteful. American cigarettes sold for just one dollar a carton in exchanges, but could be resold on the black market for more than triple their equivalent value in yen. Another common black market item was American currency, not scrip but actual five- and ten-dollar bills especially, which were so popular that they would often sell for far more than their yen value equivalent.

Even the yen itself was a commonly-traded item. This occurred because the yen was devalued four times as the occupation progressed, from being near-par value to the American dollar immediately after the war ended, to the outrageously high ratio of 360 yen to the dollar by 1949.[19] What happened was the Japanese government would proclaim

---

[19] This 360:1 yen-to-dollar exchange ratio was personally set by MacArthur, who here displayed his knowledge of antiquity: he derived the ratio from the base-sixty numbering system of ancient Babylonia, which is also the basis for the 360-degree compass rose

a currency devaluation, which would trigger hoarding of the higher-value existing yen. In order to keep currency in circulation while new bills were being printed, the government would issue special adhesive stamps, to be affixed to the existing yen notes to denote their previous higher value.

Trouble was, these stamps were easily counterfeited, and the fraudulent copies were sold on the black market to hoarders at a fraction of their true worth. The counterfeits would then be re-sold at higher prices, close to the value of the real stamps but still low enough below their implied true worth to entice buyers who would then use them on their devalued yen currency.

On the (sort of) plus side, the black market enabled Americans to become familiar with the nuances of Japanese culture. It was through the black market that Americans first sampled Japan's famed Kobe beef, where the steers are massaged by gloved hands to engender meat of exquisite tenderness. The beef quickly became a favorite of American civilian contractors because they could most afford the delicacy, then serve it to impress business contacts--a scenario that became a wry irony, because well-off Japanese participants in the black market favored *American* beefsteaks (*beefoteki*, in Japanese), T-bones most of all, which *they* also would use to impress clients. All this cross-cultural exchange of steaks from wherever by whomever for whatever made beef the most popular food item traded in the black market--if nothing else, an interesting phenomenon in the predominantly--and thus presumably vegetarian--Buddhist country.

Genuine, imported Scotch whisky was the most popular alcoholic beverage traded nefariously, and it too was devoured by both Japanese and Americans, the latter in this case including lower-rank, underage enlisted military personnel who otherwise were prohibited from buying hard liquors until age twenty-one, but could buy beer when eighteen years old.

By far the most popular items Americans sought on the black market were Japanese swords, collectively called *nihonto*, or more commonly but also somewhat erroneously *katana*, which also means a two-handed long sword, and any sword worn cutting edge-up in the bearer's *obi* (waist sash). Many varieties and grades of swords changed hands during the occupation, from impeccable antiques to cheaply made imitations, with the most coveted being the meticulously handmade swords once used by Japan's fabled samurai warriors. There were numerous types, styles, and grades of these storied weapons, each grouping usually named after its era of manufacture, with the pinnacle of the art form manifested in blades formed from multiple layers of steel lovingly folded together, using a technique developed around the eighth century.

The most plentifully-available, highest-quality swords were made in the traditional folded manner through the *gendaito* (modern sword) period, which lasted from 1876 through the last year of the war. A half-century after gendaito had begun production, Hirohito ascended the Chrysanthemum Throne, ushering in the second *Showa* (ironically, "period of enlightened peace") era , the first having run from 1312-1317, and a new generation of eponymous swords. *Showato* swords were made until 1989, the year Hirohito died--but while a scant few examples were made in the traditional manner, most showato represented a major step down in quality because their blades were shaped from just single sheets of steel.

Finally there were machine made, mass produced replicas of samurai models, cumulatively--and derisively--termed *gunto* (military sword). Production of gunto began early in the twentieth century, mainly for issue to officers in the Russo-Japan War of 1905, although some were sold abroad. Tens of thousands more were added for distribution to a new generation of officers during Japan's buildup to war in the 1930s. And for the moment setting aside the derisiveness of the term "gunto," many if not most of these swords were of exceptionally high quality in their own right, simply because of Japanese pride in the tradition.

When the occupation began, Japanese were barred for holding weapons of any sort, so thousands of gunto swords, at least, were simply dumped out in the open along with firearms. Homeward-bound American soldiers reported scooping up swords by the armload from where they had been haphazardly piled alongside awaiting troop transport ships. But once the families and other civilians plus military replacements began arriving, Japanese soon realized that, weapons ban or not, they had eager customers for the swords.

Many Japanese were so desperate just to survive they used their own and their families' inherited swords as barter currency for critically needed food and other supplies, in many cases letting even valuable antique, traditionally-made swords go for pittances. But they found such eager, malleable customers in the Americans--virtually all of whom were wholly ignorant about the exotic art form--that natural market forces of supply and demand soon took hold, and prices of all swords, from the magnificent to the mundane, rose exponentially, bringing tens of thousands of swords clattering down from otherwise sparsely-filled Japanese cupboards. Some estimates have more than a million swords eventually changing hands during the occupation, so many in any event that by 1958 it was believed that there were more nihonto of all types, styles and grades back in America than remained in Japan.

At first, because of the weapons prohibition, virtually all swords were traded on the black market. And because the swords were bought and sold under the counter, it could be extremely difficult to gauge a sword's true worth until after the transaction had been completed, and the sword taken to an expert for a frankly honest evaluation. Compounding the situation was that even some mass-produced gunto could be of exceptionally high quality in their own right. The very term gunto in fact refers not to the sword, but the metallic scabbard in which the weapon was sheathed.

And of course, there were outright counterfeits of traditional samurai swords. A blade formed from a single sheet of steel could be so exquisitely finished that an expert could not tell its composition without closely examining the tang. Even more insidious--and brazen-- a counterfeiter might take a recently-made gendaito and chisel a forgery of some centuries-past maker's signature into the tang. The result would be a work of art unto itself, an exact replica of a genuine antique, its authenticity all but impossible to discern to other than a limited number of experts.

The black market activity in swords eventually became so pervasive that MacArthur personally stepped in to halt the practice. In

1947, he met with Japan's premier sword authority, Dr. Homma Junji, who presented the general with examples of every blade from every period of Japanese history. Working with an American colonel considered the preeminent American authority on the art form, the trio separated the swords with artistic merit from the pretenders. SCAP then authorized the sale and possession of swords made in the traditional folded manner, and ordered all the gunto destroyed. Despite MacArthur's directive, underground cottage industries sprang up to turn out imitations, and they and sequestered gunto that had escaped destruction all found their way into the black market.

Today, Japanese swords of all types adorn the homes of grandchildren (and by now, likely great-grandchildren) of occupation personnel, and these present-day families are often shocked when they try to sell their keepsakes thinking they are authentic, ancient samurai weapons, only to discover to their chagrin that they are cheap twentieth century knock-offs, or at best gendaito or traditionally-made showato. Ironically, even pre-war gunto and the imitations manufactured during the occupation now have some antique value of their own because well over half a century has passed since they were first sold to gullible Americans. They routinely fetch prices of a hundred dollars or more at internet auction sites and antique arms stores.

It's impossible to even begin to list all that was traded on that black market for the obvious reason that traceable records weren't kept. But it was said that there literally was nothing that could not be traded on it. An incident that occurred in August 1946 points up this contention.

Back in the spring of that year, a combined typhus-cholera plague struck Japan; some thirty-five hundred Japanese were believed to have died from the twin scourges. Come summer, a Japanese film production company went to make a documentary about the plague.

For the production, the producers sought to film the body louse, called *shirami*, that bore the typhus bacilli, but were turned down by medical facilities and laboratories that had samples. So an enterprising production assistant got the idea of shopping for them on the black market. He went walking through the Tokyo rail station market calling out, "Shirami, shirami, who'll sell me some shirami!" Within a few minutes, the young man had collected thirty typhus-carrying body lice, for which he paid one yen apiece. *Stars and Stripes* carried the story of the incident on page one under the headline, "Even Lice Sold on Tokyo Black Market."

While the families may have excitedly bought forbidden Japanese swords on the black market, and vied with their neighbors for used American goods from homeward-bound personnel, most shopping was for everyday necessities and done at commissaries and exchanges in the usual fashion. The major exchanges generally held a fairly broad selection of products from home that American families anywhere would consider essentials that needed regular replenishment: sundries, toiletries, clothing, hardware, and basic household goods, all of which the housewife would certainly purchase. The difference was that prevailing living conditions in Japan often meant that items not considered vital necessities back in America could move to the top of a shopping list on the far western side of the Pacific, and so would be stocked in greater abundance than would be the case back home.

One such category was products meant to produce sources of light and heat should the family's local electric power grid fail, which was an expected and planned-for daily occurrence. During the war, power generating plants were a major strategic target, and many were destroyed. At the time, the electrical service industry in Japan was typified not by huge, central power plants meant to light an entire city, but rather a vast network of small coal-fired power stations, each servicing perhaps a half dozen or so nearby *chos* (neighborhoods). These plants were returned to service one-by-one throughout the occupation--but even once back on line, coal for all these power stations was a precious commodity because much had to be imported, so its distribution and use was rationed.

So to conserve fuel, conduct repairs and rebuild, power plants would shut down without notice at various times during the day. There didn't seem to be any schedule to these stoppages, and the length of time the power would be out could vary from a few minutes to several hours; but each cho could count on an interruption in electrical service at least once within any twenty-four-hour period. It was also not uncommon for a power plant to shut down for the entire six or so hours between midnight and dawn, the time when demand would be at a minimum, to conserve fuel and also conduct rebuilding and repairs.

The wrecked plants were rebuilt from a mixture of useable parts that survived bombing raids, plus other materials procured from whatever source. Power poles and lines were returned to service in the same makeshift manner, resulting in poles of varying heights and quality often leaning askew every which way with their lines drooping close to the ground, giving a column of them the look of big popsicle sticks frozen in mid-drop.

This patchwork quilt approach to power transmission meant that service could be interrupted at any unforeseen moment in addition to the usual daily blackout periods. Just a hard rain could do it; no accompanying lightning might be needed to knock out the juice. And the poles and lines were also susceptible to a feature peculiar to Japan and other land masses located along major geologic fault lines: earthquakes. Earthquakes were not that severe, but they also were not infrequent; I personally remember at least a half-dozen, and mother recalled even more. And when one struck, it was all but certain to knock down a power pole or two.

This electrical power uncertainty meant that a housewife's shopping list always included fresh batteries, candles, and kerosene fuel for lanterns and non-electrical space heaters. She would also be on the lookout for the latest in flashlights, lanterns, and heaters. Some families had their own gasoline- or kerosene-powered generators, but they were very scarce and always sold out the instant they were put on display at the exchange, if indeed they even made it to a sales counter top before being scarfed up.

For me, the sketchy power supply at times produced something akin to the frontier-like living conditions MacArthur envisioned us living under. Standard accessories in my bedroom were a flashlight, kerosene lantern, and a candle or two. If the power went out in the evening while I was reading or studying, I'd simply use the flashlight, always within reach, to help me light the lantern, then return to my study business Abe Lincoln-style, reading by lamp light. On warm nights when the power was off, the only sounds in my room would be like music: the soft, whispering hiss of the lantern harmonizing with the melodic tinkling of wind chimes that hung in my bedroom window.

The nebulous power situation also, and understandably, influenced grocery buying habits. We had a refrigerator with a small freezer compartment; all the families did. But they were poorly insulated compared with today's models, so when the power failed, it didn't take long for frozen foods to melt and fresh victuals to spoil. As a result, housewives quickly abandoned the American custom of stocking up on perishables during once-weekly visits to the supermarket, and turned instead to the continental tradition of daily trips for produce and meats meant for consumption that evening, or at the latest the following morning. My mother, for one, so enjoyed the daily shopping venture she made it a lifelong ritual, only resorting to less regular market trips once she became too infirm to drive to the grocery store every day.

After stocking up on needed electrical blackout supplies, the housewife might then see what new model radios had come in. Combination long wave-short wave radio receivers were the most treasured appliance an American home could have during the occupation, and for two reasons: they were an immediate link with life back in the United States, and the quickest source of news about Americans' activities elsewhere in Japan. The very best radios were portable, or as portable as a tube-powered, fifteen-pound-plus radio plus a full backup battery pack and a bulky external antenna could be in those days. The most preferred radios were built back in America and came equipped with AC/DC conversion apparatuses built-in, so they could be plugged in for playing.

Small, battery-powered portable radios were also available. I had my own and took it with me whenever we went on a trip. These particular radios were cheaply made, packaged in thin plastic cases, had only an AM band, operated erratically, were sold principally to Americans, and were made in Japan: fragile, tinny precursors to the country's eventual world dominance in the electronics field.

I believe my radio must have been built by Matsushita Electric Co., then and now Japan's biggest electrical company, so large and varied it is a conglomerate, or *zaibatsu*. Early in the occupation, most zaibatsu were forbidden from rebuilding and marketing as punishment for their role in arming Japan's war machine. This ban was the only form of reparation imposed directly upon Japanese industry in the wake of the war, and it riled MacArthur so much, and he argued and lobbied against reparations in general so vehemently, that in November 1945, Truman ordered him to back off, to not interfere with the prohibitions--the only specific, restrictive order the president ever gave SCAP regarding his running of the occupation.

Matsushita was the first of the handcuffed zaibatsu to break free of the restrictions, and it did so using a novelty that came with the democratization of Japan and the new constitution: organized labor. The company's new unions lobbied both its own government and the occupation administration so intensely that in 1949 Matsushita was granted the right to restart production of consumer electrical products. Radios were among their first products. My father's burdensome multi-wave radio might also have been a Matsushita product because he bought it after the company was back in operation. I probably never knew, and mother couldn't remember.

The sole English language radio transmission was provided by the Armed Forces Radio Service (AFRS), which had AM stations scattered throughout the Japanese isles, effectively covering all areas where American servicemen were stationed. Most programs were delayed broadcast recordings of American commercial programs, with Jack Benny's regular Sunday night show, the most popular radio program back in America in the late 1940s, also occupying the top slot in Japan.

Fully three-quarters of AFRS programs were entertainment re-broadcasts, followed by educational programming, which was mostly aimed at enlisted personnel. Local news and features occupied the balance of broadcast time, and these were very popular because much of their focus was upon how other American service personnel were living in Japan. Some of the news and feature stories were gotten by AFRS correspondents, but many more were simply condensed, on-air readings of stories as they first appeared in *Stars and Stripes*, the venerable service newspaper. These readings were accepted practice because AFRS was a constant presence in remote duty station locales, whereas newspapers might only be received on a weekly basis.

Because transcriptions were used and there was just one network, certain rebroadcasts were often assigned to odd time periods. Many programs that enjoyed prime time evening play back in the United States were relegated to mid-morning or afternoon time slots in Japan, although the most popular programs, like the Jack Benny Show, were rebroadcast at a time approximating their American listening hours. This haphazard program placement is still practiced by AFRTS ("T" for television) stations in Japan, Okinawa and South Korea, although the policy now applies to television programs as well as radio.

Commercial programs were rebroadcast at the same length of time as back in America, except the commercials were removed. In the early days of the occupation, this meant that the air would simply go dead for sixty seconds, or whatever time period the commercial had occupied. To account for this break in the audio stream, people left their radios permanently tuned to their local AFRS frequency so they would not have to search the dial and risk missing the station just because they tuned in to dead air. To account for the silent periods, maids were admonished never to change a station setting to ensure that AFRS, even if in a dead air interval at the time, would eventually come up when a radio was turned on. Soon enough, though, army-oriented public service announcements, usually regulations and information tidbits, were scripted and either recorded and played back or read live to fill the vacancies.

A problem with the rebroadcast policy was that sports events held back in America reached the AFRS airwaves long after the outcome of the event was known. The final score would already have been published in *Stars and Stripes*, some other periodical, or carried as part of a sports segment in a live news broadcast. Because the army attracts sports enthusiasts, this particular rebroadcast practice proved nettlesome to many servicemen, because knowing the outcome of a contest for a week or more in advance of its rebroadcast removed all suspense from a tightly-contested event. Still, sports re-broadcasts were popular with program schedulers because the events' usually long lengths relieved programmers from trying to fill air time.

It was to counter the sports event annoyance and other rebroadcast delay aggravations that virtually every American household's radio had short wave bands. Dad lugged ours with us every time we went away for a weekend or longer so he could listen to sports events back home as they occurred. However, the fourteen-hour time difference between Japan and the east coast of the United States meant that he lost a lot of sleep because he had to listen to the game during pre-dawn hours.

I remember being awakened early one November morning around four o'clock by the sounds of the 1949 Army-Navy football game. We were in a resort hotel suite at the time, so father could not listen to the radio in complete privacy, a circumstance that annoyed my mother, a lifelong light sleeper. The contest annoyed dad as well, but for a different reason: despite Army being highly favored, the game ended in a 21-all tie--coincidentally, the same score the two teams played to the day dad proposed to mom exactly twenty-three years earlier.

Yet another form of immediate communication was telephone service. This was reliable because it was established and maintained by the army's Signal Corps, and so was not subject to the same disruptions and vagaries as was electrical service. The occupation's phone service was woven in with Japan's telephone network, which meant an incoming call might or might not be from someone conversant in English. So it became an occupation custom to answer a phone not by saying "hello," but rather to use the traditional Japanese greeting, "*mushi, mushi.*"

Telephone numbers could be dialed directly within most large metropolitan areas, but long distance calls had to be placed through an operator. This procedure took several minutes because it entailed first dialing the operator to place the call, then hanging up until the operator could make a connection with the remote locale, at which point the operator would call the originator back with the requested party on the other end of the line.

A big problem with this method was that the call originator had no way of knowing whether the other party was even around to answer the phone at his or her end unless the operator called back to report there was no answer, a courtesy the operators were required to

116

perform. But this often took some time, especially if the operator had other requests to fill in the meanwhile. My mother, for one, would skirt this annoyance by placing a call, then have one of our maids monitor the single house phone, located in the downstairs hallway, while mother busied herself elsewhere.

There was also a trans-Pacific telephone linkage, initiated in January 1946 on a one-way, Japan-United States, call basis only. Two-way service was added two years later. At first, the service was reserved for official communications, although "official" was interpreted broadly. For example, calls were allowed in the case of family emergencies back in the United States. General use was permitted beginning in August 1946, although the toll charge throughout the occupation was stupendous by today's standards: a fifteen-dollar minimum for three minutes. We used the service once, for my parents to talk at some length with my married sister back in Mississippi following the birth of her first child, a daughter, in January 1950. Jeanne placed the call, so dad sent her a check to pay for the it. Mother told me the connection was not very good, that sentences were off-and-on complete, probably not unlike certain cellular phone usage today.

Mass print communications began in the fall of 1945 with regular publication of *Stars and Stripes*. Soon thereafter, the first libraries opened, with newspapers from the United States, even one- or two-week-old ones, being the most sought-after commodity. By August 1946, periodical distribution included ten thousand copies of *The New York Times* Sunday supplements and twenty-five thousand copies each of *Time* and *Newsweek* magazines. Six thousand troop information booklets were also being run off monthly by that time.

That summer also saw inauguration of the *Nippon Times*, an English language newspaper published in Tokyo that, while a civilian endeavor, was nevertheless subject to the same review and censorship rules as *Stars and Stripes*. Of the two, the latter was by far the more popular, primarily because it was service-oriented with many features on servicemen and their families, including how-to advice on living in Japan and even a Personals column. *Nippon Times*, on the other hand, endeavored to be more worldly, a thin and pale Tokyo version of the

Paris-published version of the New York *Herald-Tribune*. In late 1946, *Stars and Stripes* had a monthly circulation of some ninety thousand while *Nippon Times* had just five thousand, an 18:1 ratio that would little change for the duration of the occupation.

Back in the exchange, another regular stop would be the camera counter. The most popular cameras by far were postwar Japanese creations, and new models came on line frequently. Like my little portable radio, the cameras were a precursor of Japan's future world dominance in the industry, although back then, the cameras and their lenses were of much higher quality relatively than was my radio. The reason was because, with the short-term exception of Nikon, the Japanese optics zaibatsu were the only conglomerates not subject to reparations prohibitions. Plus they had enjoyed worldwide renown before the war, and thus soon were back in business to continue their tradition of excellence.

My father was among their eager customers. He had taken his prewar Kodak 2x2 format camera with him to Japan, but quickly abandoned it in favor of one of the new Japanese thirty-five-millimeter models, a format that at the time was uniquely appealing to Americans. Father and other Americans who snapped up cameras during the occupation likely accelerated their acceptance in the United States, because they brought them back to America gushing hosannas in praise of their compactness, reliability and performance.

The housewife, her husband and their children would find much to occupy them while in one of the larger exchanges, which could be like department stores and then some back in the United States. The huge, multi-story central exchanges in Tokyo and Yokohama, which I knew well, not only sold goods, but had beauty parlors, barber shops, tailors, lounges, shoe repair shops, florists, watch repair facilities, cosmetics bars, optical shops, souvenir stands, snack bars and possibly more.

Most of the clerks were young Japanese women, so many of not most displays of goods contained signs that appeared to be bi-lingual. I say "appeared" because the Japanese writing on the signs was not a literal translation of the English word, but rather the *kanji*-written equivalent of the *phonetic* spelling of the word. For example, a display of cameras might have attached to it a sign spelling out in kanji the equivalent of kam-er-ah, which may or may not have been the Japanese language word for a picture-taking device.

There were many and similar, here-and-there language differences that, viewed from so far back in time, may seem quaintly indicative of how conquered and conqueror daintily maneuvered around one another. For example, suppose an American wanted to buy a blue man's shirt. The Japanese word for a man's shirt is *wai-shatsu* (why-shot-su), which translates as a "white shirt." So if the person wanted a blue man's shirt, he or she would literally ask for a "blue white shirt."

Once done shopping in the exchange, the housewife would usually next visit the commissary, generally located right next door. But while shopping in the exchange might have had its moments of pleasure, the subsequent turn through the commissary could be speckled with periods of disappointment. Seasonal fresh produce was available, and it could be very good, but supplies could be limited and scooped up quickly. Fresh meats, poultry and fish were a premium commodity throughout the occupation. For the most part, families made do with frozen and canned foodstuffs, a result of differing situational sets, from shipping difficulties to health concerns to strictures and even outright prohibitions involving certain foods.

Overriding all other foodstuff availability considerations was Japan's own desperate situation at the time. The country had been a net food importer before the war, and it was in part to relieve this dependency that Japan went to war in the first place. And now that they had lost the conflict, Japan's traditional neighboring sources of food were reluctant to renew exports of their own scarce supplies to the very same country that had overrun and exploited its conquests' resources, causing food scarcities throughout Asia that prevailed for the rest of the decade and beyond.

The meagerness of homegrown Japanese food assets meant that from the occupation's very first day, the American army relied for sustenance not upon the defeated country, which had been the common practice throughout history, but rather its own imported stockpiles. Fortuitously, the Americans' non-reliance upon Japan for food supplies hastened the spread of goodwill between the former enemies, which was all well and good--but it meant that the families often had to do without food amenities they had enjoyed back in America, a situation that created a number of ironies.

Fresh poultry and eggs were one example of a food supply misfit. Japan had a thriving poultry industry before the war, and in sharp contrast to the overall grim food situation, it survived the conflict largely intact. But because of the generally desperate food situation, Americans, the families included, were honor-bound not to exploit this resource, which was another way of saying we were not to buy fresh poultry and eggs outside the commissary in order to ensure that the Japanese had a plentiful supply. As a result, frozen chickens bought in the commissary were the families' sole respectable source for poultry.

The same principle applied to fresh eggs. Fresh eggs were plentiful in Japanese markets; I personally remember seeing open cartons of them laid out, together with fresh chickens. But again, Americans were admonished to keep hands off. Fresh eggs could not be shipped in because of spoilage problems and priority considerations, so the commissaries imported and sold powdered eggs.

I clearly remember those dust-like eggs. They came in plain, cardboard cartons stenciled, "Eggs, Powdered, (X)-Dozen Equivalent." Mother would bring home a box, then the maids would whisk them up with milk, which also came powdered and had to be reconstituted, so we could have scrambled eggs at least. As a result, our family, and I would suppose most of the others, regularly faced the ironic situation of never having farm fresh eggs unless we ordered them in a Japanese restaurant, or were served them when guests in a Japanese home or at some native function.

The proprietor of a Japanese restaurant of course would be overjoyed to sell us eggs because we could readily afford them, creating the *double* irony of fresh eggs originally denied Americans in order to ensure sufficient quantities for the Japanese, finding their way into American stomachs anyway by means that were perfectly acceptable, but by a process that denied the eggs to the Japanese for whom they were originally meant.

The milk used to reconstitute powdered eggs was subject to the same local supply prohibitions as were eggs. Once again, Japan had a productive dairy industry before the war that survived the conflict largely intact--and once again, Americans were admonished not to exploit it. Reconstituted powdered milk was available in bottles, which at least looked like the fresh product--but my adamantly thrifty Midwestern-bred mother eschewed the ready-to-drink milk in favor of the powdered version, which I never came to like.

This leave-it-for-the-locals imperative similarly applied to butter, only in this case the substitute was not a reconstituted dairy product, but margarine. Starkly white margarine that was converted into a butter-looking substance by mixing in a dark yellow powder. The makeshift egg, butter and milk experiences apparently affected me greatly, for I not only vividly remember seeing them prepared, but for the rest of my childhood and to this day only accept eggs from their shells, milk from a bottle and butter that is clearly that, not some substitute.

The honor system for eggs and dairy products also applied to beef--only here, outright prohibitions were put into effect. Once again, Japan had a thriving beef industry before and after the war. But also once again, the only honorable way to have a steak dinner at home was to go to the commissary and buy it frozen, imported from either America or Australia. And trading even in frozen beefsteaks was outright prohibited because of the black market in them, a high demand that came not just from wealthy Japanese, but also from British Commonwealth personnel who were subject to the same rationing strictures that postwar Britain itself continued to endure.

At the time, a steak would sell in a commissary for just eighty or ninety cents a pound--but that same cut might easily bring *quintuple* that amount or more, almost equivalent to present-day prices, on the black market. This situation created a tempting racket for unscrupulous mess sergeants and commissary personnel, and so the penalties for under-the-counter steak vending were stiff. Black market sales of meats, steaks in particular and also imported liquors, were courts martial offenses.

Commissaries otherwise did little to make their offerings appealing to their customers. Meats, poultry and fish were frozen in bulk at their source, then broken apart in a central commissary and wrapped for single-item sale in plain white butcher paper. The package contents were merely scribbled on the wrapping paper in heavy black ink, a cursory practice that may seem indicative of the primitive product packaging of the day, except that frozen meats sold in American military commissaries in Japan, Okinawa, and South Korea today are still packaged for sale in the same, off-handed manner.

Moving along in the commissary, the housewife shopper might be pleasantly surprised at the quality and variety of fresh produce, fruits and vegetables alike. Or not. Quality and quantity would depend upon availability from an occupation-approved source.

The problem was not the scarcity of Japanese produce, a critical problem immediately after the war but one that improved markedly as the decade wore on, but rather because much Japanese produce of the period was toxic to American digestive tracts, a result of their centuries-long custom of fertilizing crops using what was delicately termed "night soil:" raw, untreated human excrement, urine and feces. The practice was not only unhealthy, studies performed during the occupation also found that the tradition depleted the soil of nutrients, eventually sterilizing it. Use of night soil was subsequently cited as a principal reason Japan had not been able to feed itself adequately, because its continued application eventually ruined crop land.

To counter this soil-depleting condition, the major bulk agricultural imports to Japan during the first postwar years, along with basic foods, were potassium- and potash-rich fertilizers, part of an overall occupation plan to change Japanese agricultural practices, including elimination of the night soil tradition. However, while agricultural reform became a hallmark of the occupation, it only plodded along because of yet another irony: the same reforms that freed Japanese farmers from serfdom also empowered them, and they mightily resisted scuttling their night soil habits. Throughout the occupation, use of human waste as a fertilizer continued to prevail, at least on the small farm plots that were the backbone of Japanese agriculture, and as a practice did not completely end until the mid-1960s. The Japanese farm bloc remains the country's most powerful lobby, often hostilely obstructing food imports it considers threatening.

I knew the night soil custom all too well. We lived at the south edge of Yokohama, just past the harbor, on an ancient, extinct volcanic ridge that in addition to large homes was dotted with small family farms that in the late 1940s still used human waste fertilizer; and during springtime, the warm, humid air reeked near-constantly of the open, raw sewage. In-ground holders for the waste were located at the very center of the family plots, and the farmers would carry individual loads of the waste throughout the vegetable rows in large, substantial wooden pails called "honey buckets."

I vividly recall my first encounter with the holding pits. I had taken a shortcut through one of these fields with a friend when we came upon a repository. Naturally curious, we lifted the top to look down and saw yellow urine with tiny worms swimming in it. Neither of us knew what we were examining. My friend volunteered, "It looks like silkworms someone peed into." I agreed. That evening, my mother set me straight while a couple of our maids stood off to one side giggling at my naivety.

In any event, fresh vegetables and fruits were a precious commodity throughout much of the occupation. Exceptions were what tropical fruits could be imported from the Philippines, including bananas for my morning cereal, and also hard produce that traveled well: onions, carrots, potatoes, hard-shell squashes, apples, melons, and the like, which were imported from Australia and possibly also New Zealand.

Fresh salad vegetables common in and important to American diets were hit-and-miss available until the occupation introduced an agricultural phenomenon new to Americans and Japanese alike: hydroponic gardening. The first of these, the 8002nd Hydroponic Farming Depot, was established in late 1946, and by mid-March 1947, its first crops were harvested: tomatoes, lettuce, scallions, onions, radishes and cucumbers, all of which became mainstays of the farms. By June of that year, nearly half a million pounds of vegetables were being harvested, and just a month later the output topped a million pounds. However, despite this huge output, there was never quite enough to go around consistently because the farms supplied the American army at large and the Commonwealth contingent in addition to the commissaries.

The Japanese immediately took to hydroponic farming, and did so far more enthusiastically than did American agriculturalists at the time. Or even today, for that matter. Japan's largely temperate climate facilitates the practice, since less artificial heat input is required. Thanks to what is by now more than a half-century of hydroponic farming, vegetables of unusual freshness and succulent taste are available in Japanese markets on a year-round basis. American service families stationed in Japan today far prefer Japanese produce to that imported and sold in commissaries. However, while the local produce is of course now perfectly safe to eat, it often is priced too outside a military family's budget to enjoy on a regular basis.

Once done with necessary grocery shopping, the housewife, like her fellow homemakers back home in America, might next stock up on treats for her family. Coca-Cola would be at the top of her list, just as it had been since the occupation's first day. Literally. The Coke machine at the American embassy was the first receptacle to be stocked when the facility was reopened, and MacArthur, his wife, and son were welcomed to their new home with a toasting of raised Cokes.

Coke became the only American product never to be in short supply for the occupation's duration, and just to make sure this remained the case, the Atlanta-based company began erecting Coca Cola bottling plants throughout Japan beginning in 1948. Coke was also one instance where the Japanese could not duplicate the American product, although they tried. Bottled Japanese soda pops were quite varied and plentiful by the time we arrived in Japan, but just like today, there were many imitators but no duplicators.

Ice cream was another treat priority, but because of the hazy electric power situation had to be consumed quickly, and so was sold primarily, often exclusively, in pint containers or simply as single servings in exchange outlets. Ice cream was not at all available when the occupation began, and priorities precluded it from being shipped over in great quantities. To remedy this, American contractors built four ice cream production plants throughout Japan. The plants were American-owned but largely staffed by Japanese, and they produced only the most popular flavors of the time: vanilla, chocolate, strawberry, and banana. It should be noted that the ice cream plants, commissaries, and perhaps even some exchange soda fountains or snack shops had their own, self-contained emergency electrical supply sources should the area power grid fail for whatever reason.

In short order, ice cream production became the occupation's principal industry, surpassing even the Coca Cola flood, with the four plants together producing some fifty-five thousand gallons of ice cream daily. Once again, though, production could not meet demand, providing a reason for Americans to test the domestic product.

I recall that single-serving Japanese ice cream came in flimsy cardboard containers with a narrow, flat stick (no spoon shape) to eat it with, and just one flavor: vanilla. But it was rich compared with what mother brought home from the commissary. The Japanese also sold fruit-flavored ices on the street and in their own markets, but I remember their flavor being bland, and I sometimes became ill from slurping them. Here, the exchanges and commissaries offered the better choice: frozen popsicles, imported from America.

Familiar American consumer items were less available to service families and other personnel stationed in remote locales, usually because the unit was not large enough to warrant setting up even a small, combination commissary-exchange. Many of these detachments had just a few score soldiers, sometimes less than fifty, and such a contingent might include just a dozen or so families.

These small, isolated detachments were also the closest thing to the frontier existence MacArthur conceptualized, and their soldiers and families most fulfilled SCAP's wishes with regard to interaction with the Japanese. More so than the rest of us, they involved themselves with the local communities on a level commensurate with the missionaries, who not infrequently would be living and ministering in the same towns and villages as the army unit. It was out there that the Americans who bothered to learn Japanese did so; they had to in order to shop and get around.

It was in these outlying regions that Americans plunged into Japanese cuisine, sometimes out of necessity, and usually suffering dietary tract trauma until they became used to it. And as an aside, here as well was the first home of one of only two American celebrities (other than MacArthur) identified with the occupation: the actress

Victoria Principal, born in 1950 in an American army hospital in Fukoka on the island of Kyushu. The other celebrity who was part of the occupation knew it at an older age: children's book author Lois Lowry, who lived with her parents (her father was an army dentist) in Tokyo 1948-'50 when she was eleven-to-thirteen years old. Ms. Lowry attended the Tokyo American School at Meguro.

The soldiers and their families stationed away from the principal troop concentrations participated in local festivals, organized charity events, taught Japanese children and adults alike about American ways, and introduced them to democracy so the natives could better understand their new constitution and its meaning. They even sponsored scholarship programs for promising Japanese scholars in American colleges and universities, although this practice was also common in the heavily populated areas.

Any marriages between Japanese women and American servicemen were most common in these outposts. Indeed, a number of the American soldiers who spent their three-year tour at a remote station, so culturally removed themselves from the dominant American presence in the Tokyo-Yokohama environment that they either stayed in Japan or returned there once their military obligation was completed.

Fortunately, accessing these remote outposts was easy thanks to Japan's extensive railway network, which had survived the war pretty much intact. This was deliberate. While the strategic bombing had laid waste to most of Japan's industrial infrastructure and scorched huge swaths of residential areas, rail lines and rolling stock were spared in order to provide transportation for the invasion that never occurred. Now in peacetime, the railways became the principal link to occupation duty stations everywhere.

To service these isolated units, special combined commissary-exchange trains were made up and made regular weekly circuits of the remote outposts. The trains were stocked with a limited supply of familiar consumer goodies like candy bars and sundries in addition to staples, American foods, and beverages. Each train was eight or so cars in length and a mixture of passenger and freight cars, modified to accommodate aisles for ready access to goods displayed on racks, in bins, and in refrigerated compartments. Necessary groceries aside, the most popular food items were snacks, sweets and sodas. Beer was also for sale, but no hard liquors.

Not surprisingly, clothing was the most popular sundry, especially among families with children. The most popular household appliance the trains carried other than the ubiquitous radios was kerosene-fired space heaters, which individual soldiers and families alike used to supplement Japanese charcoal burning heaters. Space heaters remain a highly popular item among American service personnel stationed in present-day Japan, because both sufficient insulation and central heating are still rare in Japanese dwellings, even the most modern and upscale ones.

The trains also included a car devoted to Special Services. There, soldiers and their families could relax and pick through the latest newspapers and magazines. Some periodicals were for sale, while others were meant for reading only while the train was present, which usually was for an entire day. The car also contained a mini-library, the rule being you borrowed a book on one pass of the train, then returned it the following week. Fairly recent Hollywood movies were available on the same basis: one per week for showing to the entire detachment and the families, to be returned when the train next passed through.

Some special passengers would also be aboard the trains. One was an interfaith chaplain, available for communion and counseling. There also was a medical team, normally a physician, dentist, and a couple of nurses. They worked out of a common medical-dental facility, usually set up in the Special Services car. They could perform examinations, treat some minor diseases and injuries, dispense medications, and do routine dental work like prophylaxis and fillings. Soldiers and their dependents who demanded more serious attention, pending births being the most prevalent condition, were transported back to a main base hospital for treatment, sometimes on the train; or if critical, by a medical evacuation unit that would be called in. Virtually all the personnel at the remote bases were young junior officers, non-coms and enlisted men, so chronic and geriatric diseases were not a problem.

Finally, the trains regularly transported an individual critical to occupation children who lived far distant from the heavily populated coastal regions: a certified tutor. Just as many remote bases were too small to warrant commissary and exchange facilities, they were also too modest to justify setting up a school for the unit's few youngsters. Instead, the kids were home schooled; or if one of the wives happened to have been a professional teacher, she might conduct regular classes for the all the unit's children.

Local Japanese schools were out of the question because of the language barrier. Soldiers and their families in remote outposts of necessity became more adept at Japanese than their urban brethren, but mastering the multi-nuanced tongue plus its intricate kanji, or picture writing, would have entailed years of study all by itself. So each week, a tutor would drop by to review the children's progress, give exams, hand out workbooks and other texts, counsel the teacher-wives, and in general see to it that the children were being educated in accordance with public school standards back in America. These tutors also provided the sole verbal link between the occupation and the Wild West so romanticized by MacArthur: for the occupation's duration, the roaming teachers were officially termed "circuit riders."

Education for heavy concentrations of American school age children was another matter, and more difficult to accomplish. Because occupied Japan was considered an extension of America, the same laws requiring public education applied there as back in the United States. Thing was, at the occupation's outset, public education of occupation children was ignored--literally overlooked! For all their attention to other details, occupation planners had neglected to include budgets for education of American school-age children, and to plan for an education system in general.

When the first children arrived with their mothers in 1946, there was no American school system to serve them. When the fall term began, *all* the first school-age arrivals, not just those at remote posts, were simply taught at home by their parents using guides. That same autumn, occupation planners were informed that a huge onslaught of school age children could be expected the following year. So in

January 1947, occupation planners began establishing a comprehensive, organized, certifiable, and responsible school system.

The first school buildings were simply appropriated. The school I attended the last of my fourth and all of my fifth grades was typical: *Nasugbu* Beach Elementary School, not far south of our home in Yokohama. The massive, concrete building, a gloomy, brooding gray in color, had been a prisoner-of-war facility during the war, a revelation that of course added to its mystique among us kids.

Once buildings suitable for use as schools had been seen to, they then had to be outfitted with desks, books, supplies, peripheral education paraphernalia, and not least of all, with teachers. At the beginning, occupation forces were scoured for anyone with teaching experience, housewives who had been teachers being the most obvious and exploitable resource. The rest of the teaching gap was filled with soldiers, DACs, secretaries, and anyone else who had teaching experience and could be spared from their regular duties, which was not always possible.

Persons with no teaching experience but at least real world experience with their subjects, notably mathematics and science, often taught high school classes. With the notable exception of housewives, these *ad hoc* teachers were paid for their labors. Later in the occupation, housewife teachers would be paid as well.

Some English-speaking Japanese teachers who were already on the occupation payroll as teachers in the Army Education Program (AEP) for soldiers were re-routed to the children's schools. There were limitations on what they could teach to American children: sciences, arts, and some technologies--but not religion, philosophy, geography, history, government, sociology, or psychology.

As the occupation progressed and budget allotments were expanded, teachers were hired in the United States and brought over on a two- or three-year rotation basis, a practice that is still employed. Regardless, for the primary grades at least, many of the teachers and lower-end administrators were wives of servicemen, and when their husbands' time in Japan was up, back to America they went, the favorites to the regret and consternation of us impressionable younger kids.

Schoolbooks and workbooks were an occupation budgetary problem solved by having parents buy the books for their children. This of course presented families with an expense burden they had not anticipated, and which could be especially troublesome to families of lower-rank personnel. So raising money for textbooks became community affairs.

Money for books was initially rounded up in true homespun American fashion, with families from individual schools organizing into communal groups that raised funds through community bake sales, used clothing and household goods bazaars, and just plain door-to-door canvassing. Families bound back to the States were solicited to sell their children's textbooks at discounted prices.

Even after proper funding for education was acquired, logistics remained a problem. The troop rotation schedule meant a school population that was always in flux. Planners could not tell from one school term to the next how many students of what particular grades would arrive; exact school enrollment was only known one month in advance of any particular term. Additionally, the shipping priorities that plagued families also affected school supplies: just desks, chairs, and blackboards were available in Japan. All else had to be imported from the United States, and because of the distances and priorities, ordered six months in advance.

Still another issue was the type of educational system to be used. A division was established between primary school education, first through eighth grades, and high school, grades nine through twelve. The high school students were taught using then-accepted back-home curricula and standards, which was easily done then because there was little difference from one state's polices to another.

Primary education was another matter, particularly because the families were mostly young, and elementary school age children predominated. It was decided that whatever standard was adopted for occupation elementary schools would also apply to young children of families in the remote outposts, and further that the educational method be a straightforward approach easily understood by non-professionals, the wives and mothers charged with their children's education.

The answer came from the Calvert School, a little-known but still extant and highly- regarded private primary school located in Baltimore, Maryland. The children of a high-ranking occupation officer had attended Calvert when he was stationed in the Baltimore area, and he prevailed upon the policy makers to bring Calvert officials to Japan to supervise setting up both elementary schools and home schooling based on the school's model.

Like most private schools, Calvert's method was (and is) highly didactic in structure, a characteristic that the highly-disciplined Japanese readily recognized and appreciated. The Japanese adopted the system for use by schools in their own nascent public education system--and it is still followed there to this day. The Calvert system is also still appreciated by American children of the occupation, who remember it fondly for having given them a far better education than their own children, and now grandchildren, may have received.

Chapter 7: Alice's Gate

In the late summer of 1944, World War II was reaching a crescendo. Victory could be sensed as the Allies had reversed earlier misfortunes and were gradually shoving the Axis powers back behind the extent of their conquests. In Europe, Allied forces on the western front and Soviet armies on the east were squeezing the very borders of Germany itself. In the central Pacific, Admiral Nimitz's Marines were hacking away at the farthest reaches of the Japanese empire one hard-fought archipelago at a time, and by late summer had subdued a key strategic goal: the Mariana Islands group.

The conquest of the Marianas was vitally important because it put American air forces within flying range of the Japanese home islands using the newly-delivered B-29 "Superfortress" strategic bombers. Up until then, air strikes at Japan had been merely tactical in nature, largely performed by aircraft carrier-based light bombers that were capable of here-and-there damage, but lacked the payload capacities to inflict heavy, irreversible, large-scale destruction. The B-29s filled that void; they could easily fly the nearly thirteen hundred miles to Japan's heavily-populated and -industrialized southern coast, deliver their bomb loads, up to twenty thousand pounds at a time from each aircraft, and return to Tinian Island, the northernmost of the Marianas, with fuel to spare.

A master plan to bomb Japan into total destruction or surrender, whichever would come first, was put into action. Working from pre-war maps, what aerial photographs could be gotten, intelligence from persons who had lived and worked in Japan, books and articles on Japanese industries and military bases and their locations, clandestine reports from submarines and other water craft that had spied on the coastal areas, and whatever other sources they could muster, Army Air Corps planners assembled detailed bombing raid sorties.

At first, mission concentration was upon Japanese industries and military bases, most of which were strung out along the country's conveniently exposed south-facing coastline. Incessant sorties day-and-night, thousands of them, were held over the winter and into the following spring of 1945, raining down high-explosive bombs until

Japan's ability to rearm itself was destroyed. Once virtually nothing of military or industrial value was left, and Japan remained reticent to calls for unconditional surrender, planners' attention turned to a strategy of terror: incendiary bombing of tinderbox Japanese residential areas.

This firebombing was total warfare at its most hideous. Little was spared; entire ghettos were reduced to smoldering ruins; it was estimated that some 640 thousand Japanese civilians died in the never-ending infernos. There was even a final, thousand-plane firebomb raid upon Tokyo over the two days *after* the second atomic bomb was dropped on Nagasaki.

Yet throughout this nearly year-long rain of terror, even as mission planners devised programs and designated targets for the most awesome destruction in the history of warfare, they also took the time and care to see to it that I would have a Western-style toilet seat to relax and muse upon when I came to live in Japan some three and a half years after the last bomb fell.

Hyperbole in the extreme? Of course! But true nonetheless. Our home that overlooked otherwise largely-blackened and -flattened Yokohama was in a sprawling, upscale neighborhood that intentionally was left untouched by any and all bombing. This sparing of usable housing was deliberate, practiced Japan-wide, and included much more than just housing for us conquerors.

Beginning in the summer of 1944, plans were put into action in Washington for postwar occupations of the two principal Axis powers, Germany and Japan. With respect to Japan in particular, long-range thinking held that certain desirable structures, monuments, landmarks and geographic areas deemed unsuitable, or at least minimally worthwhile, as military targets should be spared for postwar use both by the occupying victors and the vanquished foe. Railroads, harbor facilities and large utilities complexes were largely untouched for much the same reason: the occupiers would need transport means, reliable power sources, and other accouterments of a civilized society even after having destroyed many of the accomplishments of that very same society.

In a similar vein, landmarks and facilities that were of special meaning and value to the soon-to-be-former enemy, such as religious shrines and major sports venues or recreation areas, were to be spared, in this case so as not to further enrage or shame an already conquered and subdued people.

One such prominent landmark was the *Meiji* Shrine Park in Tokyo, which would become the site of the 1964 Olympics. Since before the war, the park had been the world's largest multi-sport venue, and might be still except for the gargantuan sports complexes since erected for subsequent Olympic games elsewhere. The park survived the war intact; despite its fame and prominence, no bombs touched it. The facilities included a track-and-field stadium seating sixty thousand, separate outdoor swimming and diving arenas seating fifteen thousand each, a baseball stadium with a capacity of sixty-four thousand (and with foul lines of 400 and 435 feet respectively, indicating if nothing else that the Japanese eschewed over-the-fence home runs in this particular ballpark), plus softball fields and volleyball and handball courts.

Another spared landmark was the *Kokugi Kan* Auditorium in Tokyo, then the largest indoor arena in the Orient with a capacity of nearly eighteen thousand. Down Honshu Island in the industrial city of Kobe, another prime target city, bombers spared the *Koshein* Baseball Stadium, with a capacity of one-hundred thousand the largest stadium ever built anywhere expressly for that sport.

This courtesy (so to speak) of sparing sports venues from destruction was both a nod to and a reflection of the American conquerors' own love of sports. The occupation began just before autumn's onset, which back in the United States meant time for the annual football season to commence. So it was back home--so it became in Japan in the fall of 1945. The first major recreational activity the newly-arrived Americans instituted was an inter-army football league that encompassed the entire Pacific Theater. The league began scheduled play in October and ended the season on January 27, 1946, with the Pacific Army Olympic Championship, held at Meiji. In the title game, the Eleventh Airborne Angels defeated the

Honolulu All Stars 18-0 before a packed house of mostly Japanese spectators. No admission was charged.

Select targets other than sports complexes and neighborhoods were spared as well. In downtown Tokyo stood the *Takarazva* Theater, built just before the war but instead used as a factory. This eight-story building featured a main floor theater which ceiling rose three stories and seated two thousand. Its center point was the world's largest revolving stage (and no *Les Miserables* musical yet in sight). Then above that, on the fourth floor, was a second theater seating 750, plus a library. When the occupation began, this building was returned to its theatrical intent, renamed the "Ernie Pyle Theater" after the famed war correspondent who was killed by enemy fire on the island Ie Shima in April 1945, during the Okinawa campaign.

Ernie Pyle Theater

This huge theatrical complex was denoted the centerpiece, the first stop, for all American movies and United Service Organization (USO) shows that came to Japan during the occupation. A corresponding although far less prominent theater was spared in Yokohama, not far from the New Grand Hotel and renamed "The

Octagon" after the telltale eight-sided insignia of the Eighth Army. Sometimes and to my delight, first-run movies from "Stateside," as we wistfully referred to our faraway homeland ("Zone of the Interior" was the official occupation term for the continental United States), opened simultaneously in both theaters.

Cultural sites within cities were passed by, most significantly the imperial palace grounds in Tokyo. Spared too were Japan's ancient cultural cities, Kyoto and Nara especially, which had no military target value, although Kyoto was one of the four alternate targets for the "Little Boy" atomic bomb had Hiroshima been clouded over the day of that mission. Prominent tourist sites were bypassed, notably Nikko with its many shrines; the *Hakone* district, where the sacred volcano Mount *Fujiyama* is located, and Honshu's picturesque, southern coastline that did not include military targets--with the obvious exception of Hiroshima. And not least of all, Tokyo's famed *Ginza* shopping district got a free pass, as did the lesser-known downtown commercial centers of most cities, Yokohama included.

And of course, there was the matter of the bombing having spared me from having to use a Japanese squat-style toilet while at home during the eighteen months we lived in Yokohama. This fortuitous comfort occurred because of the cho where we lived, before the war and since the occupation simply and modestly termed the "The Bluff Area" in English language references, *Yamate Cho* on Japanese maps.

The area is significant because it is the most prominent natural feature on the *Kanto* Plain, anchoring the southern extreme of that vast, flat, sweeping landscape that encompasses what is called today the Tokyo-Yokohama metroplex. Some three hundred feet high, the ridge extends almost to the water's edge in the manner of Honolulu's famed Diamond Head promontory, but with neither the dominance of that Oahu landmark nor its cachet. Like Diamond Head, the ridge is what remains of a long-extinct volcano, but one far older than its Hawaiian counterpart. It also extends much farther inland than does Diamond Head, snaking back some five miles, making it ideal as a location for hundreds of large, exclusive, Western-style homes, one of which my parents and I occupied.

The first European diplomatic delegations that came to Japan beginning in the late 1800s noticed the ridge's dominance over the surrounding landscape together with its convenience to the harbor area and correctly figured the heights would be quite suitable for impressive homesteads. Back then, the Westerners really had no choice but to live in Yokohama, for they couldn't take up residence in the capital itself. Japanese still-lingering distrust of foreigners at that time precluded legations (as opposed to official embassies) and most other foreigners from setting up businesses and occupying dwellings in Tokyo.

Diplomat's house in Bluff Area

This paranoia was evident to Commodore Perry when he visited Japan in the 1850s; he never made it to Tokyo, then called Edo. All the negotiations he conducted with the Japanese, all the American paraphernalia he demonstrated for them (including baseball and railway trains, both of which the Japanese adopted with special enthusiasm); all this was done in Yokohama, not far from the waterfront and in the shadow, such as it was, of the bluff. In any event, this barring of diplomats and others from living in Tokyo meant that they had to search elsewhere, and the Bluff Area provided an ideal spot: prominent, dignified, and with a picturesque and commanding view of the harbor.

For thirty years beginning in the 1890s, hundreds of European-style houses were built in the Bluff Area, to accommodate the diplomats and their families and also well-to-do Western traders of the time. Most of the those homes remain standing, including impressive estates and mansions now earmarked on tourist maps. A connecting road, then and now called "Ridge Road," runs along the top of the bluff linking access to the city below with dozens of fingers that reach out from the arching spine of the landmark. Indicative of the international atmosphere, a Roman Catholic church occupies a prominent spot midway along Ridge Road, as does a Frank Lloyd Wright-designed complex that during the occupation and for awhile thereafter was the Yokohama-American High School ("Yo-Hi" at the time, and today on the Internet).

Yo-Hi high school ca. 1948.

Across Ridge Road from the church is a Catholic girls' school that I knew well because it was directly across a ravine and modest athletic field from our house. At the east end of the bluff, where it drops off to the waterfront, there is a "Foreigners' Cemetery," so-marked even today on tourist maps. Close by are an Olympic-size swimming and diving pool and some tennis courts, also built by Europeans in the 1920s. I learned to swim in that pool.

Olympic pool 1947, Harbor in Background

Below the bluff and to the north, between it and the harbor, an international commercial community arose to serve the disparate foreigners. This is where the New Grand Hotel and the waterfront Yamashita Park, named for the Japanese admiral who routed the Russian fleet in 1905, and where I and the Japanese boys held our boat-sailing time together, are located. The hotel is so-named because the original Grand Hotel, built at the turn of the century on the same site, was destroyed in Japan's infamous 1923 earthquake and fire. The New Grand, an exact replica of the original, was built in 1927 and is still operating. It's also historically significant as the place where MacArthur and his entourage stayed and made their headquarters from August 30, 1945, their first evening in Japan after the surrender, until moving to Tokyo on September eighth.

GRAND HOTEL - 1947

In the 1920s, the harbor-Bluff Area was the closest thing Japan had to a multi-cultural community--and it's still pretty much that way. The large, populous Chinatown is located there. Since being settled by Westerners at the turn of the twentieth century, the area from the bluff to the harbor center has been preferred by foreign nationals who wish to set aside Japanese surroundings and culture for awhile without physically leaving the country. It's a neighborhood of European overtones not otherwise found in Japan (Tokyo has nothing comparable) with one possible exception: an Epcot-like Dutch theme park, *Huis Ten Bosch*, which centerpiece is a replica of a Dutch city center, not far from Nagasaki on the island of Kyushu.

Army Air Corps mission planners appreciated this particular area of Yokohama as much as did the European diplomats, and took pains to ensure that it would not be destroyed. This courtesy surely pleased residents of the bluff, many if not most of whom were foreigners caught in Japan for the duration of the war, and thus witnessed the bombers flying overhead to drop their payloads elsewhere on the city. Off limits to the bombers were all from the bluff to the edge of the docks themselves, which were heavily damaged but not destroyed outright. A roughly north-south rail line about a mile inland also conveniently marked a visual demarcation between the harbor-Bluff Area and the rest of Yokohama. All between the rail line and the water was largely spared; all to the west of the tracks was leveled, most particularly by a fire bomb raid by General Curtis LeMay's B-29s on May 29, 1945.

I say "largely" spared because there apparently was one inadvertent bombing. This is evidenced in a photograph my father took in early 1949, looking north from one of the bluff fingers that extends out to what remained at the time of downtown Yokohama. All in the picture beneath the bluff around the New Grand Hotel and Yamashita Park is intact, evidenced by the obviously old, still-standing buildings. However, one strip about a half mile long that runs from southeast-to-northwest beginning at the water's edge is occupied not by typical Chinese-style edifices, but by new, bland, government issue-type buildings that run westward up the middle of Chinatown.

Looking at the picture, it appears that as one B-29 approached Yokohama from the south, its bombardier got anxious and let loose his bomb load as the aircraft crossed the waterfront, accidentally taking out this particular strip before reaching the target area, which presumably was somewhere west of the railroad tracks. This one blight aside, the stark contrast at the time between the intact neighborhood to the east of the tracks and the blackened, leveled ruins to their west, a sight I could view every time I stepped outside our house's walls, will always reside in my mind as the most extreme example there could be of the phrase, "the other side of the tracks."

Bluff to Bay, 1949
Smoke is from one of many debris fires, constant then.

Our house was typical of the Bluff Area genre: a large, off-white two-story stucco structure of, as I recall, American Foursquare design. Or perhaps it was Mediterranean, because it featured high and haughty arched windows topped by a tile roof. The house wasn't a mansion by any means, but also didn't miss being so by much. It was large enough so that my parents and I each had our own sprawling corner bedrooms with private bath, my father his own den, a voluminous entry hall on the first floor that led to spacious, beautifully-appointed living and dining rooms that were elegantly suitable for the hospitality my parents were expected to render (and did so ardently), a huge kitchen, a butler's pantry, and an apartment in the rear with its own modest kitchen and bath facilities that was big enough to accommodate our trio of live-in maids, each with her own small bedroom.

The lot was not grand, but large enough in the rear for several trees and floral gardens, plus room for me to run and even play constricted football with friends. The front yard, on the other hand, was unremarkable, just a dozen or so feet deep until ending abruptly at a quite high stucco wall that enclosed the entire property. The northwest corner of the wall ended at a garage that fronted on a well-kept gravel lane just wide enough for two autos to edge past each other. The lane gave us and the other residents up-and-down the street access to Ridge Road. Halfway along that portion of the wall was the only opening to the lane, our front gate.

That gate. Sturdy, tall, imposing and imperious. As forbidding in its way as the house's main floor windows behind it; all of them together, stern and watchful sentinels. If I have a single, clear narrative memory of my time in Japan, it is of daily passing through that gate and continuing beyond.

House Gate
"Scoshi" ("Little Bit") was our family dog.

The reason my memory is so sharp about this particular routine is because the gate separated contrasts more glaringly stark than I could ever have imagined or ever experience again. Inside the gate, my surroundings were Western and familiar; comforting in their way, replete with reminders of the life I had left behind in suburban Maryland, the site of my very first memories.

But once through the gate, I entered a new world. Not right away; I'd have to walk or take a bus or a train or ride my bicycle to fully wrap myself in the mystique of that land I had never known and never would again. But I could see it, sense it, feel it, smell it, taste it, hear it... That gate was my portal to this magical, mysterious land that was at once scorched and sad, scenic and smiling. All manner of new, inviting and mysterious things to a ten-year-old boy; my doorway to infinitely exotic senses and experiences. Alice had her looking glass; I had my gate. They were one and the same, our passageways to wonderland.

I remember clearly my first time through the gate. We had moved into our house the evening before I was to catch a school bus to go to school, so I had seen nothing of whatever surrounded our house until daylight came. After breakfast, I gathered my things and strode through the gate for the first time. Just outside was the gravel lane, and on its opposite side a waist-high protective steel railing that looked out over the city. Or more accurately, what was here-and-there left of the city. Having some time, I stepped up to the railing, my eyes taking in the view I described earlier: all intact buildings of some sort and condition all the way to the double-track railway line, which ran diagonally across my line of sight from upper right to lower left, where the tracks disappeared into a tunnel cut through the ridge.

But beyond that rail line...nothing but flattened ruins. No structure of any significant height rose from the carnage, which seemed to stretch to the horizon. The bleakness of it all was broken only here-and-there by piles of debris fires, from which smoke rose listlessly in the still, morning air like blackened skeletal fingers reaching shakily upwards to graze the belly of an uncaring sky. I just stood and marveled at the sight for a few moments, then turned and began walking up the lane to Ridge Road and the corner where I would catch the bus, which was due shortly.

The lane was somewhat steep, so burdened by my load of books and papers and other paraphernalia I'd need for school, I trudged to the corner with my head down. On getting there, I paused and raised my head to look across the street--and right before me stood Mount Fuji!

I gaped at the sight open-mouthed; I almost dropped my book satchel and all else; I clearly remember doing so. Japan's sacred volcano so dominated my line of sight I at first thought I was staring at a giant billboard that had been erected just across the street. It took me a few moments to realize I was actually looking at the genuine article, the world-renowned, beautifully symmetrical, thirteen thousand-foot high active volcano, some fifty miles distant, its crest still thickly draped with snow that early in the spring, a thin wisp of steam from its bubbling hot interior wafting lackadaisically from the peak and off to one side. I also realized that my mistaken impression of the view as a billboard was because the mountain's base was shrouded in a blueish-white mist, making the bulk of the volcano seem to be floating free. Small wonder the Bluff Area was so preferred as a residential treasure; imagine seeing such a sight daily from your neighborhood.

I stood there staring for some moments, then had my concentration brusquely interrupted by a Japanese Roman Catholic nun walking quickly by, heading toward the girl's parochial school that was across the field from our house. She was followed by a train of Japanese school girls, all younger than I, and all dressed alike in starched black-and-white jumpers, following smartly and closely one behind the other in the manner of obedient ducklings, with the caboose of their pedestrian train taken up by a second nun. None of the girls seemed to take notice of me; all were singing some bouncy Japanese song. I turned from Mount Fuji to follow their path along the curb to the school, then turned back to the mountain just as the school bus pulled up, blocking my view of the peak and yanking me back to reality.

And that was the morning of my second full day in Japan. And in some form or other, it would be repeated throughout our time there. At every opportunity, I would make it a point to retrace the path I had followed that first day. Every day we were at home, I would at some time go out the front gate, step across the lane to look out at the wasted city, then turn and walk up to the corner to where Mount Fuji would be faithfully awaiting me.

The routine became a ritual: first some steps to gaze downcast at the scorched wasteland, then a turn and a few more steps up the hill to stare in wonder at the volcano's majesty. It was symbolic, a metaphor between ruin and resurrection, from hopelessness to hope. The only time the scene failed me would be on cloudy or stormy days, and even at those times I would go do something else and wait for the cloud cover to dissipate, just so I could go catch a glimpse of my personal treasure. Surely others who lived up there, perhaps including some who were my schoolmates and playmates, partook of the same view. But this particular communion was mine; I never once shared it with anyone else.

I had other rituals as well. Or at least ingrained habits. I believe all pre-adolescent children, boys and girls alike, have and faithfully follow such rituals. I remember mine from Japan not because they were special, but because I followed them in such a special place.

One of my rituals was to tarry awhile at the railing across the lane from the gate, just to see what might be going on in the field and slight woods that lay between our street and the girls' school. Most activity was performed by the schoolgirls themselves, always in their black-and-white uniforms. Depending on the season, I'd see them playing volleyball, soccer, or lacrosse, and sometimes holding hands and dancing in circles while singing *a capella*. No matter the activity, they'd always be laughing and sometimes, when playing volleyball, also singing, their voices rising in a unified lilt whenever the ball would be struck from one side of the net to the other. I'd witness this after I had returned home from school, and I recall wondering whether the activity was being done after school or if school was still in session. I never found out; we never had anything to do with the school, except to nod politely at the nuns when encountering them on Ridge Road.

When the girls weren't using the field, Japanese boys my age would often play baseball. Baseball (pronounced bay-suh-bah-roo in Japanese) of course is a major sport in Japan, but is not their national pastime as many believe; that honor belongs to *Sumo*. But those boys surely were good at the game, as I discovered when I went to join them. One summer day, I wandered down to the field, which was rudely marked off with foul lines and bases, and indicated that I'd like to play. Being ever polite, they of course invited me to join them. However, my lack of athletic prowess soon revealed itself, especially in the field where I would make throwing or catching errors. I could hit well enough, but pinch batters who did just that weren't needed. So I found myself relegated to right field, which usually doesn't get much action, but these boys were so good they could deliberately hit balls my way, which of course exposed my lack of skills all the more.

Anyway, soon enough, when I came down to join in one day, their leader, who was about my height, came up to me, frowned, shook his head and said, "You no good, Jamie-san." I remember that while I was hurt, I wasn't at all offended; I recognized that they were far more skilled. So from then on, I'd just watch their play from the side of the field or the lane railing. We still would always exchange smiles and waves. Thinking back, I also remember that their leader's words to me were the only the few English words I ever heard any of them speak with any linked coherence, other than single words like "Go!" and "Run!" and the like, which makes me wonder if the one fellow who dismissed me hadn't learned the phrase elsewhere just to be able to let me down in a way I would clearly understand.

I also learned something from the experience that I applied beneficially later on, first on my high school baseball team (junior varsity, but still...), then in my thirties during a period when I played a lot of softball. As said, I always could hit well enough (my 20/10 vision, apparently the same as Ted Williams', helped), with sufficient and dependable skill and power to be called upon fairly often to pinch-hit in high school games, and to be picked regularly to play softball despite my fielding ineptitude. Reason: I could spray hits almost at will; I could guide them to defensive gaps or weak fielders like myself. I'm sure I picked up the knack from those Japanese boys.

Those boys taught me something else before they ousted me: to shoot marbles. I had done some of that back in Silver Spring, and was fairly good at it. Under the tutelage of the boys, I got *very* good at it! So good in the school yard where I played with my classmates that I would most often walk away with the winnings, which were the marbles my sharp shooting would knock out of the ring. And some of those Japanese marbles were gorgeous! Bright and clear, often with intricate and colorful designs inside. I still have a few, and they still get admiring remarks.

A single event on that field remains vivid in my mind. One summer day in 1949, a Japanese film crew was shooting a movie scene in a corner of the field that was partially shielded by bushes and trees. I clearly remember that it was a very professional shoot, a major theatrical production. My attention was riveted by the very large, thirty-five-millimeter camera that was set upon a tracking dolly, with all manner of persons around handling lights, sound boom microphones, reflectors and other film production paraphernalia. And I definitely recall the scene, which the director, whom I quickly spotted to be the man in charge, would conduct several times. The setting featured two actors, a young man and woman, in what appeared to be a picnic setting. My memory is of several takes of the woman, who was dressed in a white *yukata*, running across the clearing to the man with her arms open wide, and that he would rise from where he was sitting on a ground cover, and they would embrace. This went on for some time, certainly well more than an hour, because I eventually become bored with the repetition and went on to something else.

Anyway, years later, I wondered if I hadn't witnessed a scene being shot of the Japanese classic *Rashomon*, the story of a murder-and-rape as told from four different perspectives: the woman, the killer, a passerby who viewed the crime unseen from a hiding place-- and the woman's slain lover, who spoke through a medium who was also the film's narrator. I've seen the film, and the woman and her costume that I saw that day, which got much of my attention and so remain sharp in my memory, certainly look like the characters in the film. And there is a scene like the one I had witnessed in the film.

So I checked out the details of *Rashomon*'s production, only to discover that it was shot in a studio in Tokyo and exterior scenes in Nara. So perhaps I was wrong. Or maybe it was just that one scene, and it didn't make the production credits. Or perhaps another film altogether that just happened to have a similar setting. Whatever, the process was interesting to watch unfold; it occupied my attention for a little while.

Much else on the bluff and around it vied for my attention, beginning with the local Japanese shopping street (such as it was at the time) that nestled into the base of the bluff's north side, just a short scramble down a ravine from our house, the *Motomachi*. The Motomachi of today is a huge, very urbane and pricey outdoor urban mall prominently identified on tourist maps; filled with restaurants, clubs and just about every high-end franchise name from around the globe one could think of. The area is so replete with *haute couture* shops butted up against one another that it is nicknamed Yokohama's "Golden Half-Mile" in a takeoff on Chicago's "Miracle Mile," that stretch of Michigan Avenue from the Chicago River north to Lake Shore Drive that's flanked on both sides by tony stores.

As a child, I of course knew an entirely different Motomachi. The area now is marked by a network of smartly paved walkways linking the various phases of the district. During the occupation, there was just a single, buckled and rutted macadam street that here-and-there oozed its blacktop way down to what was then a smelly, polluted *Nakamura* River jammed with fishing boats and cargo barges. The shops themselves, although not by any means resembling present- day stores, were sound enough in their own ramshackle way. At least, as was the case of the rest of the immediate area, the Motomachi had not been bombed. All the shops were wooden, some with corrugated metal roofs, others covered by makeshift layers of wood and tiles.

Motomachi, 1949

Three shops in particular held my interest; I'd try to visit each whenever on the street. The first was an outdoor food market that anchored the eastern end of the Motomachi, not far from a tea house that was frequented mostly by Europeans who still lived on the bluff. I'd never seen anything like it before, so was fascinated with all that produce, plus chicken, duck and pig carcasses hanging from hooks in the open air. It was in this market that I first saw (and am still awed by) the *dikon*, the absurdly (at least to me then) huge and long white radish indigenous to Japan, apparently only grown there at the time, but now a world-wide gourmet delight.

I also remember being impressed by the scores of fresh eggs on display, often piled atop one another, especially since it was our family's policy not to interfere with the marketing of that particular commodity. The sight of those eggs would cause me to salivate remembering those warm-from-the-hen eggs mother's one-time suitor would being us each morning that Michigan winter. It frustrated me not to be able to buy fresh eggs, even though I could easily afford to do so.

My next stop on my trek through the Motomachi was a fireworks' shop, a special delight to a budding pyromaniac such as I. This particular shop was on the river side of the roadway, and I remember it tilted back somewhat toward the waterway, and so required something of a leaning act to stand inside. But no matter, because the vast and varied array of fireworks, from simple sparklers to some truly impressive noise-makers, from stand-alone displays to rockets, was enough to keep me rapt for some time. I recall the shop's aged proprietor, who would sit to one side, constantly smiling and nodding his head, patiently waiting for me to buy something-or-other. I'd almost always not disappoint him. There were few restrictions on using fireworks; we'd even set them off on our grade school grounds.

A friend would sometimes join me in the Motomachi. Jay Moynahan and I first met not directly, as at school or some other children's activity environment, but through our parents, both sets of whom were ardent bridge players who first became acquainted through that past-time. Jay lived in a separate development on the western edge of the Bluff Area, so far removed from our family's location that we didn't attend the same elementary school, although we were in the same grade. I remembered Jay well enough that I tried locating him while researching this book, and we eventually did link up via Facebook.

Jay substantiated my memories of our joint visits to the Motomachi, the fireworks shop in particular, and generally of being enthralled by the sheer exoticness of the area. Neither of us could recall how he would get to the Motomachi. He would have had to take a bus or streetcar, or be driven by his mother to our house, who might have been coming over in any event to play bridge with my mother, a frequent occurrence.

I'm certain Jay and I visited other shops along the Motomachi, but don't remember any we went into together other than the fireworks shop. In fact, I can recall but a couple of other stores out of the thirty or so that comprised the Motomachi of the occupation.

One was a combination women's clothing-accessories-tailor shop my mother sometimes would (almost literally) drag me to. She had become an ardent fan of Japanese prints and the creative ways they could be stitched together, and bought a number of outfits at this particular shop. She continued to wear these items for years; I only a few years ago donated the last to charity. A light blue floral print dressing gown became a particular favorite--and happened to be the last garment she would ever wear, chosen for her last journey, at age ninety-four, to an Asheville, North Carolina, hospital just before Christmas 1997.

Mother would spend considerable time in this particular shop, sometimes with me sulking off to one side, while she went over the fashioning of this-or-that feminine thing from the colorful fabrics, silks especially. And while I obviously didn't appreciate accompanying her forays to the Motomachi, it was in this particular shop that I first encountered what I would learn years later would become one of the occupation's more egregious habits: abuse of the *presento*.

The presento was an Americanized term for the Japanese merchandiser custom of giving a token gift to a shopper just for dropping by, and never mind if the browser bought anything, at least on the initial visit. The gifted item might be something the visitor showed interest in, paused by briefly, glanced at, or even wasn't aware of. Whatever, the little gift (sometimes wrapped, other times not) was to be accepted graciously, with a courteous bow and an *arigato* (thank you), which bore a meaning beyond what we Westerners thought it meant--and likely still think it means.

It's not that arigato has two different meanings *per se*; the word does translate correctly as "thank you." But the connotation of the word can differ markedly--even severely, with consequences if used incorrectly--depending on the context in which it is employed. For example, it's quite proper to say "arigato" as a polite acknowledgment to a small favor or courtesy, say holding a door open. In health clubs, the word is commonly spoken, usually accompanied by a slight bow, to conclude a Yoga session.

But to say "arigato" on receiving a gift, even a small token item, what was called a presento in this case, is to say in effect: "Thank you for the gesture--and I shall take care to repay you in kind!" In other words, the shopkeeper would present the little gift *in anticipation* of the recipient returning the favor by buying something, if not on that particular visit at least on a subsequent stop. Thus in Japanese culture, it is extremely rude–still!–to enter a store, accept a small gift, then drop by again-and-again without buying anything. The proprietor loses face; the ignorant browser could expect to be shunned. Then of course, the presento can be refused; the shopper has the option of simply saying "No thank you" by word or gesture, and no offense (likely) will be taken.

My parents knew this custom well and made very sure I would not abuse it, because to have done so would have brought dishonor upon our family. It upset and annoyed mother greatly that the socially-active wife of one high-ranking general would abuse the custom by all but demanding a presento every time she entered a shop, on the supposition that her very presence would generate business. So I was taught always to make it a point to buy something-or-other whenever I accepted a presento.

And "accepted" was the key action. It would happen that I would be tempted by a presento, then quickly have to decide whether to accept it. For example, the vendors in the fireworks shop knew me well and would frequently offer me a presento. Thus on some visits I would accept the gift and buy something, and other times pass it by. During good weather, when I might be wandering about for some time, my allowance money could be exhausted fairly quickly. Needless to say, I was popular among the Motomachi proprietors.

Excepting the tea house, food market and fireworks and women's shops, I only clearly recall one other store along the Motomachi of the occupation, but its memory is especially vivid. Or at least a portion of this particular shop is still sharply defined. The facility was a fairly large and sprawling (to my ten-year-old eyes) affair that stood on the river side of the macadam lane, and I remember little else inside the spacious interior interested me except what was displayed along the a side wall toward the back, which in warm weather would be open to the river: an extensive, beautifully fashioned and detailed HO gauge model railroad layout.

Like many if not most small boys, I was entranced as much by toy and model trains as by the real thing. I was one of those kids who could stand in the cold at Christmastime and stare rapturously and for some time at a working train set in some department store window.

Nor did my love of trains stop with models of them. I can remember back before we moved to Japan, when I was very young, how one of my greatest joys was to take a local train ride from Washington's Union Station out to Silver Spring, Maryland, a distance of just a little over seven miles. For these occasions, my sister would see after me. We would already be downtown for some reason or other with our mother, who would drop us off at Union Station to catch the train, then drive out to the suburban station to pick us up. I would have spent the entire trip with my nose pressed against a window. And, of course, I especially recall my first ever long distance train ride: the three-day, two-night trip from Chicago across the plains and mountains of the late winter northwest to Seattle, where mother and I would get the ship to Japan.

The back wall of this one particular shop brought all my train-oriented emotions together in one gigantic, rapturous release about the topic, the pre-adolescent equivalent of an especially spectacular sexual climax with a special partner. I remember staring open-mouthed at the display, not just the first time I saw it, but on multiple subsequent visits.

The layout itself was masterfully and intricately constructed, complete with a village, roads, at least one bridge, and freight and passenger trains alike chugging this way and that. Individual pieces of rolling stock together with the modeling kits from which they were assembled were prominently displayed for sale on the wall behind the layout, plus display cases to both sides. The entire array was like nothing I had ever seen. It of course was not the equal of masterful, professionally-erected layouts like the one found at Chicago's Museum of Science and Industry. But this was then, a unique and special treat in that unique and special country. So of course, I was enthralled.

I remember as well the two Japanese men who always were present in the shop. One was an old, wrinkled and largely toothless man who would always greet me smilingly, then sit to one side continuing to smile and nod his head while mumbling this-or-that Japanese phrase over-and-over; like the proprietor of the fireworks shop, seemingly waiting for me to do something.

The other man was quite younger, no older than his twenties, and may have been the older man's son. In contrast to the older man, I don't once remember this fellow smiling at me, or even acknowledging my presence beyond a politely curt nod in my direction whenever I entered. The reason was because he was the artisan of the operation, always painstakingly working on this-or-that aspect of the display: fitting parts of a car together with the aid of a stand-supported magnifying glass, fussing about some item on the layout, wiring a locomotive...whatever it took to keep the splendid wholeness of it all in good visual and working order.

But what I most remember about the layout was that it was not a working model of Japanese railroads, which were plentiful and colorful enough in their own right, but of *American* railroads! The freight cars especially. I had seen enough of trains and railroad cars, freight and passenger alike, back Stateside to be familiar with their design and markings--and the tiny freight cars in this ramshackle building some five thousand miles from the nearest full-scale example of an American freight train were exact copies right down to the most minute detail.

Colors, graphics, railroad logos, ladders, couplers, chains--every conceivable detail, even the smallest lettering describing car characteristics, capacities, handling instructions, safety warnings and the like, were replicated exactly as I remembered them appearing on the many railroad cars I had become familiar with as a result of my amorous relationship with American railroading. The exquisite detailing was evident everywhere on these cars; nothing, it seems, was overlooked in creating perfect miniature replicas, right down to the truck assemblies, which were bolstered by tiny coil springs to enable the wheel groups to flex up-and-down to absorb shocks, just like on a full-scale freight car.

At the time, I was so mesmerized by it all that it never occurred to me how this artist, and by extension others like him, could make such wonderfully exact models in the absence of full-size examples of the genre. Years later I would discover that he and others learned what American railroad stock looked like from pictures of the subjects they had seen in American books and, more prominently, magazines, which would have been available to them or compatriots at the many American libraries and households that had sprouted throughout their homeland.

Thinking back, and without taking anything away from the talent, their accomplishments were not just masterful artistry, but also impeccable counterfeiting. The young man I always saw grimly laboring over some detail of the model trains was akin to the metallurgists who fashioned the exact replicas of the ancient samurai swords, and the artists who counterfeited the phony yen note stamps. They weren't just making copies, they were making clones. All for us "honorable conquerors," as we Americans especially were now-and-then described–but more critically, all to help them and their own families survive.

The young man would assemble HO gauge rail cars for the shop's display, and for sale in kit form. I of course bought a number of these kits, but their components were so complex and detailed, they required patient, precise motor skills just to assemble them properly. I would spend hours meticulously trying to glue the many pieces together. In the end, our houseboy, an artist of some talent in his own right, would help me construct the models in a presentable form; and over time, Yoshi and I put together a dozen or so freight cars, which I'd display on my room's book shelves. I remember bringing three or four back to the States, but lost track of them sometime during my teen years, probably a casualty of one of our family's many moves.

While I don't remember any other specific shops in the Motomachi, I vividly recall a special time of year there: Christmas. December transformed the street. Normally bleak and forbidding at night, especially in late winter, the street dazzled with color and light at Christmastide. The decorations were eerily reminiscent of what I had known in America; imagine, if you will, images of Santa Claus, but with distinctly Japanese features. These were prominently featured on rice-paper lantern globes, among other platforms. The omnipresent fireworks bore special red-and-green Christmas wraps, and there were even Nativity scenes, although as with the Santas the participants looked more Japanese than Judaean. And everywhere were candles and torches and any other form of illumination the merchants could improvise.

I spent just one Christmas in Japan, and it was magical in a way none other has been. Its sole reminder is a Japanese Santa tree light, long burnt out, which my parents gave to my sister, who in turn gave it to her younger son. The Japanese still decorate for Christmas, although not in any religious sense. From what I've read, it's just as brightly lit, noisy and colorful as the Christmas I knew there. In its way, Christmas may be the last remaining trace of the occupation in present-day Japan.

Depending on my mood, task, errand to run, person I had to meet, or whatever I had in mind or had to do, I would roam elsewhere than the Motomachi. Chinatown was just across the river, but I don't recall anything there that caught my attention. A little farther along was a large baseball park named after New York Yankee legend Lou Gehrig where we would go to watch organized army baseball teams play each other, or play Japanese teams.

The games between the American soldiers and the Japanese players always drew the bigger crowds, Japanese and Americans alike. As I recall, the Japanese teams would win more often. The stadium where they played, modestly sized for its time, is now the home field of the Yokohama *DeNA Bay Stars*, equivalent to a major league team in the United States. The revamped stadium is sleekly modern with seating for thirty thousand, making it at least ten times the capacity of the not-very-grand grandstands I knew.

This stadium is said to be one of only three in Japan that are like American baseball parks in that it has an all-grass infield and outfield, whereas typical Japanese baseball venues, including even major stadium parks, have all-dirt infields. I'm not surprised to know that the current Yokohama stadium retained its American grass infield heritage, given that the sites are identical. The other two American-type baseball stadiums are in Kobe, which also hosted a sizeable American troop contingent during the occupation; and, interestingly, Hiroshima, which, as noted, never had any casual American visitors during the occupation.

Across a small park from the baseball field once stood a combination branch library-recreation center, which I well remember because I attended children's activities there. Often after some program was done, or I had been in the library for some other reason, I'd stand beside a low brick wall just outside the building while awaiting mother to come pick me up. When my wife and I visited Yokohama in 1994, my first time back in Japan in the forty-four years since I had lived there, we were near the baseball stadium when she excused herself to use a restroom. While waiting for her to rejoin me, I sat on a convenient low brick wall--and after a few moments realized it was the very same wall! I know this for certain because the bricks were distinctive: thin, dark red, almost slab-like affairs.

This particular area of Yokohama, from the Bluff Area to the farthest reach of the waterfront docks, was just one facet of the city. The true downtown lay farther north, and included the principal shopping districts. Like Tokyo's Ginza, this particular area wasn't bombed, but neither was it missed by much. I'd go there to take in a movie at the Octagon Theater, usually riding a bus back-and-forth but sometimes walking the entire distance, even after dark. The route traversed a totally bombed-out area, which by the rubble seemed to be a mixture of commercial structures and housing.

Quite often, if I had come downtown alone to see a movie at the Octagon, I would make it a point to buy a large bag or two of popcorn on the way out, which I then would share with Japanese kids I inevitably encountered. There were usually a half-dozen or so children my age, as I recall pretty much the same ones each time, all boys, and all dressed shabbily and speaking little if any English. But we would all share smiles as I would hand over the largely still-full bags (I never have been much of a popcorn aficionado), which they would eagerly if also politely gobble up.

"DOWNTOWN" YOKOHAMA - 5TH ST - 1947

-- 155TH STA HOSP

SVC CLUB   PX

While I remember much about living in and wandering about Yokohama, one mystery of our time there eluded me until recently. When we lived on the Bluff Area, it was called "Tagatay Ridge." And on the opposite side of the bluff from the city was an area we occupationaiers called "Nasugbu Beach," where my grade school of the same name was located, and after which the school was named. The words "Tagatay" and "Nasugbu" are missing from those areas today; they aren't listed on any maps of the Yokohama area. I found this out while researching a memoir article on my childhood in Japan for the magazine, *American Heritage*.

I looked and inquired here-and-there for the sources of those names and what had happened to them; I even queried the Japanese embassy and legation, but the most anyone could guess was that the two words were proper names. There was no fully comprehensive Internet during the time I was researching the article in the mid-1990s, so deep intelligence, Google-based search terms readily available now weren't at the time. Eventually, as with much else, I came across the answer at the MacArthur Memorial. And it once again involved a long-forgotten wartime connection.

Right after Japan surrendered, American army units under General Eichelberger's command were dispatched to the country to secure vital areas. These were veteran combat divisions that had seen heavy action against Japanese troops in New Guinea, the Philippines and elsewhere.

One of these forces was the venerated First Cavalry Division, given the responsibility (and honor) of securing Tokyo. Another was the Eleventh Airborne Division, charged with securing Yokohama, plus the *Atsugi* airport where MacArthur's plane landed right after the surrender, some twenty miles due west of the harbor. But just part of the Eleventh flew into Atsugi; the main element made an amphibious landing at a beach near the prisoner-of-war facility that would become my elementary school. Once the separate elements of the division were linked up and had secured the area, they took the time to name certain portions after campaigns and battles they had fought and won against their recent enemy.

And so the beachhead the troops landed at in Yokohama was named "Nasugbu Beach" after an amphibious landing the division had held at a beach of the very same name on the western shore of the Philippine island of Luzon. The Philippine Nasugbu Beach is today an internationally-popular seaside vacation resort. And they re-named the Bluff Area after a Manila suburb named Tagatay, some twenty miles west of the Philippine capital of Manila, where the division later staged an airborne drop.

Among the people I had earlier inquired about the origin of the names was my mother, who also hadn't any idea of the name origins and didn't even hazard a guess. She's gone now, but might have been intrigued by the origin of the names during our time there. Then again, in her way, she might have just shrugged it off.

Chapter 8: The Future Was Then

Suburban sprawl is a hallmark of post-World War II America, an endemic phenomenon characterized by a trio of interdependent ingredients: housing, shopping centers to serve the housing, and the automobile as the primary–and often the sole--means of transportation connecting the people who occupy the housing with their sources of goods and services.

It is widely held that suburban sprawl began with the initial Levittown, a tract housing project in New York's Nassau County that welcomed its first home owners in the autumn of 1947. But the first, true example of the genre, with all three interacting elements intact and functioning together, did not appear on Long Island or anywhere else in the United States, but almost a year earlier and thousands of miles westward on the south side of the Bluff Area in Yokohama. We lived nearby, so I knew it well.

From the very beginning of the mission to bring servicemen's families to Japan, a primary focus---and concern--was where to house them all. As General Eichelberger's letter to his wife back in North Carolina revealed, housing for the families was at least one of the issues, if not the principal topic, MacArthur and John McCloy discussed that mid-November day in 1945 when SCAP gave the go-ahead for the wives and children to come to Japan. And it makes sense that adequate, open housing accessible to Americans and Japanese alike may have been foremost in MacArthur's mind, given his stated ambition for the Japanese to view and experience the American family home as a benevolent, meaningful guide to their own future.

Housing was not an issue in the occupation's early days, before the families began arriving. In the suburbs and hinterlands, male-only American and British army units simply did what armies have historically done and set up self-contained and -supporting tent cities. Unattached civilian occupation personnel, bachelor SCAP and FECO staff members and the like, took up residence as close to headquarters as they could manage in hotels and guest houses that had either escaped the bombings or at least incurred only minimal damage.

The most popular of the Tokyo residential hotels was the *Yuraku*, which housed single male officers and DACs. Lorena Treadway remembered the hotel had a rooftop garden with a bar and dance floor, complete with a Japanese band that one night played "Carolina Moon" over-and-over. Ms. Treadway added that mixed drinks were just a (scrip) dime each, rendering inebriation a quickly-attained state, so never mind what the band played. She also opined that single life in occupied Japan was better than she and many others had known back in the United States. She wrote, "'Never had it so good' became a popular expression after being raised in the Depression followed by four years of war."

Ms. Treadway's optimistic view of the occupation as a haven for young people of the time would have pleased planners, for such a positive outlook was exactly what they set out to elicit not only in Japan, but also and especially back in America. Among other tactics, the ten-cent-a-drink tariff was part of an occupation ploy to peg desirable goods and services at absurdly low prices in order to lure young, unattached singles to Japan as SCAP and FECO staff members. Associated draws included: full, three-course dinners for just a quarter; the afore-mentioned American cigarettes for a mere dollar a carton; and gasoline at sixteen cents a gallon, for anyone fortunate enough to have a jeep or automobile.

Once the families began arriving, they also were eligible to enjoy the same ridiculously low-cost benefits as did the singles or any other occupationaires. Families might handle the benefits differently, however. For one thing, smoking and non-smoking family members alike might buy cartons of cigarettes by the armful and use them as barter for goods and services, rather than re-sell them on the black market. None of these incentives was eliminated for the occupation's duration, and the only nod to pricing reality occurred in 1949 when the tariff for a three-course dinner was raised to forty cents.

Many of the first dependents to arrive also set up housekeeping with their husbands in hotels, but because children now were involved, this approach entailed seeking out lodgings with enough un-allotted space wherein a family could spread out over several rooms. So the families often would end up living in sumptuous resort hotels sited in rural areas that had not harbored military targets and so were untouched by the war. The Kanagawa Prefecture west of Yokohama was home to a number of such hostelries, especially in and around the town of Hakone, which was and remains a highly popular holiday destination because of its proximity to Mount Fuji.

Patricia Stackhouse Garrity knew of resort hotel housing. Ms. Garrity was nine years old when she lived with her parents and two sisters in the yet-today glamorous and desirable Fujiya Hotel in Hakone for six months in 1947, while awaiting their permanent quarters to be constructed. I also well remember the Fujiya Hotel; we often would spend a weekend or more there. But living at the hotel? If nothing else, life in such an elegant resort hotel was a markedly different kind of home life. As Ms. Garrity writes:

> *It was beautiful. All of the railings were carved in the likeness of a dragon. We were in the Flower wing. My parents had one room and my sisters and I had the room next to them. From my parents' room you could look out at the mountains. Sometimes you couldn't see anything at all because of mountain mist. The hotel was simply huge and although we had pretty much free range while we were there, it was understood that we were always to mind our manners and no running in the hallways. Which by the way smelled like slightly burnt toast...*
>
> *Dinner on the first night we arrived was our first introduction to dress codes. Father was in his dress uniform and mother was in her very best dress. Slacks were never allowed at dinner... Our waitresses were Japanese women wearing beautiful kimonos. Water was*

*poured with great flourish. Soup was
served first and it was clear. I leaned
down and smelled it, for which I
received a stern signal from my mother,
that was not allowed...*

*While waiting for the different
courses to be served, I looked over at the
quartet playing. Later that would be
something taken for granted: a piano
playing during breakfast, a harp or
violin during lunch and a quartet
playing during dinner. The dining room
was very large and during this dinner, a
first night for many (of) us, very quiet
and subdued. With the meal finished
another bowl with clear water was
placed in front of us. I leaned over to
smell it again, and this time mother told
me that this was not soup but a finger
bowl to clean our hands after the meal.
She turned to help my younger sister so I
proceeded to push up my sleeves and
shove my hands down into the water.
Those families close by started to laugh
and although mother was embarrassed
somewhat she said that the atmosphere
in the room became more relaxed.
People commented to her later how they
had all been a little intimidated by the
formality in the room...*

*There were three pools in the
Fujiya. The Mermaid Room was for
women, and then there was one for men
and one for families. You had to put your
name in to use it. The first time we went
as a family, we all wore swimsuits. When*

it was explained to my mother that Japanese families went into the pool naked, she was appalled. She did understand, however, about washing and rinsing before you got into the pool. That made sense to her...

We were in our own world there. We had activities with the kids from the other hotels nearby. The Gohra and the Fuji View. For your birthday a party was given, with all of the trimmings. There would be party hats, a cake plus an ice sculpture. There were tours to see the Daibutsu or Great Buddha in Kamakura, the Cherry Blossom Festival, the Temples of Kyoto and the monthly trips to downtown Yokohama to the Yokohama Main Exchange or PX. Santa came to see us in a rickshaw at Christmas. Pictures were always taken by a photographer of any occasion and I have quite a few of them.

While life in the resort hotels could indeed be luxurious, they were too far from business centers to be a practical daily commute to-and-from the family head's place of work. So the routine became one of the mother living in a hotel with her children during the week, while the father roomed with an associate near his work locale, or even bunked in the workplace itself: sleeping on a cot, grabbing meals when and where he could, and using public washrooms. Life during the work week for Ms. Garrity's father might have been quite different from his time in the hotel.

Such makeshift living arrangements as resort hotels quickly became untenable as the occupation presence and numbers grew and more dependents began arriving. Permanent housing convenient to work centers had to be found. But the problem was that the vast majority of the occupation troops and their wives and children, plus the families of naval and air force contingents, were concentrated around and in Japan's major metropolitan areas--and the incessant bombing missions had destroyed virtually all available housing in those cities and suburbs.

About the only exceptions to this terror bombing (and it was that) were select, upscale neighborhoods. Prime examples of desirable environs included the Bluff Area where our family lived, and the high-rent, residential-cum-shopping quarter adjacent to and partially surrounding the imperial palace grounds in Tokyo, the area that also included SCAP's Dai Ichi headquarters building and the American embassy.

But an understandable problem with these and other still-habitable residential areas was that they were already inhabited. And just as it was occupation policy not to rely upon scarce Japanese resources to feed and clothe us occupationaires, so too did it become policy not to exercise any to-the-victor-belong-the-spoils custom of ages past where housing was concerned, and simply throw the occupants out on the street. So efforts were made not to disenfranchise a Japanese individual or family from its home just because an American family needed a residence.

If the property the occupation desired had not been used by or for the disbanded Japanese military, either directly or indirectly, then the residence would be leased for a specific time period. The owner, for his part, was paid rent and, if need be, gotten comparable living facilities. This policy was executed early-on--yet after dependents had begun coming ashore, and thus in need of housing.

A SCAP Staff Memorandum dated 25 November 1946 states in part under Paragraph 2:

> *a. In residences to be taken over, the Japanese owners or residents will be permitted to occupy appropriate sections of the residence taken for occupancy by Allied personnel wherever practicable.*
>
> *b. Where it is not practicable for Japanese residents to continue to occupy a portion of the residence, suitable quarters into which they may move will be provided prior to their ejection; in which case, a fair distribution of the furniture of the residence to be taken will be made.*

This policy seems to have held regardless whether the occupier had colluded with the former enemy in some way or another, exceptions being those who had directly run Japan's war effort, most of whom by that point were either dead or on trial for war crimes. In virtually all other cases, substitute housing would be found. If the dwelling was quite spacious, the occupier might be offered a pseudo apartment elsewhere in the very same abode, and a number of occupation families dwelt in such situations, co-existing with the previous occupants. Also, in some instances, residents were, in effect, banished to other cities that had incurred little if any bomb damage, but into dwelling units commensurate with the exile's socio-economic position.

It is worth noting that the majority of these disenfranchisements were from desirable neighborhoods in the most bomb-ravaged major cities: Tokyo, Yokohama, Kobe, Nagoya and Osaka, to name the most prominent examples. Certainly our family's house had been requisitioned (to put it delicately) from some occupant, as probably had many of the other homes in the moneyed neighborhood where we lived; but of course, being a child, I was not privy to who may have lived in our house and why they were no longer there. The same ignorance about prior occupants seems to have been the norm for the adults among us as well: there was no need to know, so nothing was asked or said. One army family was moved into a sumptuous Frank Lloyd Wright-designed house in Tokyo after their original residence was destroyed in a fire, but even they apparently didn't know what affluent family had been evicted to make room for them.

This innocence--and wonder--at the housing that awaited the families varied greatly depending on the family head's rank and position in the occupation, whether part of the occupying army itself or a member of the SCAP or FECO staff, when the family members arrived, how many there were, and to what area of the country they were assigned.

Bernadine V. Lee, who came to Japan in September 1946 with 838 other service wives and children aboard the Matson Line's *Monterey* (in its time a preeminent luxury liner) on one of the earliest dependent shiploads to arrive, wrote of her family's new home in Tokyo:

> *As Cecil* (her husband, a veteran of the Pacific war) *drove us through the narrow streets of outer Tokyo, I tried to picture what kind of a shack we would call our own. The jeep pulled up in front of a western-style, two-story frame house with a garden wall--a house with gracious old trees, a yard friendly in shrugs and flowers. It might have been in Waterbury, Connecticut* (Ms. Lee's family home), *but for a large, Japanese stone lantern in the back yard...And what a house!...To my amazement I found a home ready to live in; a kitchen complete with electric stove and electric refrigerator, toaster, waffle iron, coffee peculator* (sic; she obviously meant to

write percolator), *dishes, silverware,*
table linen, and even curtains on the
windows; two bathrooms, one with a tile
bathtub; four bedrooms, one of them
Japanese style, which Babs (a daughter)
adores ...There are several stained glass
windows in the living room, parquet
hardwood floors, a telephone, and all
the necessary furniture.

– Bernadine V. Lee, "Army Wife in Tokyo,"
Army Information Digest, December 1946

Ms. Lee also wrote of the wide variance of the homes friends of
hers inhabited, from eighteen-room villas seized from wealthy
Japanese, to Quonset huts and small apartments.

Home-style manners were quite different for Margery Finn Brown
and her family. The Brown's time in Japan was a sharp exception to
the usual experience of an American family assigned to the
occupation, and in several ways: they arrived early and stayed nearly
twice the usual deployment time, from 1946 to 1951, living nearly the
entire time in a wholly Japanese neighborhood in undamaged Kyoto.
The Browns interacted mostly with Japanese friends, neighbors and
co-workers; and Ms. Brown even became a columnist for a Japanese
newspaper, although, by her own admission, she never learned to
speak or write Japanese coherently.

Ms. Brown's autobiography of her family's time in occupied
Japan, *Over a Bamboo Fence* (Charles E. Tuttle Co., 1951), was
simultaneously released in the United States and Japan. The book was
highly-regarded and -cited for her insightful views of Japanese
lifestyles and attitudes under the aegis of the occupation, although
many of her observations and opinions could today be termed racially
insensitive and condescending. It's a matter of context. Someone
wholly unfamiliar with Japan during the occupation period would
likely find certain of Ms. Brown's viewpoints the height of political
incorrectness. But someone who lived there at the time could readily
detect many truths behind the stereotyping. Interestingly (and

tellingly), Ms. Brown little mentions socializing with other Americans, and nowhere indicates she ever interacted with other American mothers in a family atmosphere, or her children with theirs.

Ms. Brown wrote lengthily and in minute detail of her family's house and the neighborhood in which they lived, which she termed a constantly teeming "alley" in central Kyoto. About the house:

> *It was a perfect gem of ugliness, a smaller Kyoto version of the* (Frank Lloyd Wright-designed) *Imperial Hotel in Tokyo, with a switch in atmosphere from Mayan tomb to Victorian hunting lodge...Directly inside the front door by a pair of Ali Baba vases was a white tiled bathroom and a white tiled kitchen, giving the heavy paneled hall the sterile chasteness of an operating room. Ahead, there was a study with a dinosaur-sized pool table. Then a dining room, and a drawing room so large that two twelve-by-fifteen rugs failed to cover its parquet floor. Up a winding stairway under a chandelier quivering with crystals was the second floor that held four bedrooms, the third floor, and a look-out from which we could see the checkerboard of Kyoto in a valley spired with frosty mountains.*

And of the neighborhood:

> *The warrens of the alley were on three sides of us, every square inch occupied with life. In every cubicle, someone eating, spitting, boiling tea,*

> *wrapping a package, washing or giving*
> *birth.*
> –Margery Finn Brown, *Over a Bamboo Fence*
> Chapter 5, "A Kyoto Alley," p. 44

I would guess that everyone who lived in a Japanese house, or a near-miss Western-style pseudo-mansion like our abode (and apparently also Ms. Brown's home), would have a differently colorful way to describe it. But such living quarters were the exception, and likely the only ones along with purely Japanese-style houses still standing. (Our family's Mediterranean-esque house is gone, as I discovered on returning to Yokohama in 1994. A sleekly modern white stucco house now occupies the space.)

The vast majority of American military families lived in conventionally-styled single-family homes, townhouses (two-flats) and apartments erected for the occasion--and with a single, notable exception, they're all gone, long ground under Japan's hugely successful reincarnation. In Tokyo and Yokohama, at least, the land upon which most of the projects stood is now occupied by skyscrapers. But in their time and place, it was these conventional American homes together with their occupants that most provided the Japanese a deep and penetrating look deep inside American culture, mores, wants and needs.

In contrast to the (presumably delicate) procedures for acquiring already occupied and desirable housing, acquiring the land for these nascent postwar housing projects was no problem: the occupation simply identified land that had supported Japan's now non-existent war machine–army camps, air force bases and the like--seized it outright, brought in bulldozers to scrape away what was left standing after the incessant bombing (not much), then went to erecting the very first examples of that uniquely American phenomenon, the subdivision.

Huge parcels of land were gathered up using this outright seizure policy, then turned into glimpses of the future suburban America. Housing for the families of commissioned and non-commissioned officers alike was taken care of by erecting on these one-time military compounds what were and remain the largest off-post living quarters developments the American military ever constructed either at home or abroad--and in their time, the largest and most inclusive (meaning including adjacent or internal shopping centers) housing projects to be found anywhere!

In all, a total ninety-two hundred detached single-family houses, two-flats, and apartment units were built during the occupation's eighty months. That number becomes strikingly significant when viewed alongside the total number of American families living in Japan at any given time during the occupation: ninety-five hundred. Comparing the two figures on a relative basis means that the total number of families awaiting housing of any type outnumbered the total number of available American-style homes by the nearly insignificant ratio of just 1.03-to-1, which in turn meant that the overwhelming number and percentage of families were billeted not in Japanese dwellings or existing Western-style houses, but in American-style homes located within what were American-style developments.

Further extrapolation of those statistics reveals that Japanese of all stripes who worked for and with American families in various capacities--maids, gardeners, handymen, mechanics, bar tenders, waiters, store clerks, soda jerks, fry cooks, commissary stockmen and -women, and on-and-on--got unprecedented, lengthy and close-up looks into just how Americans lived. Which of course was just what MacArthur wanted!

And that was not all. In certain cases where outright seizure of large swaths of land for its near-term use was concerned, occupation authorities acted with Japan's future well-being in mind. A FECO Joint Committee Minutes dated 13 February 1950 includes this prescient sentence:

> *First, the houses should be located in such areas that in the event the houses are not required by the occupation forces prior to the time the cost of construction had been amortized, they might be utilized by* (the) *Japanese*

> *indigenous economy and thus represent*
> *a capital investment for Japan.*

The first housing project, begun in early 1946 before the first dependents arrived, went up in southern Yokohama adjacent to a beach that had been determined to have been used by the Japanese army for amphibious warfare exercises, plus there was the prisoner-of-war facility nearby that would become my grade school, and so was fair game for seizure.

Housing Area 1

Accurately if uncreatively named "Housing Area Number 1," the project had five hundred mostly multi-family dwelling units plus a servants' dormitory, and was ready for occupancy by that autumn. The next April, a second and similarly-sized and -constituted project, deftly named "Housing Area Number 2," began to be constructed across a main road that separated the two projects and was completed thirteen months later. Area 2 was one of two housing projects in Yokohama where the housing units were heated by a central steam generation plant. Patricia Stackhouse Garrity's family lived in Area 2 until 1950 after leaving the Fujiya Hotel. She shared a particularly stark memory of the steam system:

> *There were small cement buildings in some of the back yards, and we were told never to go into them. My sisters and I remember there was a small boy around five who was the brother of one of our playmates who wandered into one and fell into hot steaming water. A Japanese worker grabbed him and pulled him out by wrapping his legs around one of the hot pipes. People had gathered around by then, and an ambulance took the boy to the hospital where he died. The Japanese worker who had saved the boy received severe burns on his legs. On his own he walked to a Japanese hospital for help.*

Housing Area 2

The year 1947 saw the apogee of the American housing boom in Japan. The grandest-scale housing projects went up in Tokyo, where the greatest concentration of Americans, civilian as well as military, was located. The large American presence was due to Tokyo being the headquarters of SCAP and FECO with its civilian and military employees, and also the location for the Eighth Army's single-largest unit in Japan, the First Cavalry Division, which was headquartered at Camp Drake just outside the city proper. Providing housing for the hundreds of families of these organizations thus became a high priority, and three housing projects were erected just outside Tokyo to accommodate them. The largest of these subdivisions, Grant Heights, eighteen miles out from the center of Tokyo, was begun in February 1947 and took eighteen months to complete, although it was forty percent occupied by the end of the inaugural year.

Grant Heights was created from the one-time *Narimasu* Airfield, which at the end of the war had been a training base for kamikaze pilots. The project was built around the field's main runway, that was repaved and bestowed with the all-American name, "Main Street." The name later was changed to "Narimasu Boulevard." (Interestingly, narimasu loosely translates to "changing to something else," so considering all the change that Japan had gone through and was still enduring, a very fitting name.) Bomb craters that did not have to be filled in to make way for construction were simply left open. My parents had friends who lived in Grant Heights and had children my age. A bomb crater was not far from their back porch. When we visited, we kids made a "fort" of that crater, which came complete with weed-grown debris. In our cowboys-and-Indians games, our imaginations re-exploded the crater again-and-again.

Main Street, Grant Heights

When completed, Grant Heights had a total 1,260 dependent family dwelling units, plus sixty other buildings for army use--a significant statistic in its time, because in numerical dwelling units it surpassed any housing project then going up back in the United States, including the first Levittown, which was being erected at the same time. Eventually, two other and similar, although somewhat smaller, projects would be built in the same general vicinity: Washington Heights and Pershing Heights.

Blueprint-type drawings of these houses are in the first issues of *Dependents Guide to Japan*. Shown are a simple, one-floor, ranch-style bungalow and a two-story house with single-story wings. The *Guide...* notes that nine types of houses, plus one- and two-unit apartments, were to be constructed. Descriptions elsewhere outline one type of house with a living and dining room, kitchen, three bedrooms and bath, all very much in keeping with later tract house designs of the time.

PROPOSED PLAN
OF
DEPENDENTS' HOUSING UNIT

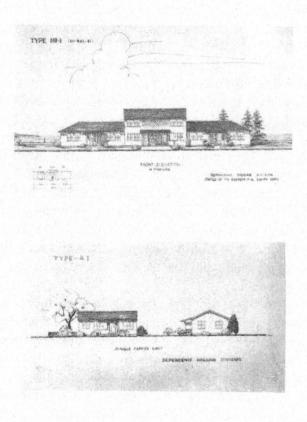

6

Completion schedules for the housing projects were delayed due to lack of building materials. Wartime destruction precluded the Japanese from supplying even such rudiments as concrete and pipe. And due to more-pressing shipping priorities, delays of up to several months were encountered for necessary building supplies, most

179

especially cement and American plumbing fixtures, all of which had to be shipped from the west coast of the United States.

When supplies did arrive, they may or may not have been in the quantities or even the type requested. This meant that a lot of backing-and-filling had to be done to make use of what supplies did manage to make it across the ocean. Dwelling units often were re-engineered in mid-construction, which here-and-there led to odd appearances not just to houses located nearby one another, but also to the exterior and interior makeup of individual dwellings. A frame house might suddenly end and be completed faced in brick or concrete block or stucco--or all three. Bricks often were mismatched, so a house begun with red bricks could be finished with blue bricks. Or bricks may be odd-shaped. Roofs often had mismatched and mis-colored shingles--or again, shingles might cease altogether and another covering, like tiles or even metal sheathing, be used to complete the job.

Inside, kitchen cabinets and bathroom fixtures may or may not have matched; I personally remember a friend's bathroom that had a blue vanity next to a pink toilet. Or maybe it was the other way around. Whichever, it was silly-looking. It was the same with doors to rooms: one room could have a paneled door, and right next to it a smooth-faced door.

Only one of these quirky-looking housing projects remains--and it's still used for family housing by the American military. Construction of the 406 ranch-style houses and two-flats that would comprise "Area X," as it was originally called, was begun in October 1947, completed just before Christmas 1948, and thankfully given the softer name "*Negishi* Heights" after the Yokohama cho at the far west end of Tagatay Ridge/Bluff Area where it is located.

Negishi Heights is the other housing development that originally featured a centrally-located steam heating system, although that has since been dismantled and replaced by individual units. The army's Camp Zama, home to the last American army presence in Japan, is nearby, and some army families live in the development, but the community chiefly houses US Navy families from the Yokosuka Naval Base. A stroll through Negishi Heights just to gaze at the oddly-mismatched ranch-style houses can be amusing; it's otherwise just another ordinary-looking subdivision. I can only suppose the interior fixtures have by this time been updated and made matching.

Japanese laborers helped erect these housing projects. They had never seen anything like them: not their concept, not their scope, not the way they went up. The layouts of some present-day Japanese suburbs--but not the houses themselves--are patterned after the American models of the occupation era. In observing and participating in this construction activity, the Japanese got their first looks at the then highly-vaunted and -exploited "American know-how."

They were especially taken by that most basic of American construction machines, the bulldozer. For whatever reason, the Japanese had never seen anything like the bulldozer despite their having built and used a similar tracked vehicle, the tank, during the war. The first Japanese-made "bulldozers" were, in fact, disarmed war surplus tanks of theirs outfitted with scraper blades. The bulldozer became a metaphor for what was then an admired American capability of getting any job done no matter the obstacles.

The dwelling units, houses and two-flats alike, even had an indirect influence on Japan's new constitution. What happened was Japanese women admired Western sit-type toilets over their traditional squat-type, because, they complained, using Japanese toilets over-developed their legs, making them musclebound and unattractive. So the women began campaigning and demonstrating to replace their traditional toilets with the type being installed in the new American houses. These campaigns in turn empowered Japanese women to campaign for more women's rights, including especially freedom to break away from their traditional roles of being bound to and subservient to their husbands. The net result was that heretofore un-imagined and un-imaginable women's rights were written into the Japanese constitution, which has more delineated women's rights than does America's own constitution.

But the significance to the Japanese of the unique and varied homes, the bulldozer as a symbol of American know-how to get the land cleared and made housing-ready, and the rapidly completed and occupied projects as the reality of that know-how, must be gathered together and weighed in the context of what the Americans erected adjacent to the housing projects, the appendixes that made them truly complete suburbs in the fullest sense of the word: shopping centers.

All the housing projects in Tokyo, Yokohama, Fukoka and Kobe included tangent shopping centers (the one in Yokohama neatly divided Housing Areas 1 and 2) that featured commissaries, exchanges, gas stations, bowling alleys, movie theaters, dry cleaners, beauty parlors, snack bars and other service establishments familiar to Americans. While shopping centers were of course known back in the United States before the war, they were to achieve their full flowering only tangentially with the postwar housing boom--and this trend was taking shape most rapidly and revealingly not in America, but in occupied Japan. A glimpse of what America was rapidly becoming in the postwar world first gained recognition for its potential not in the United States but in this alien, war-torn land.

Housing Areas 1 & 2 Shopping Mall, 1949

I very well knew the mall-like shopping center that divided housing Areas 1 and 2 in Yokohama. It was located adjacent to our Nasugbu Beach school, so of course we kids visited it almost every day. I can still visualize most of the buildings: a sizeable commissary beside an equally-large post exchange that contained Japan's first-ever American-style beauty shop, a movie theater (the "Bill Chickering Theater," another correspondent who was killed in the war), a combination snack bar/ice cream shop, a bowling alley, a dry cleaners, a cafeteria, the Neet Nac Club (spell neet-nac backwards; solely for teenagers, no grade-school kids allowed, although we'd sneak a peek through the door), a fire station, an automobile repair garage, a branch library that also included a book store, a work shop for hobbyists, and a service station.

Behind and to the left of the shopping center was our school, a playground, an athletic field marked off for baseball and football, and a chapel. Just west of the school was a horse race track, converted during the occupation into a golf driving range. Directly behind the mall and snugged up against a hillside was a hut-like building where I first joined the Cub Scouts, and nearby a much larger building used for meetings and assemblies. A Christmas pageant was held in that building. There are pictures of the mall on the Internet that were taken as late as the mid-1970s, before it and Areas 1 and 2 were demolished in the early 1980s, and it still looked very much as I remember it. I could closely date the picture from the look of the cars in the parking lot.

Even more significantly--and perhaps also curiously--exactly how Americans would use the shopping center was here most clearly and indelibly first put on display: the American penchant for utilizing (not to ignore *over*-utilizing) the automobile for every imaginable mission or errand, no matter how trivial, regardless of whether a car was even needed in the first place to attain the goal.

Americans of all stripes operated cars flagrantly in postwar Japan. Virtually all the American families, and bachelor service personnel as well, had a car or a jeep. If you didn't have a car, you devoted as much energy as you could to getting one. If you couldn't afford a car, if you were a young, low-ranking enlisted man, you'd quickly ally yourself with someone who did have a car. If you were a mid- to high-ranking officer, your car could be shipped to Japan as part of your housing allotment. If you were of a lower rank, you could buy a car from someone homeward bound.

Surplus jeeps were sold to occupation personnel who had applied for their dependents to join them. The jeeps were classified as "good," "fair" and "poor used" (the last usually a euphemism for combat-damaged), and sold for 525, 375 and 225 dollars, respectively. The jeeps were bought from army surplus stocks and sold through post exchanges.

War-battered or not, jeeps became a precious commodity. Lorena Treadway noted that a jeep's side curtains would be transferred from one jeep to another whenever the former vehicle was no longer operable. The curtains were flimsy and offered scant protection from severe weather, but they at least provided some cover. She also wrote that jeeps were so easy to start and steal (no ignition key required), that it was common practice to open the hood and remove the distributor cap whenever the vehicle would be parked out-of-sight for any period of time.

A few Americans even took a chance (and it really was that) on pre-war Japanese autos that somehow had managed to survive the incessant bombing or weren't otherwise tenaciously guarded by their owners. Among these were electric cars and light trucks, and three- and four-wheeled vehicles powered by wood or charcoal. Charcoal-powered autos especially were very common; I vividly remember seeing them pulled onto a roadside, their drivers animatedly stoking the rear-mounted burners while the noxious fumes from their efforts roiled across the roadway.

Americans took advantage of this lust to have a drivable...something...no matter what. Our by then ten-year-old Chevrolet that dad had shipped to Japan had been bought new for six hundred dollars. When we left Japan in the late summer of 1950, he sold it for five hundred dollars to the army corporal driver of his official car. That's a depreciation rate of not quite seventeen percent over a decade for a very ordinary automobile. By comparison, it's equivalent to a car selling new today for thirty thousand dollars being resold ten years later for just under twenty-five thousand. I'm unsure what the mileage on our car was by 1950 (mother couldn't remember), but even accounting for wartime rationing and limited driving conditions in Japan, it must have been flirting with seventy-five thousand or so. Mother did make a point of saying that dad's driver was willing to pay us what we had paid for "Elmer" (my parents' name for our car) new, but dad refused him.

Due to adverse road conditions, automobiles rarely if ever were used for very long trips, trains being the preferred and recommended way to travel. Also, it was chancy getting service or even gasoline for a private automobile once removed from a major population center. Mother or dad always made a point of filling Elmer before we ventured far from Yokohama.

Gasoline supplies for private vehicles never were plentiful. Early in the occupation, there was a severe shortage of eighty-octane gasoline, the standard for autos then, that was overcome by blending one hundred-octane aviation fuel with "kitchen range" fuel, otherwise known as kerosene. And throughout the occupation, gasoline was rationed to a degree, with the supply preference nodded to occupation personnel and their families. The color of your vehicle's license plate dictated where you could buy gasoline: yellow for all occupation personnel, white for foreign traders not otherwise associated with the occupation. The exchange outlet gas stations served yellow plate holders only, and they usually had adequate quantities.

Area 1 & 2 Service Station, ca. 1948

Gasoline constrictions aside, private cars were used for virtually all errands, including even short junkets from home to commissary just to pick up a single item that could have been gotten as part of some subsequent trip. And cars were almost always used for the relative short weekend jaunts to Mount Fuji and to Nikko, the exquisite, mountainous shrine-cum-resort area north of Tokyo. And why not? Gasoline was cheap despite being now-and-then in short supply, parking was free and plentiful, traffic jams were extremely rare, roads were being repaired and rebuilt--and blatant flaunting of the automobile, a privilege largely denied home-front Americans during the war due to gasoline and tire rationing, provided another link back to the United States.

The Japanese not only saw all this, they became intimate participants in the scene. Servants rode along with housewives to help lug bags of groceries from commissary to car to home. The household help took long weekend trips with their American employers, offering more opportunities to see exactly how far these Americans carried their love affair with this conveyance. Japanese pumped gasoline at service stations, performed lube jobs, changed oil and learned to repair

American cars to the point of major re-assemblies following accidents. Japanese valets at officers' clubs parked cars.

There were even drive-up snack bars, precursors of McDonald's *et al*, where Japanese attendants took orders and handed back paper sacks of hamburgers and milk shakes. An especially popular drive-in lunch stand, named "Drive-Inn," stood on the highway between Tokyo and Yokohama, and so was a refreshing break on the then-arduous drive through the carnage of the Kawasaki industrial district.

"Drive Inn" 1949

The procedure was you would park, and remain in your car until a young woman attendant would come take your order. Then while she was having your order filled, you would go inside to show your identification card and pay. Finally, you would return to your car, get back in, receive your order, and consume it while still seated in your auto. When you were done, you would remain in your car until the female attendant returned to take away your trash. And eventually, you would resume your journey. "Drive-Inn" was close enough to the main Yokohama railway station to serve passengers who chose to ride over by taxi or streetcar. They usually would give their order at a convenient take-out window, then eat their food back at the station or even take it aboard a train.

As a bonus (so to speak), Japanese got the opportunity to view American cars in what was a near-total American automobile environment, one almost completely devoid of their own automobiles. This occurred because very few Japanese autos were around to compete for the viewer's attention. For one thing, the country never did have many automobiles; a pre-war estimate noted there was just one automobile per four thousand persons.

The war of course didn't help that statistic. A survey taken in late 1945, right after the war ended and before Americans other than soldiers began arriving, revealed that there were just 11,467 operable automobiles in the entire country! At the time, Japan's population was about seventy-two million, resulting in a persons-to-driveable car ratio of nearly 6,300-to-1! Extrapolate that extreme proportion to some present-day venue and you get, for example, the equivalent of just six hundred-odd automobiles in all of metropolitan Los Angeles, which in turn figures out to just forty or so cars on Los Angeles's notorious Interstate 405 freeway at the height of an evening rush hour.

Now imagine those same forty-odd Japanese cars in the present-day Los Angeles rush hour example, only now wholly surrounded from one end of the metropolitan area to the other with nothing but American automobiles. That is exactly what the Japanese saw in the mid-late 1940s: a handful of their native cars squirming their way among choking phalanxes of American cars.

And these weren't just American cars that occupation personnel had brought over with them. Beginning in 1948, the Ford Motor Company began importing brand new, postwar autos to Japan. Then to make sure the American car presence kept growing, it was made policy that anyone who brought a car in free-of-charge as part of a household goods shipping allotment either had to leave the car in Japan or pay to have it shipped home. Small wonder the natives came to know American cars so well; they were inundated by them, if not intimidated by them. Lorena Treadway mused that there were so many American cars, jeeps and other non-Japanese vehicles running around, that all an American woman (at least) had to do to hitch a ride was stand on a street corner as if waiting for a light to change, no thumbing was necessary.

Automobile production resumed slowly; American cars would remain overwhelmingly predominant throughout the occupation. One problem with getting Japanese auto production re-started of course was rebuilding the destroyed components of the industry; another was re-assembling surviving elements of automobile manufacture so production could resume. For example, most Toyota production equipment, including precious machine tools, had been dismantled and scattered in remote rural areas to escape the incessant bombing, and rounding up everything was time-consuming.

Priorities were still another stumbling block to resumption of automobile production. But there were priorities–and then there were *priorities*! And when it came to restarting automobile production, itself a priority, you first had to get the materials and tools together to build automobiles, which required ceding the automobile production priority to another class of motor vehicles: trucks. Trucks to ferry machine tools and parts and factory components...and everything else needed to restart automobile production. Trucks had to be built first.

So throughout the occupation, most effort went into building trucks. Toyota, for one, had made automobiles before the war, but during the occupation, mostly produced freight haulers collectively termed "Toyopets:" light-duty trucks, and a small, three-wheeled oddity fitted with a flat bed for hauling modest cargo. Toyota did introduce a modest two-door sedan, the SA, in 1947, after SCAP approved limited production (three hundred vehicles annually) of gasoline-powered automobiles, but only a few were ever made due to the truck priorities. Most automobiles made during the occupation were electric- or diesel-powered.

Toyota Truck and Model SA Sedan, 1948

Altogether, the housing projects, shopping centers and automobile omnipresence gave the Japanese a first-hand, in-depth look at *exactly* what postwar America would be like--and they got it before Americans back home were even fully aware of what was going on! In the America of the late 1940s, train travel still ruled for long-distance trips; the Interstate Highway System was a decade away before it even began taking shape; far-flung suburbs with adjacent shopping centers were even further on the horizon. Exactly how and to what degree the automobile would affect the United States' future remained wholly unrealized and largely un-envisioned.

But in Japan in the late 1940s, it was already happening. True, there were almost no four-lane road stretches, you drove on the left (a challenging act to Americans made all the more so because of the prevailing left-hand-drive American cars), and direction signs were scarce and only bilingual when the Americans got around to changing them. Road conditions ranged from quite good in urban areas that escaped the incessant bombardments, to so dreadfully potholed and rubble-strewn that my father, for one, when we were driving away from Yokohama, would yearn for the paved road to end so he could drive on a constantly-level surface of crushed stone, gravel or just plain dirt.

Really! The drive to Hakone from Yokohama was like that, a distance of just some sixty miles that could take an adventurous three or more hours. Weaving through traffic while avoiding pedestrians, bicycles, rickshaws, clanking streetcars and smoky, wheezing, charcoal-powered pre-war cars was challenging. And everything about driving added together precluded anything remotely approaching high speeds.

Then atop all this, there was the traffic accident rate, which, to put it gently, was atrocious. Not surprisingly, the constant availability of absurdly cheap alcohol coupled with unfamiliarity with Japanese driving customs coupled with a proliferation of young people anxious to be free to roam coupled with a lack of restrictions coupled with wide-open, traffic-free roads created a runaway train destined to rack up impressive, if also highly negative, statistics.

For example, in 1947 alone, with the car culture still just edging its way into the occupation, more than *two thousand* traffic citations were issued just in the Tokyo-Yokohama area to occupation personnel. Not surprisingly, most of these tickets, more than seventy percent, were for driving on the wrong side of the road–but the tickets for that particular offense were not so expressed in those words. Instead, and to avoid having the offender seen to be flouting Japanese traffic regulations, the right-hand-side driving offense would be written up using the couched term, "assuming right-of-way." Driving on the right was also the second leading cause, behind speeding, of traffic accidents.

That said, it shouldn't come as another surprise to learn that the first fatal traffic accident involving Americans occurred in Tokyo in March 1946, three months before the first dependents arrived. The tragedy involved a young army lieutenant driving a young woman employee of headquarters back to her quarters after an evening of partying, when, at high speed and on the wrong side of the road, he crashed his jeep into a traffic island, killing his passenger and severely injuring himself.

But with all that, it was all there: a glimpse of the future set in what often could seem a satire of an auto expo nestled between sharp contrasts of exquisitely delicate beauty and grotesquely wanton destruction. Yet they who would later build and market Hondas and Toyotas and Nissans and Subarus and all else the world has grabbed onto obviously learned from it all. Small wonder that when Japan reached eastward across the Pacific and began marketing automobiles twenty years later that they knew American psyches so well, and were able to exploit our love affair with the automobile so successfully and adroitly.

Maurice Howe saw it coming; he sensed early-on that the Japanese had tapped into an especially sensitive and exploitable American nerve. Reared on a farm in Missouri, Mr. Howe was just nineteen years old when he stepped off a troopship in Yokohama on Christmas Day 1949. He had joined the army after a year-and-a-half of college, and in short order found himself in occupied Japan as a member of an elite group of soldiers who held *the* most coveted job an enlisted man (Mr. Howe was a corporal) could have in the occupation: he was a member of General MacArthur's Honor Guard. A lot of perks came with being one of those responsible for SCAP's well-being: head-of-the-line presence at mess halls, restaurants, shows and elsewhere; miscellaneous special treats, perks and entertainment. Corporal Howe had just about everything except...a car he could call his own.

So he set about getting one. And he documented the process. Corporal Howe would write a letter or two home almost every night. When his tour in Asia was done (he was to see duty in the Korean War as well), and he was back in America and discharged from the army, Mr. Howe gathered together all the letters he had written and had them published in a book, *Maurice's Letters Home*.

His account of the car-buying venture included observations about transportation in general and cars in particular, plus he speculated on what Japan's future might be like with respect to the automobile and other factors. His narrative covered a series of letters; prescience on cars and transportation plus other topics was woven throughout many of them:

> *The transportation arena here in*
> *Japan is one of the most interesting to be*

seen anywhere. A great many of the automobiles are converted to operate on fumes supplied by charcoal burners attached to the rear bumper. They are somewhat unsightly, but they are much less expensive to operate than gasoline or diesel powered cars. Electric cars are also popular here. Some manufacturers (such as Datsun) make both gasoline and electric models. A few American and European cars are converted to electricity, but I'd guess that these must be quite expensive. The majority of cars in Japan are American brands, although many of them are modified to the extent that it's hard to recognize them...Almost all of the vehicles made in Japan are copies of brands made in other countries. They have got the Chevrolet motor down pat in a car that looks a lot like the old Chrysler Airflow of about 1938, if you remember. I cite this instance because it is so very obvious, but there are many other examples.

Corporal Howe worked with a Japanese friend to find a car of his own. He took advantage of this offer, because the purchase of large native goods, like a car, could not be done directly with Japanese, but had to be conducted through a central purchasing office, which would buy the object for you on commission. This requirement was skirted by the friend putting Corporal Howe in direct touch with a party anxious to sell a car. Corporal Howe detailed his test drive:

Yesterday, Saturday, I drove an Austin car. The owner (a businessman here in Tokyo) wanted to show me what a wonderful automobile it really was. It has most of the advantages of large cars: cushion seats, practical design inside and out, sufficient power, with the features of a small car; maneuverability, easy parking, etc., but none of the tinny construction of the American Crosley and some other Japanese cars. They interest me.

(The Austin Corporal Howe drove likely was a Japanese pre-war version of the English Austin Company's hallmark automobile of the time, the Austin *Seven*. Around 1930, the Japanese car manufacturer Datsun, which later would become Nissan, began infringing on Austin's patents to create its own version of the *Seven*. These patent violation issues were resolved in 1934 with Austin licensing Datsun to build the *Seven*, plus develop other models for the Asian market. The agreement was the catalyst that launched Datsun/Nissan as an international motor vehicle manufacturer.)

Mr. Howe later linked the car-buying experience with other observations he had made about Japanese ingenuity with respect to automobiles and the country's future. As he wrote home:

The automobiles and trucks here show better than anything else the ingenuity and skill of the Japanese. The incentive was the critical need of economical transportation, built as quickly and cheaply as possible. It's important to note this aspect of post-war Japan because without this level of initiative and invention, the recovery from war would be FAR slower and much more costly, worldwide, because huge amounts of foreign capital are being poured into this country to bring it

> *back from total defeat and make it a*
> *productive and prosperous nation*
> *among nations...I can't help wondering*
> *how today's Japanese innovations will*
> *influence the rest of the world 20 or 30*
> *years from now. Products and services*
> *have advanced exponentially in the 20*
> *years since I was born* (in 1930).
> *Imagine what things will be like in 1960,*
> *1970 and beyond! Like it or not, Japan*
> *is bound to play a major role; a peaceful*
> *one, we hope.*

Mr. Howe was discharged from the army after returning home from the Korean War, moved to Kansas City, and in 1955 took a position with IBM. He rose quickly with the firm, advancing in step with computer technology itself, holding positions in engineering, problems-solving, processing, programming, programming analysis, and publications, eventually ending up in New York State where he retired after thirty-five years with the company. The Missouri farm boy never did buy the Austin or any other car while still in Japan. "Too much of a hassle," he told me.

The entire concept of suburbs as America came to build them never fully took hold in Japan, as it really could not, what with their unique culture and space limitations. Maurice Howe had other thoughts on why the Japanese eschewed American-style housing, as he said in another letter home:

> *The Japanese are very interested in*
> *American housing, but they really don't*
> *have the capital to exploit their*
> *interests...The main objection to*
> *American housing is the great need for*
> *fuel. The Japanese house uses about as*
> *much a day as it would take your living*
> *room stove going good.*

Yet to the Japanese, American housing and the way it was planned and erected was so different, so encompassing and so uniquely American that the Japanese equated the entire concept with the American way of life--a dead-on assumption as matters turned out. History has shown that the Japanese, in their ability to recognize what was coming even before we did, fields used this knowledge in several fields to exploit Americans equal to and even beyond their own abilities to do so.

Chapter 9: Made in Occupied Japan

All families have traditions, rituals meant for the family members only for whatever purpose: enjoyment, entertainment, education or just to bring everyone close. Our family was no exception. I only remember one ritual of our family from our time in Japan, and we'd carry it out most mornings when we were all home. What made it special was that the participants weren't just mother, dad and me; our three maids joined in as well. In fact, the maids made the ritual special.

The event would be held in the kitchen of our house. It was a quite large kitchen, and not just as seen through the eyes of a ten-year-old boy. It was large, period! It took even my father several paces to walk from its outside wall to the counter on the opposite wall. Were someone today to ask me its dimensions, I'd say twelve-by-twenty feet or so. The point is that the kitchen's size contributed to making the ritual so special. The basic effect itself? That could be held anywhere, even in a closet. But the distance involved, well...That's what made it fun!

The ritual would be held just before the maids served breakfast. We'd sit at the dining room table, patiently awaiting one of the maids to peek her head through the door that led into the kitchen, and smilingly beckon us to follow her. We'd get up, and file in to stand with our backs against the kitchen wall adjoining the dining room.

Across the room was a small, brightly-painted wooden table set beneath a kitchen window. On the table was a single appliance: a shiny metallic, conventional-looking, two-slice pop-up toaster. But the toaster wasn't set flat on the table. Rather, its far side was raised on a thin block of wood, so the top of the toaster was aimed at a sixty-degree (or so) angle across the room to where we were standing. One of the maids would load the toaster with a couple of slices of bread. She would do this with a flourish; waving and arcing the bread slices like a magician with a deck of cards, smiling the while and getting smiles in return. Finally she would push the handle of the toaster down, check to make sure the bread was toasting, then scamper to join the rest of us on the far side of the room from the toaster.

Now the three maids would step forward slightly and spread their aprons wide. A few moments more, then...the two slices of toast would explode from the toaster! The device would *fling* the browned slices high and across the room with a fairly loud *boing!* sound and enough kick to make the toaster jump, sometimes off its wooden block.. The maids would maneuver this-way-and-that to catch the flying toast in their aprons, sometimes bumping into one another in their haste, now-and-then fumbling a catch, all of us laughing and giggling all the while.

Next a couple more slices of bread would be loaded into our toaster-cum-sling shot, down would go the lever, an anxious few seconds as the toaster did its, well, toasting; and the maids once again would scamper around with aprons held wide to catch the soaring toast. Perhaps another round, and we'd return to the dining room to have breakfast, by now with a stack of freshly-margarined (there never was any butter) projectiled toast accompanying us.

The toaster was made in Japan by some Japanese company or special assembly enterprise or perhaps even some mom-and-pop shop. It came with the house, and otherwise toasted bread just fine, so the toaster's origin didn't matter because we weren't seeking a replacement. When the device first revealed its idiosyncrasy, dad briefly thought of trading it for another. But then the humor of the thing struck him and mother, so the toaster remained. I'm sure other families also had weirdly-performing this-and-that among their kitchen appliances, or at least somewhere among the Japanese-provided and - manufactured goods that came with their homes. As the cliché stock line says, it comes with the territory.

Did it ever! A lot more came with the territory; occupation administrators saw to it. When the occupation began, planners looked around for what was available in the way of large appliances, machines and tools that Americans might be familiar with and perhaps could use. Then when it became known that we dependents would be coming over, the search was expanded to include everyday household appliances and gadgets, the kind of stuff Americans took for granted and could be found in any hardware or supermarket in the USA, from small apparatuses like toasters to large appliances like washing machines to much more mundane things like everyday cooking and eating utensils.

Altogether, the planners operated like newlyweds setting up a household for the very first time: they made lists of items commonly found in the corners and crannies, cabinets and cupboards, closets and crawl spaces, of the typical American home. Next, they researched which of those items common to American homes were also common in Japanese homes–and what they found was that the gulf between Japanese and American household cultures was at least as great as the ocean separating the two countries. The typical households were found to be so far apart that when the planners' shopping list extravaganza was done and parsed out, they had a total 222 items commonly found in American homes that weren't at all common to Japanese homes. Or in many cases, even known in Japan.

Many of these homemaking items of course might have been commonly found in the homes of the few Europeans and other Westerners who had set up housekeeping in Japan. The persons who had occupied our house may well have been one of those families. The point is the residents' Western-style appliances, tools and utensils would have been known to, and here-and-there used by, Japanese who had regular, ongoing contact with those households. Domestic staffs, for example, might have been very familiar with toasters, vacuum cleaners and coffee percolators, to name just three items that were generally unknown in Japan.

But the larger point is that the items would have been scarce enough, and Japanese contact with and use of such items scant and scattered enough, as to preclude establishing a widespread culture of familiarity with such items. It would take the far greater mass of the occupation families to do that, to create such a huge demand for the familiar household goods of American culture that the sheer number and variety and uses of the goods would be implanted on the Japanese conscience.

Some of these items were ordinary, easily substituted or otherwise covered by some similar object. Examples were such everyday kitchen utensils as cooking knives and forks, tongs, ceramic mixing bowls, and so on. Many other items were more critical; no substitute would do. At the top of this list were any and all devices that entailed *measuring* something-or-other: rulers, measuring cups and spoons, thermometers, pedometers, odometers, speedometers, tape measures, scales...et cetera. Everything that involved determining a precise volume, weight, temperature, length, breadth, depth or distance had to be replicated from either metrics or the Japanese *shakkan-hō* (*shaku*, a unit of length; *kan*, a mass measurement) to America's so-called *customary* units (inches, feet, ounces, pounds, pints, quarts and the like), as derived from the British Imperial Units.

Much more than American-style measuring apparatuses were either unknown or extremely rare in Japan and had to be replicated in some form or other. Included were such as spatulas, egg beaters, flour sifters, toasters (conventional toaster-ready wheat bread was unknown in the Japan of the time), fry pans (griddles were what Japanese used), double boilers, drinking cups with handles, pressure cookers, shot glasses, cocktail shakers, whisk brooms, dustpans, rolling pins, toilet seats (the toilets themselves would have to come from America), vacuum cleaners, curling irons, steam irons, flat irons, waffle irons, all manner of glass cookware such as casserole dishes and the aforesaid measuring cups, egg separators and poachers (ironic, given that we were supposed to be consuming just powdered eggs), barbeque cookers bigger than Japanese hibachis, anything and everything associated with making coffee, complete cutlery sets (flatware knives and spoons were of course common in Japan, but not forks), Western-style mattress and box spring sets (futons were what Japanese slept on and still do), water heaters (known but not widely employed; same with washing machines), hair curlers, fly swatters, curtain rods, padlocks, window locks, chain locks...the list went on.

Over time, many of the items would be made back in America by the usual and familiar household name companies, then shipped over and stocked in the exchanges for sale just like in any present-day Target or Walmart or Kmart or any other type of -mart. Initially, however, shipping priorities elsewhere meant that many of these common household goods would have to be manufactured in Japan by sources that may or may not have been familiar with the items, unfamiliarity usually being the case. And it happened that American sources never did fill the requirement gap; throughout the occupation, many goods common to American households had to be made locally.

This lack of purely American household goods was the case no matter the household's status, our family's position being one example. My father was one of the higher-ranking officers; we were members of the occupation elite; we lived grandly; we were at the top of any priorities list. Plus we were relative late comers to the occupation; a lot of American-made goods were in the exchanges by the late 1940s. Yet with all this status, our toaster was made in Japan, as was much else we used. Or at least resigned ourselves to using.

So the question became: Who was going to make all this stuff? What sources in Japan were to be charged with manufacturing everything from toilet brushes to American-style toilets? Large, established Japanese corporate conglomerates, the zaibatsu, were, in the beginning at least, by-and-large out of the question. War destruction was one reason, reparations were another, and priorities were still another. Against MacArthur's protests, Japan was forced to ship forty million dollars' worth of industrial equipment to China, the Philippines, Great Britain and the Netherlands, all of which had assets either destroyed or seized by Japan during the war. Then in addition, Japan was made to cede to those same nations plus others three billion dollars' worth of industrial equipment and other assets it had previously shipped to or already held in other countries.

Some of these obligations were scaled back after it became clear that Japan was not again going to stir up trouble, but instead could contribute to the region's recovery. Still, Japan's economy was a shambles, the Asian countries Japan had overrun wanted revenge, and rebuilding the Nippon economy would take time, energy and investment. So, one-by-one, the zaibatsu were restored, retooled, re-staffed (many qualified workers had fled heavily-bombed coastal areas for remote regions and were content to stay there), and restarted once it was shown they were vital to Japan's overall recovery and could benefit the occupation.

Matsushita, the giant electric products zaibatsu, was hastily returned to its former glory because, among other electrical components, it made vitally-needed electric motors compatible with

Japan's direct current electrical system. Motors of all sizes, capacities and uses; because among other requirements, the occupation needed all manner of electric motors to drive appliances being installed in the brand-new houses springing up in the subdivisions and elsewhere the families lived. Included here were washing machines, clothes dryers (rare then, even back in the United States), sewing machines, vacuum cleaners, food mixers, power tools of all sizes and uses, pumps, and even electric alarm clocks. Mechanical alarm clocks were also made for issue or sale to occupationaires, but by other concerns.

The optics zaibatsu were another example of parsing the reparations. The leading companies involved here are still household names: Canon, Nikon and Olympus. Of this trio, only Nikon had been a primary supplier to Japan's war machine, having provided binoculars, submarine periscopes, lenses and bomb sights; so its return to full-scale production was held back. Olympus, for its part, had made only cameras and microscopes, so was returned to full production quickly.

Canon was to become the major postwar factor, the initial production leader on an international scale. During the war, it just made cameras–but as it happened, its products included a revolutionary camera. For it was Canon who, in the early 1930s, had developed the world's first focal plane shutter-equipped thirty-five millimeter camera. Canon also successfully copied the appearance of the already-popular German-made Leica thirty-five millimeter rangefinder camera, a familiarity that doubtlessly helped Canon's world-wide acceptance. It was a Canon my father eagerly bought soon after disembarking in Japan.

Another conglomerate hastened back into full-scale production, in this case understandably so as a morale-booster, was the beer zaibatsu. This group consisted of just a single, gigantic, two-part brewery monopoly, the *Dai Nippon* Brewing Company, which the occupation summarily split apart. Japan's familiar *Ashai* Beer was a result of this breakup.

Everyday household needs were another matter altogether. To satisfy these demands, the manufacture of common household necessities was parceled out not to conglomerates, but to a conglomeration of widely and wildly varying sources. These providers ranged from mom-and-pop shops that may have shown a particular facility for, say, extruding wire and forming it into coat hangers (once shown what an American-style coat hanger even looked like, that is); to small- to medium-size cottage industries that were experienced with particular trade skills, like metal working or wood finishing; to fairly large enterprises that specialized in some vitally-needed consumer product, like washing machine assembly.

The facilities where these sources performed their work varied from near shacks where everything was done by hand with the simplest of tools, to quite respectable small factories using complex machine-powered devices, to sizeable manufacturing plants that had escaped destruction. In the beginning, many of the products made by these concerns were purchased by the occupation at a net loss, a deliberate undertaking in recognition of the role the enterprises played in providing employment opportunities for the impoverished country. Resource-stretching was also employed. For example, it was widely known (if reluctantly accepted) that hard liquors were often watered-down in order to gin up (so to speak) even more sales of alcoholic beverages.

What amounted to a two-way chain-of-command was established to oversee production and distribution not just of goods destined for American households, but also for products to be sold at large in Japan, and eventually for worldwide distribution once Japan got back up to full production speed. At the top were the so-called "Heavy Industries," the grand capital-goods companies, represented largely, but not entirely, by zaibatsu: steel mills, utilities, coal mines, ship builders, truck and car manufacturers, wood mills...breweries. Generally speaking, these were the concerns charged with providing the primary raw materials for the finished goods, which were manufactured elsewhere. So right under the capital goods providers were grouped "Light Industries," which included pretty much everyone else involved in making or providing something-or-other for the occupation and the country, and perhaps also or eventually for export.

Under this plan, occupation administrators could track the logical flow of, say, the steel used to build a washing machine from a Heavy Industries steel fabricator to a washing machine assembler and marketer, which would be classified under Light Industries. Similarly, while Matsushita, to name one example, was grouped under Heavy Industries for its sheer size and scope of electrical products, likely subset users of its products were classified under Light Industries under headings that included Sewing Machine Manufacturing and Light Electrical Equipment and Supply Manufacturing. Other Light Industries included Pulp and Paper Manufacturers, Bicycle Makers, Watch and Clock Makers, and Agricultural Equipment Manufacturers.

Obviously, a lot of crisscrossing of services and goods were at work here for any range of products in various stages of production. For example, a motor vehicle manufacturer, classified among Heavy Industries, would at some point in a vehicle's assembly need finished seats, which coverings might be provided by a Light Industries-classified fabrics house, which might use a truck made by another auto manufacturer to deliver the materials...and on and on. The point is that all this manufacturing re-structuring and activity was simultaneously a main line by which Japanese versions of American goods came to penetrate American homes, and also one more way the Japanese came to learn more about Americans and their way of life.

It's perhaps a cliché to say so, but in many if not most ways, it was the little things that mattered. Our family's squirrely toaster was an example of this phenomenon: it was something a *family* would need, but not a large organization such as SCAP (the bureaucracy in this case) or FECO or the occupying army. Soldiers eat toast, or at least American and British soldiers do. But an army mess kitchen requires a machine that toasts bread by dozens of slices at a time to feed a continuing stream of hungry soldiers; it has no need for a consumer-oriented, two-slice toaster meant for an American family of three or four.

And that's where all these myriad, often neophyte Japanese enterprises stepped in: they provided goods American families knew and needed. An arriving family would become aware of the products almost from the moment they stepped off the boat, because their new home would come fully equipped with many of the various necessities, kitchen utensils and appliances especially. Then whatever else the family needed would be issued by an official supply source, or purchased at an exchange, or procured by cash, barter or bribe on the black market, or any or all of the above.

Beginning in 1948, more and more varied American-made family necessities began pouring in, to be displayed and sold in the exchanges right alongside the locally-produced renditions of the very same products. The Japanese version of any particular good almost always sold for less price than its American counterpart, for the obvious reason that it didn't have to be shipped in from across a wide ocean but was made locally and more cheaply, plus it may have been bought and stocked at below its fair market price as part of the strategy to pump up the local economies.

Which is not to say that consumer goods production ran smoothly. The recent war created nagging postwar obstacles. Raw materials, for one, were in short supply, steel most especially. Most of Japan's steel had gone into the country's war machine, and so was scattered across Southeast Asia and the Pacific basin, including a considerable amount at the bottom of the ocean itself.

To rectify this situation in one major industrial field, motor vehicle production, the occupation army in 1948 inaugurated the BIG-5 program, named after the Eighth Army's Ordnance Section's Industrial Group, Fifth Echelon. The initial goal of this program was a whopping Pacific-wide salvage operation focused on bringing home abandoned and wrecked motor vehicles, tools and spare parts, and using the scrap to rebuild the automobile industry.

This salvage recovery mission was accomplished successfully. An article written by a Captain Robert D. Connolly in June 1950 entitled "Men and Machines in Occupied Japan," published in the *Army Information Digest*, noted that by 1950 two automobile rebuilding plants, one for sedans and the other for buses, were up and operating in Nagoya. These factories were supported by engine and power train plants, tire suppliers, and manufacturers of such as safety glass and other components exclusively meant for motor vehicles.

It was elsewhere noted that as the program progressed, enough steel scrap was recovered to have provided material for consumer goods, including especially the various appliances, pots and pans and other household articles eventually used by occupation families. In other words, our eccentric toaster may once have been part of a truck, or even a warplane or some other metallic war relic.

Another occupation-long persistent shortage problem was sufficient coal to power industries. Japan once had a thriving coal mining industry, another zaibatsu. But beginning in the 1930s, Korean laborers were cajoled, enslaved and otherwise forced to work in the Japanese coal mines, virtually all of which are in the harsh northern islands, and so were among the first victims of Japan's atrocities to be repatriated back to their homeland, leaving few volunteers able, qualified or willing to take their place.

But the biggest and most unsettling problem with respect to Japanese renditions of American consumer products was quality. Unfortunately, many of the products assembled by workers unfamiliar with American goods and production methods were of such poor quality as to cast a pall that would adversely affect worldwide acceptance of Japanese exports for some years after the occupation ended. Far too much Japanese-origin household merchandise issued or sold to American families was shoddy, needed frequent repair, broke down quickly, or just didn't function correctly in the first place. Electrical appliances were a principal culprit, but ordinary household items, for example something as simple as a manual can opener, could also be vexing.

Things got so bad that the phrase "made in occupied Japan" became a cautionary pejorative ("Watch out for that lamp! It was made in occupied Japan, y'know."), and was often used as an insult ("Straighten up, soldier! Quit acting like you were made in occupied Japan."). Late in her life, my mother laughingly recalled how she would often teasingly admonish me to do something-or-other using the phrase, for example, "Go look in the mirror and comb your hair; it looks like it was made in occupied Japan."

The sub-par goods otherwise incurred the usual epithets: "shoddy," "junky," "piece of crap," et cetera. One contemptuous sneer that seemed to have been used more often than any other was the same aspersion Maurice Howe cast to describe the American-made Crosley automobile: "tinny." I recall using that word often because my radio neatly fit the description in appearance as well as sound quality. I wasn't alone in this regard. Adults and playmates alike would use "tinny" to describe just about any Japanese-made metallic device, usually but not necessarily something electric. "Tinny" encapsulated both the appearance and sound of Japanese-made radios and phonographs of the period.

Shocks were commonplace where any electric appliance was concerned. I can still picture my father jumping back, shaking his hand and cursing whenever he would try to fiddle with a desk lamp or radio. Poor insulation was a major cause; for whatever reason, perhaps heat, insulation often frayed easily, exposing the wiring itself. I recall sometimes getting shocks from my bedroom reading light's metal frame when I would shift it one way or another. Fortunately, Japan's low-voltage electric current system usually would mean just a minor jolt.

While poor quality can be attributed to ignorance about American goods combined with poor or at least questionable manufacturing facilities and procedures, another major contributing factor was inferior raw materials. The most egregious examples of this aggravation were products containing steel, which as noted could often be war surplus scrap. Among other potential defects, improperly alloyed or otherwise incorrectly treated steel would quickly rust in sea-bound Japan's humid environment. Mechanical watches and clocks with their complex, often extremely small elements that must engage precisely with one another were especially affected by inferior steel components. This particular blight was officially noticed by the occupation; the watch-and-clock quality issue gets special mention in select documents.

I also noticed the clock quality problem. I recall the mechanical alarm clock in my room failing to keep time, rust probably being the cause. The issue must have been especially depressing to the Japanese, for their prewar timepiece industry was highly regarded world-wide. But then it flip-flopped. The postwar quality problem with mechanical watches and clocks was so egregious that the industry never recovered until the advent of electronic time-keeping devices, a field in which Japan came to excel, becoming the global leader.

Clocks for Home and Export, 1946

The steel quality problem also affected the optics industry, as reflected in cameras. My father's Canon eventually rusted out some dozen years later. His experience wasn't isolated. Numerous present-day Internet on-line comments mention how the lens housing elements of Japanese cameras from the 1950s and late -40s were prone to rust. The rust problem was also aggravating–and damaging to Japan's reputation–where products incorporating electrical components were involved, as contact points and other critical metallic parts would rust and disengage. I remember once looking on closely as our houseboy painstakingly re-soldered the contacts of a small electric appliance of some sort, perhaps my radio.

Wood products were also prone to poor or insufficient treatment or curing; they would warp, often to such extreme degrees they became useless. I particularly remember a beautifully inlaid jewelry box that my mother treasured, then one day threw out with a look of disgust and dismay because it had warped so badly the hinged lid couldn't even lower very much, let alone close and be latched.

There were other reasons for this contagion of poor quality. At the top was the hurry-up impetus to get goods out the door and into homes and exchanges, coupled with Japanese lack of familiarity with design and production of American products. Any kind of American product. I remember an example of this from our own kitchen: the egg beater; it jammed repeatedly. Mother would throw up her hands and stomp away in frustration after trying to use the device, whereas our maids simply eschewed the contraption altogether, relying instead on their familiar whisks to mix ingredients.

A portion of Captain Connolly's article on the BIG-5 program sheds some light on why Japanese products of the time may have been of poor quality. Speaking of the program with respect to revival of Japan's auto industry, he noted:

> *In many instances, because progress in Japanese manufacturing had been stalemated for years, it was also necessary to teach the Japanese industrialists the latest production methods.*
>
> *This backwardness in technological development was due largely to the Imperial Edict of 1939 prohibiting Japanese industrialists from participating in ideas and developments of other countries. The war did the rest. In order to get quality and quantity production from Japanese contractors who were still operating on a 1939*

basis, Stateside methods had to be introduced.

In the early days of its operation, BIG-5 encountered antipathy toward mass production methods by both Japanese manufacturers and workmen. Much time and effort was required to dispel misunderstanding and ignorance. Ultimately, the problems were worked out with the Japanese workmen, technicians and engineers in the shops, in the laboratories and at the drawing boards.

Captain Connolly went on to say how Japanese workers, men and women alike, eventually came to be enthusiastic about their work in step with acceptance of the new (to them) production methods, at least as they applied to production of automobiles and motor vehicle support elements. It should also be noted that the 1950 publication date of the article was toward the end of the occupation, and thus after many of the poor quality goods had been distributed, used up, thrown out, or otherwise replaced.

And to be sure (and fair), not all Japanese versions of American goods were inferior or performed poorly. Numerous items available in exchanges were in fact quite popular because of their low price, and also because they were equal to or better than their American-made counterparts. Among these were fishing tackle, golf bags, furs, certain clothing items including lingerie, towels, furs, rugs and rattan furniture. And hibachis! The compact grills, perfect for cramped spaces where the much larger and bulkier American grills could be downright hazardous, were first popularized back in America by families returning from the occupation.

By-and-large, it was items that were meant to *perform* in some way, usually mechanically or electrically, that were frustrating and drew contempt. Still, it seemed no general categorizations could be made. Fishing reels, for example, were mechanical devices, and for the most part performed excellently. A wooden box, on the other hand, isn't mechanical at all; it just sits there. But they could warp. And that fishing reel might rust out eventually, for that matter.

Altogether, the quality problem was a convoluted mixture of suspect raw materials, inadequate production methods and facilities, and unfamiliarity with American tastes, products, and degrees of tolerance. Whatever the source or cause, the results didn't just annoy us, they also puzzled us, adults and children alike, because we had expected more. Far more. War recovery struggles aside, we simply couldn't understand why Japanese industry was struggling so with American products, given the country's talents, traditions and background.

First was the fact that Japan had been a world-class economy before the war, a major player in international trade, providing widely-sought and -respected goods. Second, and despite their humiliating defeat, the country had fielded a modern, well-equipped and -trained military machine that had conquered most of Asia before being turned back.

But the third and most striking conundrum in light of the poor workmanship where products for the families and other occupationaires were concerned, was the fact that individual craftsmanship by Japanese artisans could be nothing short of superb, as the intricately-detailed model trains I coveted clearly showed. In fact, one of the few compliments that could be culled from the general glut of criticism about the goods we were issued or otherwise acquired was that the Japanese talent for imitation was breath-taking.

We frankly stood in awe of this ability of Japanese craftsmen to imitate at least the appearance if not the performance of familiar American products. Console radios and phonographs were an example of this art, with radio cabinets, for one, often being indistinguishable from their American counterparts. Some imitators even went so far as to recreate the logos of leading American manufacturers of the time, like Philco, Westinghouse and RCA, on the cabinets.

Beyond imitations, outright counterfeiting of American products was rampant. Lorena Treadway wrote of how the locally-produced, foul-tasting cigarettes were sold in packs cleverly made up to resemble

Lucky Strike cigarette packaging. Likewise, inferior Japanese whisky was sold in bottles dressed up with look-alike American whisky labels. One of these imitators was found out by the bottle's label, which read, "Famous in Philadelphia since 1486." Cigarette lighters were sold engraved with the buyer's name, and one line of lighters featured so astoundingly accurate a facsimile of the front and back of a hundred-dollar bill that the US Secret Service stepped in to have occupation authorities ban the product and its practitioners.

And special mention for ingenious *chutzpah* has to go to the small city of *Usa* in the *Ōita* prefecture on the northern coast of Kyushu. Products from this municipality came blatantly labeled, "MADE IN USA." Needless to say, occupation authorities put a stop to this practice fairly quickly. The town is otherwise famous and visited for the Usa Shrine, erected in the year 725, and the lead shrine of all *Hachiman* shrines in Japan.

Our bewilderment about annoyingly-inferior Japanese products vis-a-vis remarkable works of art from the same people was augmented by the low-quality items often being displayed in the exchanges literally just around the corner from superbly-crafted *objects d'art* and souvenirs. These desirable items were sold in special sections of the exchanges, or just outside under awnings, but so superior to the humdrum household necessities that it frankly awed us that the same people who foisted off inferior goods could also produce such exquisite works of art.

Among the items might be finely-detailed geisha dolls, intricately-carved miniature temple bells, scrupulously-detailed carvings of temples and shrines, artistically detailed *faux* samurai swords, ancient warrior dolls in colorful medieval costumes, art prints and originals, jewelry, amulets, vases, artificial flowers, charms and bracelets...all manner of bric-à-brac. And this cornucopia wasn't all Japanese in origin. As the occupation progressed, native craft merchandise was imported from elsewhere in the Far East, in particular the Philippines and Southeast Asia, Vietnam and Thailand most especially.

During the Christmas season, these stalls became especially colorful and animated, especially so in the eyes of a young boy. I remember being transfixed by the displays lining the block outside the main exchange in the Tokyo Ginza, just staring open-mouthed while moving slowly from one often-animated exhibit to another until mother would come pull me away. Just as back home in America, sales promotions were heaviest leading up to Christmas week. One seasonal marketing jingle, sung over the AFRS radio stations, simultaneously acknowledged our aversion to certain Japanese products while urging listeners to buy up local goods for shipment back Stateside:

> *Though Nippon gifts may leave you cold,*
> *The home folks love 'em more than gold.*
> *Your Christmas gift fund should be spent*
> *On treasures from the Orient.*

I fortunately still have some of these special souvenirs that my parents acquired. Among them is a painstakingly-carved miniature brass temple bell my mother would use at mealtime to signal the maids. Across the room from the bell are a quartet of three-inch-high ivory peasants: a fisherman with his catch, a farmer holding a rooster, a fat woman plopped astride an elephant, and a priest holding a pineapple aloft. The four are so lifelike in their excruciatingly intricate detail that age lines and calluses are carved into the soles of the subjects' bare feet. Our family also once had, but somewhere lost over the decades, what was otherwise cited as the most popular of these tiny ivory figurines: a peasant farmer stooped under the burden of a yoke across his shoulders from which hung a pair of matched honey buckets. It was said each of these figurines differed, if ever so slightly, from the many other renditions of the same subject.

The remaining carvings stand atop an exquisitely-carved four-tiered step table set which lacquer coating is a little cracked but otherwise somehow never warped, perhaps because of the cedar wood from which it is made. And the four figurines surround a tall, subtly-decorated vase holding a bouquet of artificial chrysanthemums that look like they were just picked–while the vase itself is indicative of the special treatment Japanese porcelains received during the occupation.

Very special. Whether as works of art or everyday household commodities, ceramics of all stripes were unhesitatingly singled-out as critically-needed elements in Japan's recovery. But as with much else where postwar resources were concerned, there were limitations and considerations–plus with respect to ceramics exclusively, there was the two-faced nature of the resource, each demanding attention, each the worthy equal of the other. On the one hand, artistic; on the other, pragmatic. Uniquely beautiful vases here, ordinary functional toilets there. So given the limited resources, the occupation was beholden to solicit what amounted to a Solomon's Choice, wherein some type of split decision as to priorities would have to be rendered by some authority.

The artful porcelains--vases and dinnerware and statues and much more--were functional or merely decorative *objects d'art* collectively termed "china" because the art form had been introduced into Japan from its mainland neighbor and rival some thirteen hundred years earlier. Such porcelains merited special attention because they were, and perhaps still are, Japan's most coveted art export. Japanese-origin china had been known to the West for at least four centuries; the goods were among the artifacts the Jesuit missionaries brought back to Portugal. So getting the porcelain component of the ceramic industry up and exporting once again was early-on identified as one of the primal, critical keys to Japan's resurrection in international trade.

But it wasn't just porcelains that merited special attention; there was the other face of this ceramic Janus to consider. The occupation had a critical need for commonplace ceramics in the families' housing, for use as tile floors, bathroom fixtures, counter tops, kitchenware and more. Plus Japan itself of course needed construction-grade ceramics for similar practical applications in rebuilding the country's homes, and for other structures and uses. Interestingly, and despite ceramics' size, scope and criticality, this key industry was not a zaibatsu, and so was classified by the occupation as another Light Industry.

In addition, as with much else when it came to getting Japan up and running again, there were obstacles. First, ceramics manufacturing requires high heat, the kind of heat that only a coal-fired furnace can provide; and as previously noted, Japan's coal industry was suffering,

214

with the commodity being rationed. Second, the porcelains at the time were commonly decorated with gold, and little gold was available in Japan until 1950, which meant that the initial postwar porcelains would by-and-large have to be absent gold trim.

The third issue was the matter of the *amakusa* stone, which at the time was cited by the occupation as being "best for ceramics," meaning porcelain art in particular. This stone, found only in the *Kumamoto* Prefecture on the western side of Kyushu, is today renowned and sought for its superior knife sharpening characteristics; no mention is made of it still being used in porcelain creations. But during the occupation, the stone was treasured for porcelain artifacts. And it might be still, were it not for the resource scarcity problem that eventually led to a necessary shift in product ingredients. In addition, just when porcelains were needed most, the miners of the stone and related ceramic earths threatened to strike in protest of abominable working conditions.

So faced with all the problems and hurdles and demands and priorities facing re-starting ceramics production, coupled with the two competing, critical demands for ceramic goods, those responsible for seeing that things got done solicited a Solomon's Choice judgment from the occupation's resident Solomon, General MacArthur.

SCAP began settling the issue by settling the threatened strike; he personally got the stone miners more food rations, improved working conditions, more reliable transportation, more fuel, and higher pay. That done, the general zeroed in on the porcelain art works side of the issue. In 1948, he ordered that only the finest-quality ceramic art works be designated for export, this in order to restart Japan's porcelain market abroad with what amounted to a can't-top-this, best-in-show effort. MacArthur linked this decision with an order that effectively slammed the door on any other terra cotta wares from leaving the country for sale elsewhere by declaring all other ceramics, porcelains and everyday pottery and fixtures alike, as "unsuitable for export."

Were my mother still alive, she might cringe at this revelation. This is because she acquired numerous porcelains while we were in Japan, and learning her selections might have been lower in quality (and we're speaking quite relatively here) than those that were exported would have bruised her ego with respect to her ability to judge artistic worth. Among other vases and dishes and bowls and what-not mother scooped up were three large sets of the legendary *Noritake* china tableware: one as a latent (I would go so far as to say reluctant) wedding gift for my sister, which she shipped back home and Jeanne used well into her old age; one for formal occasions that Jeanne inherited but rarely used and so gave to her daughter-in-law; and a classic blue willow pattern for everyday use, the few remnants of which I ended up with and still have.

And as matters turned out, it wasn't just our and others' porcelain purchases that were affected by SCAP's "unsuitable for export" edict. The order applied to much else manufactured for export during the occupation: the best was sent abroad, the second best kept in Japan.

Whether exported for sale or sold in Japan, virtually all porcelains manufactured during the occupation, select pieces from multi-purpose sets of china tableware included, were stamped or otherwise emblazoned "Made in Occupied Japan" or simply "Occupied Japan," as opposed to simply "Made in Japan." The qualifier adjective was added in order to help ensure stronger product acceptance abroad, the feeling being that residual hostilities toward the recent Axis power could be assuaged by *de facto* stating on the product that someone else was now in charge. The policy is most evident on porcelains, but was applied to many other exported consumer goods as well.

One visible result of MacArthur's Solomon-esque way of doling out the precious ceramics resource was evident in porcelains manufactured then and continues still: metallic oxides began to be used more prevalently; complex silicates, feldspars and clays were scaled back. The effect of favoring metallic oxides over silicates can be clearly discerned, often starkly so, between pre- and postwar Japanese porcelains. Items made with the oxides predominating are characterized by exceptional translucence and whiteness, with outstanding glaze texture. Put another way, there's nothing subtle about them: they stand out; colors especially can be vividly distinct. Prewar and older porcelains, on the other hand, are subdued. In a way, it's like the difference between viewing Vincent Van Gogh's famous

"Sunflowers" painting, and an artistically-scaled and -lit digital camera image of a bowl of sunflowers as projected on a modern, high definition television screen. Both renderings are works of art; it's just that they are poles apart in emphasis and perspective.

Finally, in order to definitely ensure that the ceramics industry would rebound successfully and contribute substantially to Japan's resurrection, the United States Government became the world's major buyer of the industry's varied goods, purchasing forty percent of the country's total ceramics production during the course of the occupation. The same can be said about much else Japan produced during that period.

Chapter 10: The Grand Tour

I'm certain most of us can remember the first time he or she kissed a member of the opposite sex who was not a relative. I certainly can! My memory of the kiss, right down to the brief dialogue that led up to it, is one of the most vivid from the time we lived in Japan. The reason is because the seminal osculation occasion occurred in so classically romantic a setting that it's a shame the whole event was wasted on a pair of eleven-year-olds.

We had gone to the Fuji View Hotel (still open, still sumptuous) to spend a weekend in the spring of 1950. The hotel is accurately named, offering a fully glorious view of Mount Fuji. The sacred mountain's summit is scarcely ten miles directly south of the resort–yet the hotel's title remained a family joke for years to come. This was because rooms at the Fuji View and all other "rest hotels," as the occupation authorities termed such retreats, were allocated on the basis of rank during any given stay period. And on this particular occasion, while my father's rank certainly was high enough to get us a suite of rooms, our suite was located on the *north* side of the hotel, a revelation that both disappointed and embarrassed my father.

Before the trip, dad described to mother and me how we would wake up each morning to Japan's sacred mountain awaiting just outside our windows. He knew of this view because he had briefly stayed at the Fuji View before mother and I arrived in Japan. So we get to the hotel, but instead of being assigned a preferred south-facing suite with its view of Mount Fuji, we were greeted each morning with a view of elegant gardens and a parking lot. We were still to get a morning look at Mount Fuji, but had to have breakfast in the south-facing dining room to do so.

(I of course never knew who was occupying the south-facing suite or suites, probably some general or visiting dignitary. Not getting a south-facing suite was doubly embarrassing to my father because, in his position as chief quartermaster of the occupying army, he was in a position to pinpoint the exact dates he would be ranking officer at the hotel. So it appears he may have been outranked at the last moment.)

Anyway, on our first full day at the hotel, I became friendly with this attractive girl who was a few months older and slightly taller than I. We immediately liked each other because we had the same reading tastes and liked to talk about the same subjects, plus we enjoyed riding horses and tentatively playing tennis, both of which were available at the hotel. She also, like I, had no siblings, or at least none in Japan. I forget her name or where she lived in Japan with her family; I only remember that her father and mine must have been about the same rank because they spoke comfortably and casually with each other.

Nothing much transpired between us in what remained of the first day we were together. The next morning, however, we quickly spotted each other at breakfast, and ended up spending the whole day together, mostly walking about, conversing about this-and-that. Our respective parents noticed how friendly the two of us had become, so that evening began with our families, the six of us, having dinner together, the girl and I seated beside each other, our parents looking on indulgently and approvingly.

After dinner, our parents went off to play bridge, leaving the girl and I alone. So with darkness descending, we walked out the south side of the hotel, to the edge of a large pond upon which were sleeping swans, and in the distance that splendid view of Mount Fuji. The night was clear, leaving the iconic volcano bathed in moonlight with perhaps a few wispy clouds hanging around the summit, and at our feet the mountain's reflection shimmering lightly in the stillness of the pond. To add to the scene, the time of year was such that the upper slopes of the volcano were still covered with streaks of snow, presenting the white-capped classic image of Fuji, the appearance most preferred by artists and romantics.

At the edge of the pond was a large flat rock, just big enough to accommodate a couple wishing to tarry a bit and take in the picture-perfect scene. So we sat upon the rock, close together and not speaking, but just gazing straight south across the pond and the swans at the perfectly symmetrical mountain beyond. It was now quite dark, and somehow our hands fell softly together, lingering for a few moments. Then while still looking straight ahead she asked, "Have you ever kissed a girl?"

I flinched. "No," I managed to stammer while trying to concentrate on also continuing to stare straight ahead, then, "Have you ever been kissed?"

"Once," she replied, causing me to twinge a little. She paused for a long moment, then turned slowly to me and asked, "Would you like to kiss me?"

"Yes," I responded, not daring to look directly at her. By this time I was shimmering more than the water on the pond.

At my answer, she lifted her chin, smiled warmly and closed her eyes. I hesitated momentarily, then nervously leaned over to let my lips brush her cheek, at which she turned a bit more to me so that I ended up kissing her full on the lips. The contact was such we both pulled back. The girl flashed me another warm smile, then unhesitatingly leaned forward and kissed me full on the mouth in return, her lips lingering on mine at bit longer than mine had rested on hers. She now withdrew slightly, and gave me yet another warm smile...

Then suddenly, without another word or signal or sign or motion– she leapt to her feet, and as fast as she could ran off in the darkness toward the hotel!

I was stunned, stupefied; all I could do, I clearly recall, was to look aghast after her fast-disappearing form in open-mouthed wonder and shame and self-questioning and self-doubt. What had I done wrong; what could I have done wrong? This whole kissing thing was all her idea–and now she was gone; like an apparition from a Greek comedy, a nymph who flirts and teases, then vanishes. And all of it in this stupendously romantic setting, seated before one of the world's most famous geological features complete with moonlight, snow atop the mountain, reflections on the water--and even sleeping swans.

Artists have captured this setting of Mount Fuji countless times over the centuries; it's been the subject of too many paintings and watercolors and photos to count; the scene must hang upon thousands of walls; I'm certain hundreds of pairs of lovers have sat upon the same rock and exchanged long, passionate kisses and embraces and gropings and fondlings and maybe quite a bit more after it was dark enough and late enough.

And here I was, sitting alone, trying to put together and understand what was going on inside me; how to handle the strange feelings slowly ebbing through me like some kind of sludge that was at once alien and scary, yet also intriguing and appealing. I mean, after all, she was just a *girl*! At least three or more years would pass before I would again exchange kisses with a girl, by which time I knew (well, sort of knew; I don't think anyone, any male especially, ever truly knows) what it was all about. The difference is I don't recall that second or third or whenever with whomever kissing times; just the one, the first, in that incredibly picturesque, swan-studded setting, augmented by the wonder about what was going on inside me.

After a bit, I slunk back to our suite, head down, afraid I had done something shameful for which I'd be punished. I didn't look for the girl and never did tell my parents what we did. At some point, I guess I must have inquired about where the family lived, but I don't remember doing so; perhaps I was too embarrassed about what happened.

I never saw the girl again, not her nor her parents. I surreptitiously looked around for her the next morning. Nothing! No sign. Mother eventually told me that the family had checked out and left early. We stayed one more night before going home. I didn't bother going outside that last evening; I didn't see the point in doing so. Nor do I remember staying again at the Fuji View Hotel, although I suppose we may have at some point. But there are some things in life that are so special, so unique and lasting, that they overshadow all other memories.

I hope that girl is still around, probably a grandmother by now, maybe even a great-grandmother by this time. It would be nice if she too remembers the evening, and now-and-then smiles about it to herself. I would also hope she remembers our brief conversation as well. For my part, the words we exchanged are the only "sound bite," if you will, I recall verbatim from the time we lived in Japan. That and my Japanese playmate's curt rebuff to my scant baseball-playing athleticism ("Jamie-san no good!"). It's too bad both were kiss-offs, the one literally so.

The Fuji View Hotel itself is otherwise a vague memory; I had to look it up on the Internet to remind me of details. I had to do the same with the Fujiya Hotel, even though we stayed there more often than any of the other resorts. The Fujiya was (and still is) a sprawling luxury retreat, with magnificently varied meandering gardens and a host of recreational outlets, including a golf course for my parents, and fishing and boating for me. But what I most remember about the Fujiya were our accommodations there.

Each time we stayed in the Lily of the Valley Suite, at the farthest end of a remote wing, with its own garden. My parents had their room and I had mine, separated from theirs by a common room. My room was inordinately huge, larger than at home, and magnificently appointed. The room came with its own servant, each time the same, a quietly deferential teenage girl who would appear at odd moments to inquire, in halting English, whether there was anything I needed. As with our household servants, my duty was always to reply in the negative.

While we usually had dinner with other Americans and their families in the public dining room, we always had breakfast in our suite, announced by a maid tapping lightly on my door. Like so much else in this land of rituals, breakfast was no casual affair, but an exquisitely sumptuous, artfully arranged version of a typical American eye-opener of the time. This may seem an odd thing to remember so vividly, but then you tend to savor mornings that begin in a room opened to dewy, perfumed air, a glass of apricot nectar and a freshly cut chrysanthemum served on fine china beside that rarity-of-rarities for us occupationaires, fresh eggs.

I also remember the cocktail hour in our room in the late afternoon: for the tea sandwiches, my first experience with same--and also for Ritz crackers! Obviously, certain common American package goods were finding their way to Japanese shelves by the time we got there. My presence was required whenever my parents entertained Japanese guests (but not necessarily American ones). I could otherwise scarf down Ritz crackers and also peanuts just about anywhere else; bowls of them dotted the public rooms.

The gardens and general luxury of the resort aside, my only other memory of the Fujiya Hotel is the same as Patricia Stackhouse Garrity's: our respective first-time experiences with a public bath. Like she, a parent, in my case (of course) my father, had to coax me into setting my modesty aside and just enjoy the experience. Our companions in the bath were Japanese men and boys; I don't recall any other Caucasians. I also found out that the idea of gender-separated public baths was an occupation-ordered policy just for the appropriated rest hotels. Other, Japanese-exclusive resorts (there were plenty to go around) supposedly featured baths open to both sexes.

And the cost for all this sumptuous extravagance, in a remote and exquisite resort with all manner of amenities, wonderful cuisines and fawning attendants everywhere? While I'm sure meals and refreshments and recreation were extra, the charge for the suite itself is forever sealed in my memory: fifty cents a night. The Fujiya today lists plain double rooms at several hundred dollars nightly, with suites going for over a thousand. And, yes, the Lily of the Valley Suite is still listed. Looks the same, too.

Such retreats as the Fujiya and Fuji View Hotels were another area the Americans focused on intently early in the occupation. On one level, they were meant for troops and their families to go on weekend retreats and vacations; relief not just from work and the routine of everyday events, but also from the poverty and shambles that were otherwise so evident. On quite another level, they played a key tactical role in that they were part of the plan to have the dependents consider their tour in Japan a *de facto* extended vacation in an exotic land.

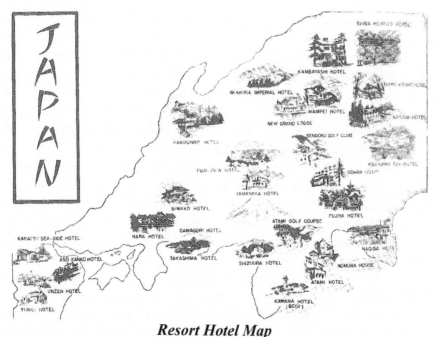

Resort Hotel Map
Part of welcoming kit along with "Dependents Guide…"

Before the war, these resorts were largely meant for Japanese nobility and so were quite grand. Some still exist and remain suitably luxurious; the Fuji View and Fujiyama, to name just the two I knew well, garner five-star ratings on Trip Advisor and other Internet travel sites. Other resorts seem to have fallen from their once lofty status in favor of more modern, equally luxurious resorts. Whatever the present-day status, the settings for the resorts are far more commercialized now than was the case during the occupation.

Like the scenic rural areas they occupied, these resorts were also deliberately not bombed. Thirty-two of the lavish retreats were appropriated for use by occupation forces, then refurbished to American standards (one major change: yet more Western sit-type in place of Japanese squat-type toilets) before being reopened. The hotels had a total capacity of some twenty-five hundred persons, which for booking purposes the army arbitrarily divided into an allotted guest ratio of six-to-one, non-commissioned officers and enlisted men-to-officers.

From the beginning, the Americans took to the hotels passionately. All were back in operation by the end of May 1946--and by the end of summer, nearly nine thousand officers and forty-four thousand enlisted men, some with their families, had stayed in the resorts, a running statistic that would bulge exponentially as the occupation progressed and more dependents came over.

The resorts had different amenities and themes depending on where they were located. The *Aso Kanko*, a rest hotel on Kyushu, featured an American "wild west" theme with horseback riding using western tack in addition to the regular golf, swimming and hiking. There was a hot springs pool labeled "Rustlers' Gulch," and the hotel bar was named "Silver Dollar."

A prominent local feature of that area is the Mount Aso volcano, the most active volcano in the world. At the time, it could be toured: you stood at the crater's rim and looked down into the bubbling cauldron. Juanita Larimore of Santa Rosa, California, remembers standing with her parents at the volcano's edge as a ten-year-old in 1950 and seeing at the far side of the cauldron the bodies of a man and woman who had committed suicide by throwing themselves into the fiery pit. The volcano erupted several times during the occupation, and a blowout in 1954, shortly after the occupation ended, destroyed the Aso Kanko Hotel. Mount Aso has gotten even more active since.

At the other end of the country was the *Akakura*, a rest hotel near Sapporo, on Hokkaido, then as now popular for its skiing and other wintertime sports activities, plus a hot springs. The British occupation contingent had its own rest hotels. A seaside resort of theirs, the *Kawana*, located southeast of Yokohama on the Izu Peninsula, featured an all-Japanese staff, all of whom were trained to speak English using upper-class English accents.

The occupation also seized a number of regular transient hotels in cities and elsewhere and redid at least portions of them to accommodate Western customs and expectations. In some cases, bed frames might be lengthened to accommodate American males, who by-and-large were significantly taller than Japanese men of the time.

Toilets, on the other hand, might be left alone due to the costly replacement expense.

Actual operation and staffing of the appropriated resorts and hotels were left in Japanese hands, but under the supervision of army detachments consisting of two officers and five enlisted men each. The only exceptions, apparently rare except in Tokyo and other congested cities, were close-together clusters of transient hotels. There, a single seven-man contingent might cover several hotels. Wherever and however, these units literally went by the book and followed American military doctrine to achieve proscribed standards, which in most cases dovetailed with regular American civilian laws, advisories, specifications and regulations for hostelries.

A major problem area was food handling, preparation and disposal, where many Japanese procedures were considered unhealthy by Western standards. For example, even the washing of hands after going to the lavatory was considered an elective process in Japanese hotels, so was often ignored before arrival of the Americans. Sewage disposal systems were medieval in the literal sense, with garbage usually being thrown out a door (whenever workers even got around to doing so). Drains often didn't have traps--when sinks even had drains in the first place. Open catch basins usually sufficed, and they often overflowed onto the floor.

Perhaps surprisingly, the water that flowed into these sinks (and most everywhere else, for that matter) was perfectly safe to drink right from the tap. Chalk this up to the Japanese penchant (some would say passion) for personal cleanliness, epitomized by the ritual--and it is that--of the daily bath, which in this water-rich land demands a lot of clean, fresh water. It may seem curious that the Japanese were so concerned with external corporeal cleanliness that they paid more heed to what they poured over their bodies than what was ingested into them. But that's the way it was.

The food choices themselves varied widely depending on whether the meal was at one of the rest hotels or a transient hotel. Menus at the rest hotels were varied and lavish, with multiple choices and courses, for the reason that dining was an alternative, a separate operation where the meal charges were apart from the room rate. So, you paid more, often excessively more, than the twenty-five-cum-forty cents levied back at the SCAP and FECO headquarters dining halls.

At the transient hostels, on the other hand, the prevailing policy was to include meals in the lodging fee, the so-called American Plan, which made for a boarding house atmosphere: you got what you got. For example, the Sunday dinner offering at the Kyoto Hotel the evening of November 19, 1947, was pea soup, southern fried chicken with giblet gravy, mashed potatoes, buttered asparagus, hot rolls with butter, chilled apricots for dessert, and coffee. Period. If you wanted something not on the menu, you had to go out. Or pay more to order off the hotel's regular menu, if the hostelry was even large enough to offer a variety of menu choices, which usually was not the case unless you were okay just with Japanese food. Also worth noting is that the card with the above menu printed thereon is bilingual, yet another indicator of how American and Japanese cultures were subtly nudged toward each other.

The fried chicken entree that evening makes for interesting speculation today, because Japan is the third largest market, after China and the United States, for Louisville, Kentucky-based KFC, the largest foreign fast food franchise in the country. Fried chicken bought exclusively at KFC outlets has become a traditional Christmas Day meal in Japan, stemming from a publicity campaign in 1974 called *kurisumasu ni wa kentakkii* ("Kentucky for Christmas").

The custom begins on Christmas Eve with people waiting in lines reportedly for up to two hours at KFC stores to buy hordes of fried chicken, then lugged home for celebratory-style consumption Christmas Day, accompanied by cake and champagne. It would be interesting to know if Japan's love affair with American fried chicken didn't get started that cold January night in 1947 at a hotel in Kyoto. Or at some other Americanized hotel the same evening, because that night's menu at the Kyoto Hotel likely was repeated at all the other transient hotels the occupation had appropriated, for the simple reason of economy of mass supplying of the victuals. My quartermaster father would have approved of that strategy. Come to think of it, he may have ordered it.

While the resorts were all but completely redone to American hotel standards (including especially American menus), they were never meant for use by occupation personnel and dependents exclusively. As is obvious from the public bath experience, well-to-do and middle class Japanese frequented them as well. This policy too was part of the deliberate strategy to have conquerors and conquered assimilate unfettered with one another, for it forced (as it were) Americans who otherwise might have kept to their enclaves to mingle closely with Japanese of their stature. It was all part of the master plan to have the two societies, the indigenous and the interlopers, come together amicably in all manner of environments, and for some duration.

What the planners did not count on was how enthusiastically the Japanese, for their part, would take to the rest hotels with their Americanized amenities. Japanese guests savored especially the opportunity to dine on American-style steak dinners; throughout the occupation, far and away the most popular entree choice in resort restaurants as well as American and British Commonwealth military clubs. And Japanese women quickly came to favor Western toilets--to this day a contentious issue in Japan, with young women especially preferring the sit-type.

The detachments that oversaw hotel operations came from the occupying army's Special Services section, which otherwise set up and ran very much else about the occupation that was non-military in nature. Included here were all recreational activities, installations and league play: baseball, football, basketball, track, swimming, skiing (snow and water), ice skating and boxing. The section also set up and administered the many hobby and handicraft shops, movie theaters, and the more than one hundred libraries, which capacities ranged from five hundred or so titles plus periodicals at remote outposts, to more than thirteen thousand volumes at the main library in Tokyo.

One recreational activity operated by Special Services merited special attention: golf. But with a hitch. The open-door policy of the resorts and other leisure time outlets notwithstanding, certain golf courses remained segregated for the occupation's duration--but not in the usual racial, gender or religious sense.

British expatriates had introduced golf into Japan in 1903, but the sport didn't take hold at first; just twenty-three courses were open when the war broke out, and they were available only to nobility and similar members of the hierarchy. The occupation and democracy changed all that. The number of courses more than tripled to seventy-two in the decade following war's end, and have been adding since. Golf is second only to baseball in popularity of Western sports introduced into the country, and may have more participants.

But the segregation policy didn't bar Japanese. Just like today, the natives could play whenever they could get a tee time, plus, as the occupation progressed, they got more of their own courses. It's just that during the occupation and the urgent need to focus on rebuilding the shattered country, very few Japanese bothered with the time-consuming recreation.

Nor was the segregation a gender or race issue. My mother played a lot; she even belonged to a regular women's foursome. She once hit me with an errant tee shot--while I was standing at a nearly-precise ninety-degree angle to her stance some fifteen feet away! And African-American servicemen had access to the very same courses, this at a time when the American military itself was still segregated, a long-standing policy that President Truman erased by Executive Order during the latter days of the occupation, in 1949.

Rather, golf courses as independent facilities, those not attached to hotel resorts, were kept segregated by *military* class. Specifically, officers had their own courses, and the non-commissioned officers together with enlisted personnel had theirs. Separate but equal, a half-dozen courses each.

The separation policy was instituted in this instance in order to retain the service custom of commissioned officers having their own private clubs, and NCOs having theirs. Again, it's a military thing: officers and non-coms simply don't socialize with one another. Or at least they didn't then. And since a clubhouse atmosphere with its peer group camaraderie is part-and-parcel to the traditional golfing round experience, it was only natural and expected to keep the two military classes apart in what was overwhelmingly a tightly-knit, all-male atmosphere.

The same policy applied to occupation women, dependents and female employees alike. Women could also play golf on the same courses not connected with a resort, but they had to do so within the same status guidelines: wives and children on the courses contingent with their husband's rank and status, unattached women on courses matching their boss's rank or position. Perhaps as a result of this separation policy, golf courses and the resort hotels were by-and-large kept separate. Wherever, there was always a separate clubhouse building to hold a nineteenth hole ritual.

Golf and the resort hotels were just two aspects, if arguably the two most popular for adults, of occupation recreational outlets. Flat-out tourism was another: the myriad opportunities to fulfill the welcoming brochure's admonition to drink in all this exotic land had to offer.

When it came to tourism, just getting somewhere could be an adventure. Or not. Much depended on where you lived relative to the tourist site you wished to access, and how much time you were willing to spend getting there. For the majority of occupationaires, those living within the Tokyo-Yokohama metroplex, the most sought-after destinations were Kamakura, Nikko and Mount Fuji and their surrounding attractions. I knew them well. Those lures are still Japan's principal tourist draws, and they were all within a daylight drive of Tokyo: Nikko and Mount Fuji and their surroundings each just seventy-odd miles from downtown Tokyo, Kamakura about half that distance.

But when it came to accessing a far-flung destination, defined as any trip involving at least one en route overnight stay, how you got there depended on how much time you were willing to spend along the way. For example, the beautiful, historic (and bombing-spared) tourist-oriented cities Kyoto and Nara. They're nearly three hundred miles from Tokyo, and the internationally-famous *Mikimoto* Pearl Island (then just trumpeted as the Mikimoto Pearl Farm) more than two hundred miles away. Back then, long before Japan's first four-lane superhighways, it could take two or three arduously long days to drive between Tokyo and Kyoto.

Mikimoto Pearl Oyster Fishers, 1949

To be sure, the journey wasn't hard accommodations-wise; there were always the rest hotels or otherwise perfectly fine Special Services-recommended hostelries along the way. So a drive could be fun, adventurous and rewarding in and of itself. On the other hand, if the traveler had time constraints, then the best option was to go by rail. By train, it was just a long day trip or no more than a single overnight between, say, Tokyo and Kyoto.

For most of us, trains were the way to go. In Japan, railroads were far more than just another way for people to get from here-to-there; they were Japan's principal transportation mode for people and freight alike from the late nineteenth century until the 1960s, when the country's burgeoning wealth led more citizens to afford private automobiles. Still, the percentage of travelers in Japan who get around by rail is the highest among modern, industrialized states.

So fortunately for the occupation and everyone else, Japan's rail network survived the war relatively unscathed. A survey conducted as the occupation began showed that ninety percent of the system, freight and passenger service alike, was operable. Evidence of this resilience was starkly visible at the very depth of Japan's ruination when the war ended: with all else in the country mired in despair, desperation and humiliation, trains kept running.

Or at least one did. This was shown by color motion picture footage taken by a British journalist, William Courtenay, who had accompanied MacArthur throughout his Southwest Pacific campaign, and was part of SCAP'S entourage that first landing in Japan on August 30, 1945. Courtenay shot footage of the countryside from SCAP's motorcade as it drove from the Atsugi airstrip into Yokohama. At one point in the city, when the column was surrounded by nothing else but the flattened and still-smoldering city-scape and other wreckage, the procession paused to allow a multi-car passenger train to pass by. Courtenay let his camera role, and caught the train filled with passengers looking like everyday work-bound commuters, many gazing nonchalantly out the coach windows as if nothing out of the ordinary was going on or had just happened! Or that they were just a few yards from the man who had recently presided over the conquest of their country and would reshape its destiny for untold decades to come.

The railway system the occupation inherited of course wasn't the sublimely sleek realm of the *Shinkansen* (Japanese for "New Trunk Line"), route of the "bullet trains" (*dangan ressha* in Japanese, the system's nickname) Japan is heralded for today. Far from it. Like much of the rest of the country, most railway components, passenger cars especially, were in need of rehabilitation or repair, and in general were ill-kempt and shabby.

In addition, steam locomotives were the only power source available to haul trains, which meant the railroads had to compete with other priorities for the scarce, rationed coal supplies, which in turn meant severely limited scheduling. To counter this power source obstacle, electrification of the railways was begun during the occupation and gradually caught on. Present-day Japanese railways are seventy-two percent electrified, which in percentage terms ranks Japan in high-up sixth place among the forty-four countries with electrified rail systems. (Water power-rich Switzerland heads the list with one hundred percent rail electrification.)

While rail equipment needed rehabilitation, railroad trackage itself honeycombed the entire country; even the most insignificant hamlet either had its own train station, or was within a reasonable bicycling distance of one. The principal system, excepting the *Shinkansen* lines, which are Standard Gauge, is three-foot, six-inch narrow gauge rail, called "Cape Gauge" after the Cape Colony in South Africa where it was first developed. The narrow gauge was used for easier maneuvering in Japan's largely mountainous terrain. New Zealand's railways are also Cape Gauge for much the same reason.

Japan today boasts one of the world's most comprehensive passenger rail services, and it was just as all-encompassing then. There was even a two-and-a-quarter-mile railway tunnel beneath the Kanmon Straits separating the main island of Honshu from Kyushu. This engineering feat opened in 1942 when the Japanese Empire was enjoying the zenith of its conquests. Today, *three* separate, somewhat adjacent and parallel tunnels connect the two islands: the original railway tunnel, which handles freight and conventional passenger traffic; a nearby four-lane roadway tunnel, opened in 1958; and the *Shin-Kanmon* Tunnel for the *Sanyo Shinkansen* rapid-fire trains between Osaka and Fukoka that zip through their exclusive eleven-and-a-quarter-mile tube in under four minutes.

The occupation approached the railroad situation by burrowing into it here-and-there: seizing rolling stock for its own use, passenger and freight cars alike, then coupling them into regularly-scheduled Japanese railway consists. No time was wasted doing this; the Third Transportation Military Railway Service (TMRS) was created in October 1945, when the occupation was just a month old. A companion army postal service, the Twelfth Postal Regulating Section, Kobe, was added the following January, together with the launch of regular, train-borne mail service southwest from Yokohama to Fukuoka, on Kyushu, and from Tokyo north to Sapporo, on Hokkaido.

Rehabilitation focused on passenger cars, adapting them for American use and comfort. First priority was cushions and padding on chairs and benches, which usually had just been bare wood, plus more upholstery generally on bulkheads and elsewhere. Bunks in sleeping cars were torn apart, lengthened from four-to-six inches to accommodate the taller Americans, and dressed with Western bedding. Toilet closets were refitted to suit American tastes, together with plumbing and water fountains. Entire coaches were stripped of their seats, then converted to dining-cum-club cars, complete with bars, kitchens, richly cushioned lounge chairs, dining sets with white linen, fine china and silverware--everything to make a lengthy train trip relaxing and enjoyable.

Allied Forces Railcar, ca. 1947

Operation of trains themselves remained in Japanese hands. Today, several dozen separate companies run Japan's trains; back then, railroad operations had been privately-owned and -operated before the war, but all were nationalized during the war. So the occupation had the convenience of a single source for all equipment, services and personnel: from major reconstruction, acquisition and repair projects to the smallest dining car paraphernalia, and anyone and everyone to operate it all. The TMRS, for its part, served as the system's traffic cop and control agency, which made sense given the heavy demands the occupation would put on the railways.

Trains had special reserved sections for occupation personnel where uniformed military members and their accompanying families rode free of charge, but all others had to pay. At first, a section of one coach in a train, or perhaps an entire coach, would be designated for occupation personnel in every third train. Once the families began arriving and were scattered throughout the country, rail operations expanded to include several occupation-only cars in trains, then wholly American army train consists.

The commissary trains discussed earlier were an example of these all-American trains, and likely the principal illustration of the genre. As noted, they hauled everything a military outpost with families might need: food, clothing, mail, medical and dental facilities and personnel, building supplies, appliances, teachers, clergymen, libraries, movies, replacements, guests, contractors, construction equipment, payroll clerks, bureaucrats...everything.

Whether part of a regularly-scheduled Japanese passenger train or a wholly occupation-designated train, TMRS passenger cars were strictly for the occupation's military and civilian personnel and their families, plus select--but by no means all--official visitors and contractors. No Japanese were allowed to occupy seats or berths in the TMRS cars or the cordoned-off portions of regular coaches, making those particular conveyances one of the few Japanese-origin facilities-- the equipment had been theirs, after all--that were out-of-bounds to the natives during the occupation.

There seems to have been no specific reason for this exclusion policy. It could have been a cautionary decision, instituted to avoid risk of occupiers-versus-occupied "incidents" in the often-crowded, closely-quartered, time-consuming atmosphere of a lengthy train ride. Also, the occupation component of trains often included a kitchen-cum-dining car section that prepared and served American-style meals free of charge to service personnel. These were complete, multi-course repasts at breakfast, lunch and dinner done in the same manner as the transient hotel meals mentioned earlier: set menu items, no side dishes. Plus there frequently was a bar service in a lounge-furnished and - decorated atmosphere, but all passengers had to pay for their drinks and snacks.

This particular segregation policy does not seem also to have applied to African-American soldiers prior to President Truman's de-segregation of the armed forces in 1949. I personally remember seeing uniformed American Caucasian and Negro soldiers together mingling around trains and boarding them.

While some trains had special cars and sections for us occupationaires, we also rode on all-Japanese trains, and some of us paid the fare to do so even though we didn't have to, because the occupation picked up the cost. But I paid the fare anyway because my parents told me it looked good, made me feel I was helping the hosts in some small way, and in any event was inexpensive.

Pretty much the same policy was in place for riding buses and streetcars in Tokyo and Yokohama. Technically, we didn't have to pay a fare because the occupation subsidized the services, and the conductors always smilingly waved us past the fare box. But I was admonished always to pay the fare in any event, again because it supposedly left a good impression. And besides, a streetcar ride of any distance was ridiculously cheap: just five yen, the exchange equivalent of not even a cent-and-a-half.

My most common train trip alone was between home and Kamakura, where my friend Larry Prather lived, and which cost the yen equivalent of about fifty cents round-trip. The journey involved taking two trains: from the *Ishikawacho* Station at the end of the Motomachi on the *Negishi* Line to Ofuna, where I would change to a Yokosuka Line train that dropped me off at Kamakura. And never mind whether I rode in TMRS-designated coaches, because more often than not, I hopped aboard purely Japanese trains.

The trip itself would be akin to the polite way to ride a present-day subway in that it was culturally understood there would be no unnecessary, casual communication between oneself and the other passengers--further understandable in this case, since my fellow passengers usually spoke little if any English. But not always! Sometimes it would happen that a Japanese man (never a woman!) would sidle up to me, bow graciously, then engage me in rudimentary English conversation: "Good morning." "Ry-kah you Japan?" "Riv-uh you where in 'Merica?" Things like that.

It was during these rudimentary exchanges, on trains and elsewhere, that I learned that when speaking English with someone trying to understand our language to keep words simple, look directly at the person, speak slowly and distinctly, and--very important--never use contractions, slang or idiomatic expressions. Otherwise when on a train or streetcar and I would be the only "round eye," as we were sometimes termed, I'd just smile and maybe bow a bit and go about looking out the window or reading or doing some homework. Like I said: just like riding a subway.

I took that home-Kamakura trip so often it became ingrained. When I returned to Japan in 1994 for the first time since living there, I found I didn't have to consult a present-day map or tourist guide to find the same route to Kamakura I used as a child. After touring the present-day Motomachi, which included a trek up the ridge to where our house once stood, I instinctively knew the way to the Ishikawacho Station, caught a train to Ofuna, and once there still knew to go one platform over from where I was let off to await the next Kamakura-bound train.

(Ofuna is familiar to readers of Laura Hillenbrand's *Unbroken*, the compelling account of American airman Louis Zamperini's ordeal as a prisoner-of-war of the Japanese. It was at a camp apparently just a short walk from the Ofuna station that Zamperini and his fellow POWs endured much of the abuse from their captors. I of course didn't know of any of this at the time, which is just as well, because I'd sometimes be waiting at that station after dark for a train home, and so likely would have been haunted by spirits from that time.)

My short, personal trips aside, watching other Americans step on-and-off long-distance TMRS railroad cars was the closest I ever got to my own trip aboard one of the regular overnight passenger trains--for the reason that when it came to long-distance journeys, our family always traveled in our own private railway car!

I owe this singular fortuity to my father's position with the occupation. During our first few months in Japan, when dad was the Eighth Army's Procurement Officer, he often had to travel considerable distances to negotiate with Japanese businessmen and royalty for supplies and facilities the occupation needed. Then in August 1949, he was made the army's Comptroller (chief financial officer), a position that still required he travel around the country in the elegant private car. And these trips often included mother and me because dad's business often was conducted in the Japanese tradition of the families of the negotiators also becoming acquainted.

And so we traveled in this elaborately-outfitted, -decorated and -staffed rolling hotel suite. Actually, several suites. Usually just mom, dad and me, but sometimes with one other couple and their son, who was about my age. This other officer was an associate of my father, which I know because they would often huddle together in the office section of the car for long periods of time going over papers and figures while mother and the other officer's wife would chat or play cards. The situation certainly wasn't crowded. Even on the rare occasions when the other family would join the journey, there was always plenty of room. I had my own private stateroom with its own wash stand and toilet. A maid made up our rooms and otherwise made it known she was available to satisfy any whims I might have (none; never allowed).

The car had a kitchen manned by a resident cook and steward who saw to a spacious and gracious dining area at the rear, plus a bar and observation lounge. All meals were proper dress-up-and-sit-up-straight affairs. Dinner was always elegant, featuring haughtily ornate china, intimidating crystal, and hefty silver flatware that clanked together ominously with the rocking of the car when our train was moving.

Private Rail Car

The car itself was a meticulously-maintained Edwardian-era relic, probably from Europe or perhaps the United States, that was either built for Japan's narrow gauge tracks in the first place, or had its chassis retrofitted from Standard Gauge to Cape Gauge in what is called in railroading talk a "bogie exchange." I feel certain the vehicle wasn't Japanese in origin because the decor featured elaborately-carved moldings and dark paneling wholly out of keeping and character with what I remember not necessarily from Japanese railroad cars, which by-and-large were featureless, but from art schemes in general. There was not a single hint of a Japanese artistic motif anywhere on the car, not so much as a print on a stateroom wall. James Zobel opined that the vehicle may have been MacArthur's own designated private car, which he not once used, so it was just released for whatever dignitary or official might need it.

We took some long, sometimes strenuous trips in the car and so appreciated the car's luxury all the more. My mother especially remembered the time, in the dead of winter, we rode it aboard a ferry from Honshu to the northern island of Hokkaido, and how what she termed a "swarm" of Japanese laborers, perhaps more than fifty, with no power machinery whatsoever that she could recall, struggled to maneuver the car from the land-bound tracks to the pitching ferryboat. They got the lead pair of trucks aboard the ferry, but then the lurching boat kept causing the tracks to mis-align, leaving the car to skew back and forth while the Japanese struggled to inch it forward while simultaneously trying to control the heaving ferry.

I have a vague recollection of this occasion. I better remember being bored once on Hokkaido, waiting with my mother in the public rooms of some hugely grim, near-empty and very chilly hotel, sleet falling outside, while my father did his business elsewhere. He did return later that evening, and we went back to the private car, spent the night aboard it, and early the next morning headed home. Altogether, a five-day journey for a six-hour business meeting.

On several occasions, we rode the car overnight to Kyoto, for my father to conduct business with a member of the Japanese royal family, a Count Hirohashi. On these particular sojourns we stayed with the nobleman and his family, who lived in this large, extremely elegant home set amongst lush evergreen trees, and with a spacious Mediterranean-style inner garden that featured a fountain centerpiece. The count had a son who was some two or three years older than I, perhaps thirteen, and noticeably taller. The boy was polite enough to me, but impatient to go elsewhere to be with his friends, which was understandable. So as was often the case on these trips, I would end up amusing myself.

Count Hirohashi had gone to college in the United States, so spoke impeccable English, while his wife and son managed admirably. Mrs. (Countess?) Hirohashi was especially indulgent of me. Before dinner, we all would gather on a garden terrace for appetizers and cocktails, where Mrs. Hirohashi always had a special treat for me: Ritz Crackers that she would smilingly serve me straight from the box. And to wash the crackers down, a Coca Cola poured right from the then-world renowned, contour-shaped, six-and-a-half-ounce green bottle.

The Hirohashi's of course couldn't go into a commissary or exchange to buy Ritz Crackers and Cokes, so it would appear they and a variety of other American package goods were being imported and sold in upscale Japanese markets by that time, in addition to their being available in the resort hotels. Count Hirohashi and my father became close friends and exchanged fairly pricey gifts.

My only other clear memory of being on the private car was the time we inadvertently stopped in Hiroshima, and for what seemed several hours. Mother recalled that we were sidetracked both because track repairs were ongoing, and to let regular traffic bypass us. Most times, our private car was hitched to the rear of some regularly-scheduled passenger train, but at others it was coupled either right behind the locomotive, or perhaps with just a freight or baggage car to comprise its own, complete consist. So I'm guessing this particular delay was one of those times when we were on our own, and so were expendable scheduling-wise.

Because the totally-flattened city was off limits to occupation personnel unless you had official business, dad became quite agitated about being there: I remember him pacing back-and-forth, impatient to get underway. It of course was not his fault we were stuck there for some reason, but he was that way: he always followed the rules. And this rule said keep away, and never mind you may temporarily not have control of the situation. I also recall wanting to alight from the car to take a look around the devastated city for myself, and father sharply and impatiently ordering me to stay aboard.

So I simply nestled into one of the plush chairs in the lounge of our ornately-appointed private railway car and stared out the window at the most extensive, wanton destruction I was to see during our time in Japan or any time since. Yes, I know, there was the view of the damage across the railroad tracks I everyday saw from the lane outside our house, and I would often walk through rubble-strewn streets between the Bluff Area and downtown Yokohama.

But this carnage was different. It's one thing to state off-handedly that such-and-such a city is bombed flat; it's quite another to look out upon what just half a decade earlier must have been a quite attractive seaside metropolis and see literally that: nothing but flattened rubble all the way to the horizon. No people, no roads, no structures still struggling to remain upright. Just mish-mashed remnants of what once were buildings, now a jumble of twisted metal, broken concrete forms now just various-size and -shaped chunks, perhaps a charred wooden beam or two...

I just stared at it for what seemed like a long time. Then eventually our train began moving, so I turned my attention to something else. Exactly what I've no idea; I only know those images of what remained of Hiroshima are all I recall from that particular trip.

Chapter 11: The Grand Life

Our family got to see a lot of Japan as a result of my father's open, high-level position. And perhaps because of all that travel, we never once took a vacation in the usual sense of the word, which is to say a week or two at some exotic destination or at least a different country. And as it happened, many if not most others there at the time treated their leave time the same way. After all, why spend extra money, time and trouble traveling to some exotic locale where every day brings something new and unique, when we were already living in such an environment, where just about every day brought something new and unique?

The British Commonwealth occupiers (they didn't care for us Americans' "occupationaires" label) did visit Hong Kong and Singapore, Britain's southeastern Asia overseas holdings at the time, and also perhaps India. This was only natural and understanding, because most of these expatriates had lived in those colonies but lost their homes and freedoms when the Japanese invaded. The few Australians and New Zealanders who participated in the occupation also may have flown home now-and-then, although the distances involved were quite great, especially for the Kiwis.

As for other regional travel possibilities: mainland China and Korea were out of the question because of the turmoil on the mainland that of course eventually led to a new war there. And as for Malaysia, Indonesia, Southeast Asia, the Philippines and the other island groups in the Western Pacific: recovery from the war would be slow and arduous. It would be years before their sun-drenched beach resorts, mystically beautiful temples and myriad other tourist attractions would be open for business.

There were regular commercial flights between Tokyo and Honolulu at the time, but in those pre-jet airliner days, the thirty-eight hundred-mile trip took some fourteen hours, plus a lengthy refueling stopover in Wake Island, and must have been quite costly.

(I know this tiring Tokyo-Honolulu jaunt for a fact because I took that very flight, the first airplane trip I was to make. Mother and I flew it back to America when we left Japan in early September 1950. The aircraft was a Pan American Airways flagship of the time that had just entered service, a double-decker Boeing 377 *Stratocruiser*. Just the two of us occupied a private cabin on the lower deck, adjacent to the forward port side entry. I remember we took off from Tokyo's *Haneda* Airport early in the morning, flew over a quite active volcano, perhaps Mount Aso, got to Wake shortly after noon (had lunch on the plane there), then finally arrived in Honolulu well after dark. We stayed two days in Honolulu, in some dreary transients' quarters at the air base as I recall, then flew from Honolulu to San Francisco on a different type of aircraft. So, at age eleven, my very first air journey involved two airliners covering just over six thousand miles, nearly a quarter of the way around the world.)

But with respect to vacation travel outside Japan at the time? It may seem the cruelest of all ironies, yet it is so: the best place to be in the war-ravaged Western Pacific region in the late 1940s and into the following decade was in the very country that had been responsible for all the problems. So virtually all us occupationaires stayed put when vacation time came around.

Our family was no exception to this stay-at-home practice. Dad got thirty days' leave annually; all military personnel did and still do. But he would sprinkle his leave time throughout the year rather than take it in an all-encompassing chunk somewhere-or-other. No problem! Even in its war-damaged condition, Japan enjoyed a plethora of wondrous sights, sites and enthralling things to do in and around them.

Just for example, Japan's famed hot springs, her *onsen*, can be found scattered here-and-there throughout the country. It would happen we would be out exploring somewhere and just come across a nest of the steaming wonders. I remember lolling in them with dad for what would seem like hours, with mother lounging nearby and even trying the waters herself.

Other than the regions around Mount Fuji and our business-associated trips to Kyoto and Nara, I mostly remember Nikko as a favorite, oft-visited tourist site. Nikko was quite a drive for us, some one-hundred, twenty-miles north of the Bluff Area in Yokohama, the longest trip we would take by car, usually if not always involving an overnight stop at some transient hotel. We could have taken a train; Nikko is the final stop on the line named for the site. But we needed a car once there.

So just getting to Nikko could take some effort, but very much worth the trip. The area and town, a national park, is the site of *Toshogu*, Japan's most lavishly-decorated shrine. Included in the shrine's ornate artwork are the world-famous, so-called Three Wise Monkeys, bas-relief renderings of the proverbial "see no evil, hear no evil and speak no evil" adage. Other, not dissimilar monuments and shrines adorn the area, including what most be one of the world's most ornate mausoleums. The region altogether has been a major, central worship site for Japan's two principal religions, Buddhism and Shintoism, for centuries, making the area a sort-of Eastern equivalent of tri-faith Jerusalem.

We visited Mikimoto's Pearl Farm on at least two occasions, where we witnessed the comely female pearl divers plunging away, then surfacing with baskets of oysters. We would then follow the baskets to a workshop to watch delicate-fingered artisans remove the bivalve's valued irritation. Once pearls were cleaned and lightly polished, they were ready for market. Presentos were of course offered and accepted, so mother ended up buying several pearls, loose and in jewelry form, usually as a necklace. I still have one of the pearls, an especially large one set in a gold ring.

Extracting Pearl at Mikimoto's

We were also treated to the Japanese tradition of cormorant fishing, once only a royal indulgence. This custom occurred (still occurs) at night. We were put out in skiffs with the fishers and their large, gawky-looking, seemingly ungainly black birds, three or four per skiff, each on a leash and with a broad band around its neck. The fishers would release the birds, who would fly up a little, then plunge head-first into the water, to emerge a few seconds later, each with a fish in its beak. The fishers would then reel in the cormorants and retrieve the fish, which the birds would have been prevented from swallowing because of the collars around their necks. The birds did get their rewards, however.

After the fishing was done for the evening, our party would indulge in a lavish *sukiyaki* dinner alongside the water (the fish were bound for the next day's markets), while the birds would mill around nearby, gobbling up their share of the night's catch. It was at one of these outings that I was allowed my first-ever drink of an alcoholic beverage: a short glass of *saki*, the renowned Japanese rice wine. I remember that the wine was warm and that I didn't care for it; I've changed since.

Waterfowl of another species were the subject of an age-old, popular royal indulgence: duck netting. This unique treat was for adults only; I couldn't participate. But my parents regaled me for days afterwards about the outing, and dad took scores of pictures.

This custom took place--and still takes place--on one of the emperor's rural estates, the *Saitama* Imperial Wild Duck Preserve. A berm some eight or ten feet high would have been semi-permanently in place at one end of an open field that would feature a huge inviting pond, all kinds of wild grains, and additionally be seeded with different varieties of duck feed. The whole field was really a setup, a sting operation, a lushly-rich trap for the ducks, tens of thousands of which are still known to feed in the preserve annually.

The event would start with what was termed a "Judas duck," a live, squawking bird, being released into the pond as a "plant" to attract others. Once there were ducks on the pond, this willing traitor, this quacking Quisling, would obligingly paddle toward the berm, and of course the flock would follow. And when this action got going, once the ducks were berm-bound, beaters armed with large, bamboo fans would scamper into the meadow from the opposite side, flailing the grasses and yelling the whole time, which of course would frighten the ducks and cause them to take off away from the racket, in the direction of the berm.

Duck Netting Party

All this time, guests who chose to participate would be crouched behind the berm along with attendants, all outfitted with huge, long-handled, two-handed nets. Then as the panic-stricken ducks flew over the berm, all would leap up and snare the feathered dupes in the nets. The ducks, scores of them, would then be butchered and dressed, and the day would end with everyone enjoying barbecued duck and, to hear mother tell it, way too much hot saki.

The duck netting was held in the autumn. On the opposite side of the calendar was another eagerly-anticipated imperial event: the emperor's cherry blossom festival, held on the imperial palace grounds early each spring, when the blossoms are out and colorful, but almost every other flora is still huddled away from the weather. We attended two of these events, and on both occasions, I rode a horse unescorted, so took the opportunity to ride close by a chariot bearing Emperor Hirohito and his wife to get a good look. They both smiled and nodded

in acknowledgment of me tipping my cap. At least, it seemed that way.
I sat up extra-straight and puffed my chest out in any event.

Author at Cherry Blossom Festival, 1950

Mother rode in a horse-drawn carriage with some lady friends. I
don't remember seeing my father during the festival other than when
we were first dropped off. He would then disappear with some of his
friends and colleagues. It was good that on such occasions we were

251

attending on so-called official business (there was a lot of that), as formal representatives of the occupation, and so were driven to the event in dad's staff car. The drive back to Yokohama was always fun, as my father was a highly amiable inebriate: very talkative, always full of often humorous-laden accounts of what he and his friends had been doing, or his observations of what had been going on.

So there were recreations and outings and trips and special events for whole families. And for adults only. And also for children only. Which brings me--finally--to my accounting (to take a cue from my father) of how it came to pass that I one afternoon happened to play musical chairs with Douglas MacArthur.

The party where the game occurred was held in a large room, probably a reception hall of some sort, in the American Embassy in Tokyo, where, as noted, the MacArthurs lived throughout the occupation. The embassy wasn't needed for diplomatic purposes, because the United States did not resume diplomatic relations with Japan until after the peace treaty was signed in 1952, formally ending the occupation.

I had thought the event was a birthday party for Arthur MacArthur IV, who is exactly a year and a week older than I. I figured this was the case because I distinctly remember bringing a gift-wrapped, shoe box-size present to the party. But in researching this project at the MacArthur Memorial, archivist James Zobel and I went through hundreds of pictures of the family together with notes and asides from MacArthur's wife Jean, and couldn't find a single reference to a large-scale birthday party attended by dozens of kids. But there were pictures of other parties with lots of kids (and, yes, I looked for pictures of me). So I'm guessing it was some occasion that required exchange of presents between the guests, or perhaps for some charity Mrs. MacArthur was sponsoring, and there were scores of those.

I do remember that this party was the one and only time I was driven to an event alone in my father's staff car by his personal driver. And it must have been a pretty big deal, because I wore a suit. And I must have been briefed thoroughly beforehand, and been impressed that I was to be on my best behavior, because I remember sitting smack dab, bolt upright in the middle of the sedan's back seat for the entire hour-long drive to Tokyo, never smiling, clutching the present protectively, always looking straight ahead.

The party itself may not have been for Arthur's birthday, but it had all the other trappings of same: cake and ice cream, colorful decorations, lively music, et cetera. There was a brief receiving line with Arthur and his mother, so I got to meet him and shake his hand. And that was that; I don't remember him taking part in any of the games, although he may have at some point, it being his party (I think).

In any event, at one point, we all began playing musical chairs. I remember Mrs. MacArthur standing off against one wall, smiling and nodding her head to the music. I had seen her on several previous occasions at our house, which she visited now-and-then. Jean MacArthur was a superb bridge player, a fanatic for the game, as was my mother. So when Mrs. MacArthur would cast about for bridge players of her caliber, it was only natural that a player as good as my mother would be included in her coterie. And as my mother reminded me late in her life, this bridge contingent would meet regularly in a rotating fashion at the different homes of the players. So it would happen that mother would sometimes go to Tokyo to play bridge, and also that Mrs. MacArthur would now-and-then make an appearance at our house for the same purpose.

(Jean MacArthur was a tiny lady, barely five feet tall, extremely gracious and outgoing. She was her husband's representative at what must have been every social occasion and official function that was not strictly military in nature. It was she who taught my mother the presento acceptance custom. She lived to age 101.)

Anyway, while still playing the game, I saw this older guy, wearing a plain, khaki, open-collared shirt and trousers, enter through a side door, pause and chat for a few moments with a maid, who giggled and nodded her head at whatever the general was whispering to her. Then with a self-conscious grin and exaggerated snapping of his fingers, MacArthur joined in the sweeping round of the game.

The music continued for a full twenty seconds or so; I distinctly recall seeing him carefully shuffling along with us kids from one chair to another. Then the music suddenly stopped, and the girl who was beside him quickly nudged him with her hip, then plopped into the vacant chair, leaving SCAP standing there with no place to sit. He stood there momentarily, then gave an exaggerated "darn it!" expression, and quickly walked off the floor, and back out the door through which he had entered.

I of course knew who the interloper was; I'm sure we all did. And I'm equally sure none of us ever gave a thought to making a fuss over him making an appearance. For after all, he was our ultimate father figure, a feature of the landscape. No big deal. Restart the music!

And that was it. The closest I ever got to General MacArthur, which at least was closer and for a somewhat longer time period than my parents together ever got. As I emphasized earlier, SCAP wanted a distinct separation between his office and mission and the occupying army. So he was only dad's boss in the broadest possible sense in that he also was in charge of *everything* in the Western Pacific ocean in the latter half of the 1940s.

Which is all a way of saying that the only time my parents ever even saw MacArthur in an informal setting (dad would see him at formal military events) was early one summer evening in Tokyo. They were walking along the sidewalk outside the Dai Ichi building, and as they came up to a particular black Cadillac limousine with a sergeant standing alongside holding a rear door open, they saw MacArthur, attired in trench coat, quickly exit the building, hustle into the back seat of the awaiting car, and be driven off.

My mother told me that account along with much else in the lengthy, multi-layered interview I had with her late in her life. She didn't embellish that story or any other. She didn't even make a big thing of her frequent socializing with Jean MacArthur; I had to prod her for details. Nor did she boast about her acquaintance with any other important person, for that matter. It was her way.

Chapter 12 - The Silent Enigma

In many ways, the occupation of Japan was an illusion. And I don't just mean an illusion for a ten- and eleven-year-old boy, but an aberration for all of us who were there then. Many times, and again in many ways, things just really weren't what they seemed.

To cite just one example: my father loved his scotch whisky. Perhaps it was his Scottish heritage (his father, my paternal grandfather, was a native Scotsman), but when dad came home after a day at the office, he wouldn't consider himself ready for dinner or the evening fit for relaxed enjoyment until after he had his traditional scotch-on-the-rocks.

Dad likely relished this habit before my arrival in the family; he certainly continued to enjoy it during our time in Japan and subsequently. And at one point late in his life, long after he had retired from the army and my parents had moved to Asheville, North Carolina, he told me that he especially enjoyed the scotch whisky he obtained during the occupation. Favored it so much he made it his brand of choice for the rest of his life. He told me this one evening while I was visiting my parents in Asheville, and we were just sitting around before dinner, sharing a scotch together.

Which makes me wonder whether I would have told him then what I know now about that scotch he so enjoyed in Japan: that it likely was watered-down whenever and wherever he enjoyed his scotch in the company of fellow officers, meaning in the bar of an officers' club, which was his favorite situation. It was also occupation policy to water-down domestically-produced hard liquors, including Japan's notable *Suntory* whisky, the most sought-after locally-produced brand then and still a world-wide favorite. The policy also extended to imported liquors destined for by-the-drink sales at officers' and NCO clubs for American and British Commonwealth personnel alike, and also at the rest hotels and aboard TMRS trains.

The official purpose for the practice was the same no matter the liquor or its source: stretch limited supplies in order to bring in more income. In its way, the policy was similar to the practice mentioned earlier about cutting gasoline with kerosene in order to stretch supplies. And the process was simple enough: bottles were opened, water added, then re-sealed using official occupation seals. The excess diluted liquor would be bottled anew and similarly labeled and sealed, then sent out to the bars.

Unofficially, but nonetheless mentioned in ex-officio documents, by-the-drink liquor sales were watered-down to account for the fact that a lot of alcoholic consumption was being done by American service personnel who weren't legally old enough to buy hard liquor back in the United States; where, then as now, age twenty-one was the cutoff line in most jurisdictions. In Japan, on the other hand, the legal drinking age apparently was lower than the country's current twenty years of age, although most bar tenders ignored even that figure and served at least beer and wine (what wine there was then, usually saki) to whomever had the yen or scrip and otherwise didn't yet show signs of having consumed too much.

So bar liquor was diluted in the hope that youthful imbibers would quickly fill up on the stuff or run out of money to buy more, or both, before becoming too intoxicated to cause embarrassment or trouble. Occupation crime and traffic accident statistics indicate the policy might not have worked all that well, especially where operating motor vehicles or even pedaling bicycles was concerned.

Imported and domestic liquors meant for exchange sale, plus such other alcoholic beverages like beer and wine, didn't have to be opened, altered and re-sealed because exchange outlets operated under the minimum age of twenty-one rule predominant back Stateside. And just like at any store back in America, a purchaser of questionable age would have to show an identification card with his or her age revealed thereon before making a buy.

But there were still nefarious activities where liquor sales were concerned. For example, the highly-popular scotch whisky that was purloined or hijacked and resold on the black market at outrageous prices to whomever had the yen. Or had the dollars–and I don't necessarily mean dollars in scrip form either, but rather the real, green backed thing. It didn't take nearly as many authentic dollars vis-a-vis scrip dollars to make a black market purchase.

Still, the product could have been opened, watered-down, then re-corked with a counterfeit seal before being released on the black market or elsewhere as full-strength booze. The leftover diluted whisky would be re-bottled into like containers fitted with counterfeit labels in addition to phony seals for subsequent sale. I'm not saying my father ever bought liquor on the black market; in his position, he wouldn't ever have had to. But still, with all the underhanded activities going on, it's possible he might have received a bottle of watered-down scotch by some means or other, perhaps as a gift.

There were many other illusions of course. And deceptions. All manner of things that weren't what they seemed to be: the phony ancient samurai swords, the counterfeited yen value stamps, the foul-tasting cigarettes done up in Lucky Strike packs, mother's treasured trifecta of Noritake china place settings that weren't the finest examples of the genre...Like so much else, the list goes on. And on and on. My personal favorite is the miscellaneous goods that came from the city of Usa stamped, honestly enough, "MADE IN USA." I wish I could say I remember having examples of those products, but honestly cannot. That said, the goods were so profligate, chances are I did pick up one-or-two here-and-there.

And then there was the greatest illusion of all: the Japanese people themselves. On the surface, all seemed normal and open: the faces we saw, the courtesies we honored and returned, the conversations we exchanged, the persons we knew and dealt with closely and personally that were from extremely varied positions in life; in our family's case, literally from servants to royalty. At the time, it was all so sincere, so real, so the-way-things-are-and-supposed-to-be, especially to my boyish innocence. But was it really?

I sought an answer from my mother. One of the principal questions I asked her in the lengthy, multi-day interview I conducted with her in 1994 was, "What did the Japanese really think of us?" She drew back a bit at the question, in the manner of someone who at some point expected the query, and had a reply at hand, but still didn't like being put on the spot to have to answer it. And so the reply came fairly quickly. She looked straight at me and said matter-of-factly, "We never really knew."

Mother's bewilderment about what the Japanese really thought of us occupationaires seems to have been common among most of us who lived there then, including even people who might at some point have claimed or even demonstrated otherwise. The same goes for Japanese attitudes, culture and customs in general; the ignorance about the double-entendre meaning of "arigato," the word for thank-you and how it's meant when accepting a present, being just one example.

My Mother (right) with Friend and Guide

The only exceptions I can think of with respect to this cloud of ignorance would be the families assigned to remote outposts, where getting to know the locals and getting along in general was necessary. Plus, the missionaries and teachers who chose to practice among the Japanese would of course be well-schooled in the language and customs. But as for the families in general, I would have to say that when it comes to knowing what the Japanese really thought of us, that most respondents would have the same nonplused response as did my mother.

Then of course, this cultural wall had two sides. As hard as the Japanese would try, there were always barriers between us and them of one sort or another, language of course being just one of them. And it could get frustrating for all involved. As Margery Finn Brown in *Over a Bamboo Fence* wrote in exasperation:

> *We had five servants in the house who didn't know a word of English. They were hungry and anxious to please. They loved to arrange flowers. But the most fundamental routines of an American house were deep mysteries: nobody knew how to set a table, fry an egg, make a bed, or shoe a baby. We communicated by glistening smiles and pantomime at which they were adept. Not I! Faced with the prospect of miming, "Cook-san, pour not the honorable hot coffee on the honorable cold jello," or "Boy-san, (adjust) G-string of you cover with clothes," I usually lost my nerve.*
> – Margery Finn Brown, *Over a Bamboo Fence*
> Chapter 3, "Service with a Bow," p. 28

I would say Brown here innocently betrays her own resilience to understanding and dealing with the Japanese during the occupation,

259

this despite her having lived there for so long, and having been a columnist for a Japanese periodical. This is revealed in the offhanded and dismissive way she *assumes* that a servant girl would have known instinctively how to fry an egg. But as I point out in the "Made in Occupied Japan" chapter, conventional fry pans and their accompanying spatulas as Americans know them were all but unknown in the Japan of the time. So in all fairness, how could Brown reasonably expect a servant girl to automatically know how to fry an egg in the American manner, when she might not even have known which utensils to use? If indeed the tools were even available in the Brown household.

Speaking just of the language barrier, English must have been as hard for them as Japanese was for us. For example, consider that there are no inflections in spoken Japanese; it's not, Hee-ROW-she-muh, or Hee-row-SHE-muh, but Here-oh-shu-muh. Nor are there verb tenses; everything is communicated in a qualified or modified present tense. It is still common for Japanese to speak English using just qualified present tense, for example, "We go Disneyland Monday next week." or "We eat pizza now two days past." Learning when and how to employ English's half-dozen verb tenses must be as hard for a Japanese as our learning the how's, when's and why's of French's *fourteen* verb tenses. In the end, it's more comfortable and expedient to make yourself known by expressing the foreign language in familiar, recognizable structural and grammatical terms. You may at least get credit for trying.

Communication with the servants in our particular household was of no concern, for the simple reason that our head maid spoke perfect English--which was understandable, because she was an American citizen! Horiko had been living in Hawaii before the war broke out, but I don't recall, and neither could mother, whether she was Nisei or a naturalized American citizen. What mother and I both did remember was that Horiko had been the victim of what can only be described as a classic case of bad timing: in late-November 1941, she sailed from Honolulu to Japan to visit relatives, arriving around the first of December, then of course was caught for the war's duration following the Pearl Harbor attack the first of the next week.

Why Horiko was still in Japan four years after the war had ended and was not yet repatriated is something of a mystery. American citizens, prisoners-of-war especially but not exclusively, were among the first persons held by the Japanese to be returned to their home country. But repatriations were delayed and in some cases disallowed for Americans who were known to have cooperated or even collaborated with the Japanese in one way or another. The sheer volume of foreigners caught in Japan who were desperate to return home slowed the repatriation process for everyone. Something like two-and-a-quarter million fellow Asians alone wandered the islands; the estimates see-sawed and were never nailed down.

Then again, perhaps Horiko had found a better life back in Japan with her cousins than she was experiencing in Hawaii and decided to stay. The point is that despite Horiko's perfect command of both languages and history of living in both cultures, my insightful, frank and fair-minded mother was never able to penetrate even her shell, and so was at a loss to explain what the Japanese really thought of us.

Many other Americans there at the time apparently had the same frustrating experience, Margery Finn Brown among them. But she at least took several stabs at bridging the understanding gap. At another point in *Over a Bamboo Fence*, she even tried looking at us from the Japanese point of view:

> *What sort of people are these foreigners anyway? Americans smoke cigarettes, read newspapers, bear children as we Japanese do. But their standards are so different (her italics). They fritter their lives searching for happiness when duty, obedience and passivity are the things that endure. They haven't the wisdom to accept gracefully what the gods choose to send. A materialistic, excitable people with strange customs! But we shall see! Before we accept them, we'll stare,*

appraise and gossip. There, they've gone...Wouldn't you think the mother would sit in the back seat with the children where she belongs, instead of up in front with the father...?
     –Ibid. Chapter 5, "A Kyoto Alley," p. 47

From my viewpoint and experience, that's a pretty fair analysis--in the context of the Japanese cultural mind-set that was present and predominant during the occupation! The portrait Brown paints of the Japanese character she encountered daily and in multiple situations, from dealing with maids to arguing with editors and all in between, oozes shikata ga nai–a term she understood and uses elsewhere in her book. Only in this particular observation of hers, the passive acceptance-of-fate nature of that characteristic is sprinkled with what appears to be a fairy dusting of mono-no-aware, a glint of self-assurance and -awareness. Nowhere to be seen is the extreme pessimism of ensei, the feeling that life is no longer worth living.

Brown elsewhere notes that working with her column's editors was very much a peer level undertaking; no passive submission there! But overall, she seems to have captured the prevailing national mood of the occupation period. In a way, it's too bad she was gone from the occupation before it ended, so never witnessed the complete shift of the Japanese national character away from passivity and grudging acceptance of fate, to prideful optimism plus unabashed positivity and aggressiveness.

The shift in Japanese character to a more optimistic and opportunistic nature parallels a cultural retreat of sorts on the part of us occupationaires after the Korean War broke out in June 1950, and more so after the occupation itself ended less than two years later. Most tellingly, it is evident that Americans, at least, became more insular, more removed from contact with the Japanese, as the 1950s wore on.

This withdrawal trend on the part of occupation families is revealed in a 1954 edition of *Dependents Guide to Japan*. The first two issues, published in 1946 and 1948 respectively, when the occupation was new, unique and most intriguing, lead with terse, if also friendly, welcome-to-Japan introductions. Their messages are a sharp contrast to the edition published in 1954, two years after the occupation had ended but while there was still a strong American military presence in Japan. This later issue's foreword includes the admonition:

> *Two types of service wives come to Japan. The first group arrives with a very narrow-minded attitude. They fully expect that everything here in a foreign land will be exactly like it was in Kansas City or Philadelphia. It isn't! They are guaranteed a miserable time and they hate every moment of the time that they are here...The other group understands that they are coming to a strange land with customs much different from those in their own country. They accept Japan as it is, participate in its activities, and have a most enjoyable time.*

This verbal finger wagging is a clear indication that too many wives, presumably but not necessarily occupation late-comers, and by extension entire family units, eschewed experiencing travel and culture during most if not all their entire tenure in the host country. They apparently didn't let so much as the colorful rays from a delicately-carved figurine permeate their cloud of disinterest, and maybe also distrust. For example, one family reported, upon returning to American shores, that the only time during their three years in Japan they ate Japanese food was at the Tokyo airport while awaiting the flight that would return them to American soil.

Of this example and others that were similar, Donna Alvah wrote, in reporting on *all* postwar occupation locales, in Germany and elsewhere in addition to Japan:

> *On-base developments that housed hundreds of American families came to be known as "Little Americas" whose occupants drew criticism from civilian as well as military Americans for allegedly not venturing out of their self-contained communities to interact with residents of occupied and host countries.*
> – Donna Alvah, *Unofficial Ambassadors: American Families Overseas and the Cold War,* p. 34

There were several possible reasons for this insularity on the part of the families in Japan. First and foremost is the fact that once the occupation ended in 1952, and the Japanese cast off the last vestments of shikata ga nai together with regaining rule of their land, that post-occupation families would have encountered a different type of Japanese personality, notably one that would be less deferential and more confident and assertive, perhaps at times aggressively so.

This post-occupation character shift is shown in two separate polls from the era that Donna Alvah also reported on, a random sampling of Japanese citizens. The first poll, taken in 1950 at the height of the occupation, showed that fifty-five percent of Japanese respondents favored alliance with the United States, twenty-two percent were neutral, and less than one percent wanted alliance with the Soviet Union. Three years later, just after the occupation ended, the same poll now showed just thirty-three percent of respondents in favor of a alliance with the United States, thirty-eight percent neutral, and the same minus one percent favoring an alliance with the USSR.

A second factor was that a war was ongoing in nearby Korea until mid-1953, and that together with the communist takeover of China meant that Cold War tensions persisted in the neighborhood for years after. Third, communism was, if not rampant, at least often open and vocal in Japan throughout the often-paranoid Cold War time of the 1950s and into the -60s, and the demonstrations could be very intimidating, even scary.

Fourth and perhaps most significantly, our mentor, our sponsor and leader, the example we all followed, was gone, summarily fired by his Commander-in-Chief for insubordination in his conduct of the Korean War and long returned to the United States and retirement like any man. Only the legend of MacArthur remained; *paterfamilias* himself had abandoned his family.

Yet the very insularity shown by the family, and certainly others that had never sampled Japanese food or culture, not only made it possible for Japanese to look deeply inside the American home, but magnified and intensified the experience. In addition to our good points and materialistic needs and desires, Japanese got to witness Americans' fears and prejudices--*exactly* as American families then lived them.

This post-occupation Japanese character change and a lot more was what John Dower met with, interviewed and reported on in his Pulitzer Prize-winning *Embracing Defeat*, published in 1999. Present-day Japanese can be quite vocal in their resentment about excesses, real and perceived, of the occupation as exercised by individual foreigners, Americans of course included, often especially so. Hubris, jingoism, ridicule, cheating, disparagement, racism, thievery, cheating, threats, rape, assault, murder...At one time or other and to varying degrees of severity, we occupationaires did it all! And to be sure, the concurrent occupation of Okinawa was–and still is--especially acrimonious and ridden with excesses; incidents of rape, assault and even murder are still not uncommon.

Small wonder Dower at one time accuses us American occupiers of having been "colonial viceroys." I personally resent how in two words Dower dismisses MacArthur's rationale for establishing and managing the occupation in the manner he did: eschewing the British tradition and following his father's egalitarian model instead, which if nothing else was aimed expressly at avoiding that particularly insulting label. And I know that virtually all of us who were there as children most definitely refute the label. Interestingly–and perhaps tellingly– much of the latter-day castigation is expressed elsewhere, if not in Dower's account, by persons who were too young at the time to have been fully aware of what was going on, or weren't even born yet.

Criminal transgressions by occupation personnel for the most part are duly noted in official transcripts of the occupation--but at the time were often ignored for coverage in *Stars and Stripes* and elsewhere. Which of course could be part of the problem, a primary reason for the present-day resentment. Japanese bitterness at having constantly to bow literally and figuratively before the conquerors is also expressed. And that's understandable. But it's also important to recognize that Japan was practicing revisionist history with regard to their role in the war during the time Dower was researching his book: who was responsible for what and to what degree, who did what to whom and why, and so on down the line.

And it continues! In many ways, the Japanese view of its wartime role is an ongoing internal conscience struggle that sometimes is dealt with honestly and openly, and at others is either ignored or downplayed. The issue of the so-called Korean "comfort women" is an example of this avoidance of responsibility. The Japanese don't deny it happened, and have paid out more than three hundred million dollars compensation to the victims or their survivors. But they can be dismissive of the consequences of the practice, and have been reluctant to express apologies.

What it comes down to is, the Japanese the reader encounters in Brown's book are all but absent from Dower's account, so far removed from Japan's present-day culture they might as well be museum exhibits. Flipping from one book to the other is like observing a step-by-step evolutionary progression, where the subject can be seen divesting itself bit-by-bit of the vestiges of being under the thumb of a foreign power.

Thrown over the side are all those conversions to Christianity done just to please MacArthur and the missionaries, tossed in the garbage is the groveling acquiescence to those stupid, arrogant and demanding generals' wives who never bothered to learn what arigato meant, dumped in the gutter is the patient, smiling indulgence of the whims of some nosy grade school kid who won't stop fiddling with stuff and asking silly questions... At least it seems that way to me. I nod my head in agreeable recognition reading Brown's descriptions of the people then; they were the Japanese I knew. And I would guess most occupationaires knew in one way or another.

It does not appear that Dower ever spoke with Brown, consulted her work or even heard about it or her subsequent book on the same topic, *A Westerner Looks at Japan*, published in 1953. At least there are no citations, index marks or bibliographic references to her works or her person in *Embracing Defeat*. It's too bad the two never met, for that would have been a fascinating discussion to eavesdrop on: opposing sociological observations of not some primitive tribe, but of one of the leading societies of the modern industrial age. And it would have been very possible for them to have gotten together during the time Dower was working on his book, because Brown didn't die until 2010, having lived to age ninety-seven.

What Dower did do was cite the observations of the (still!) preeminently acknowledged Western authority on Japanese culture, Ruth Benedict. It's not much, just a paragraph, but it's there–and in my opinion, encapsulates a lot:

> *As suggested most famously by the cultural anthropologist Ruth Benedict, a member of the OWI intelligence team, the Japanese were said to behave in accordance with situational or particularistic ethics, as opposed to so-called universal values as in the Western tradition. The same person might be polite and generous under some circumstances, harsh and callous under others. What mattered was the social context and the individual's prescribed role in each and every situation. In exceptional circumstances, where roles and constraints had not been defined, the individual had no core values, no clear subjectified self, to fall back on.*

– John Dower, *Embracing Defeat*, Chapter 6 "Neo-Colonial Revolution," p. 219.

The Japanese acquiescence at the time, their seeming to stand patiently to one side whilst awaiting an occupationaire to do something-or-other, also struck Lorena Treadway and Maurice Howe, among others. I can relate to that. Quite often, unless the American took the initiative, the situation might take on an us-versus-them connotation, but absent any animosity. Call it a Mexican Standoff as directed by Mel Brooks: two adversaries facing each other, and neither makes a move. Or even worse, we would seem to be considering the Japanese invisible men: shadows, non-persons, images not worthy of attention. Howe commented on this unfortunate habitual occurrence in one of his letters home:

> *I suppose it does pay off to be humanitarian to the Japanese. With all the association I have had with them, I have never had a bitter word spoken against me. At the Embassy, there are only a few GIs who try to be nice or even courteous to the Japanese employees. In public, most GIs ignore the natives completely. I do not, and everywhere I see any of them, here or downtown, whether I recognize them or not, they speak to me, but they shun (as much as possible) the guys that generally consider themselves superior to the Japanese people. It means a lot to anyone to realize that the people we are here to rule (because we won the war), respect him for being what he is, instead of being the bully that they would fear rather than like or respect....I do believe, though, that all efforts toward closer bonds between Americans and Japanese are to be well rewarded.*

As for Lorena Treadway, generally so light-hearted when it came to the whole occupation thing, she had this comment on Stateside Americans' misunderstanding of the occupation:

> *Many of the folks back home have no concept of Japan or our life here. Some individuals who have no problem separating Nazis from the German people in their minds still think all Japanese men, women and children personally participated in the Bataan Death March. Many think our lives are difficult despite our letters to the contrary. One newly married young woman wrote to a friend that she was expecting a baby, and the friend wrote back, "Your news is wonderful, but how can you raise a child without hot water?"*

Then in 1991, forty years after she had returned to the US, she opined this:

> *Their work habits as we saw them and as depicted in Teahouse of the August Moon* (a Pulitzer Prize-winning play about Okinawa produced after the occupation was over) *are just the opposite of the industry and resourcefulness the Japanese have shown in the forty years since then. In retrospect, I feel that their seemingly carefree attitude at that time was owing to the fact that they had lost their pre-war and wartime sense of purpose and fanatic zeal, and they had not yet developed the new sense of purpose that*

would bring them worldwide economic
success. They were being taken care of
by MacArthur and the Allied forces. The
occupation years, in my opinion, were
the only years in their recent history that
the Japanese people could relax.

And then there was Nancy Echols, author of *Innocence Abroad*,
who lived in Tokyo with her husband, a public affairs officer with the
FECOM office, for three years beginning in 1947. In her book, she
writes questioningly and with puzzlement about the Japanese and
American relations with each other.

At one point she recalls a servant woman who had an attack of
appendicitis one night and needed to be taken to the hospital
posthaste–but that the daughter of the woman wouldn't awaken Echols
to take her to the hospital, but instead just let her sleep until she awoke
in any event, when it was almost too late to get her mother to the
hospital (it wasn't, but just barely). Echols seizes on this example and
others to fault the Japanese for, as she put it, "...their lack of initiative--
their unwillingness to take personal responsibility." Echols then mused
on this and other matters relating to occupatonaires' relationship with
the Japanese:

I wonder if we are wasting time
worrying about one another. Maybe it is
better to concede our basic differences
and merely like one another... It's not
that I don't appreciate the value of
studying an alien culture, nor do I think
we shouldn't try to understand one
another. I only mean that we don't have
to understand one another to have
mutual liking and respect...And I do
think that we must remember how
different we are when we try to teach
Japan any of our western ideas. No

> *matter how beautiful this western*
> *vegetation is, we must realize that it is to*
> *go into Japanese soil and that it will be*
> *pruned and bent according to Japanese*
> *ideals of beauty and will be subject to*
> *Far Eastern weather conditions. The*
> *resultant bloom may differ from the*
> *original, but it will suit the Japanese and*
> *it will have roots deep enough to*
> *withstand any rude or contrary winds.*

Then noting how the lack of intimate contact between us occupationaires and the Japanese inhibited even the liking of one another, she notes ruefully:

> *What a shame that is for all*
> *concerned. How misleading are these*
> *rare and impersonal contacts. What can*
> *one learn of the culture, the opinions,*
> *the dreams of a people in this way?*
> *Almost nothing, I should say--or even*
> *worse, misconceptions, guesses, mis-*
> *understandings of one another.*

Maybe. Because in large measure, while we never learned to like or understand each other, at least we dependents did take the time here-and-there to be courteous and considerate. And somehow and with all its faults it worked, and the world today is much different for it. And perhaps it all began with something MacArthur did just as the occupation began that seems to have made a deep and lasting impression, but somehow got lost in the shuffle. But now it has resurfaced, thanks to one Hisahiko Okazaki who stated in an article published in the *Daily Yomiuri* in January 2003:

> *When a food crisis occurred, relief*
> *arrived in the form of emergency food*

271

*supplies imported on MacArthur's
orders. This left a deep impression on
many Japanese at the time, who felt
Japan as a nation could not match U.S.
beneficence... "To give food to a country
that lost the war? We don't understand
America," thought the Japanese people
at the time. They felt more and more
strongly, "This is not just any country
we are dealing with."*

So maybe that's it! Maybe the whole occupation succeeded
because MacArthur launched on a giant and unprecedented scale what
amounted to a series of presentos that were passed back-and-forth as
the occupation progressed, just like visiting and re-visiting one of
those trinket shops on the Motomachi I knew so well! And it happened
this way:

First, the Japanese surrendered. "Arigato!" said the victorious
Allies, "Thank you for ending the bloodshed and carnage. And now to
repay your courtesy, not only will we not pillage your ravaged country
further, we will send in food and supplies and start to rebuild you."

To this, Japan replied, "Arigato! Thank you for not plundering our
country. And to repay you in kind, we shall not resist your occupation;
we will bow to your wishes and serve you as you please."

"Arigato!" now said the Allies. "Thank you for that courtesy; it
erases all concerns we may have had. And to repay you in kind, we
shall help you restore the democratic principles you once tried to hold,
and guide you again into the company of nations."

"Arigato!" exclaimed Japan. "Thank you so much for that. And to
repay you, we shall embrace democracy and begin to create for the
world to behold a society that will revolutionize consumerism."

And so it goes. And went. *Arigato!*

*A man walking toward a dark shape
far in the distance thinks to himself:
What is that strange thing? It must be a*

wild and dangerous animal. No, as I get nearer, to see that it is a man, but I am sure that he is an enemy. However, I shall go up to him and speak kindly to him. Ah, now I see his face. Why, he is my brother!

– Japanese proverb

Acknowledgments

James Zobel, Archivist, **MacArthur Memorial**, Norfolk, VA
For taking the time to guide me to all manner of interesting, often not heretofore surveyed, documents, and in general acquainting me with aspects of the occupation I never knew.

US Army History Center, Fort McNair, Washington, DC.
For opening all manner of records of the occupation, including especially monographs and official logs, and also for guiding me to much long-ignored or -forgotten material.

Harry S Truman Presidential Library and Museum, Independence, MO.
For providing background information and insight on the president's relation with MacArthur, and activity surrounding the Potsdam Declaration.

Jay Moynahan, Ann Cook Crossley, Patricia Stackhouse Garrity, Sally Amos Graessler and others who were children in Japan during that special time who shared their memories with me on-line, via email and regular mail, and at Yo-Hi (Yokohama-American High School) reunions.

Wikimedia, for being a ready-up source for background information on all manner of facts, in- depth and trivial, I felt needed reminders, detail, further comment or substantiation.

Yo-Hi, a great on-line reminder source of names, places, maps and pictures of where I lived, learned, wandered and generally called home.

Google Maps, another on-line source of reminders, this time of distances and places relationships to one another.

Turner Classic Movies, for showing the short documentary film *Hitler Lives*, providing me a visible, contrasting touchstone to the concurrent occupation of Germany.

Mark Jones and **Marcus Porpora** for the invaluable information about samurai swords.

Stars and Stripes newspaper archive, for all manner of tidbits, feature items, asides, and yet more reminders of my time in Japan.

Bibliography

American Caesar, William Manchester

Beneath the Eagle's Wings: Americans in Occupied Japan, John Curtis Perry

By the Grace of God and MacArthur: A Department of the Army Civilian in Occupied Japan, Lorena Treadway

Embracing Defeat and *War Without Mercy*, John Dower

Innocence Abroad, Nancy Echols

MacArthur: His Rendezvous with History, Courtney Whitney

Maurice's Letters Home, Maurice Howe

Memoirs of an American Family in Occupied Japan, John and Marion Allison

Over a Bamboo Fence and *A Westerner Looks at Japan*, Margery Finn Brown

Reminiscences, Douglas MacArthur

The Allied Occupation of Japan and Japanese Religions, William P. Woodard

The Chrysanthemum and the Sword, Ruth Benedict

The End: The Defiance and Destruction of Hitler's Germany, 1944-45, Ian Kershaw

The Rising Sun, John Toland

Unconditional Democracy: Education and Politics in Occupied Japan, 1945-1952, Toshiro Nishi

Unofficial Ambassadors: American Military Families Overseas and the Cold War, Donna Alvah

CPSIA information can be obtained
at www.ICGtesting.com
Printed in the USA
BVOW09s0721160617
486874BV00001B/105/P